HOOLIGANS ABROAD

D0851293

To Don & Judy,
from Eric
with love & fond
memories.

The Authors

A graduate of the University of Leicester, **John Williams** worked for three years (1979-82) on a research project on football hooliganism in the domestic context. He now works as Fieldwork Director in the Leicester Department of Sociology on a project for the Football Trust.

Eric Dunning has lectured in Sociology at the University of Leicester since 1962. He has also held visiting lectureships at the Universities of Nottingham and Warwick, and taught in the United States at Washington University, Brooklyn College, the University of Minnesota, and the State University of New York at Buffalo. In addition, he has lectured extensively in Germany and the Netherlands. He is Vice-President of the International Committee for the Sociology of Sport.

Patrick Murphy has lectured in Sociology at the University of Leicester since 1974. His particular areas of interest are the Sociology of Crime and Deviance, and Comparative Sociology.

HOOLIGANS ABROAD

THE BEHAVIOUR AND CONTROL OF ENGLISH FANS IN CONTINENTAL EUROPE

John Williams, Eric Dunning
and Patrick Murphy
Department of Sociology
University of Leicester

Routledge & Kegan Paul
London, Boston, Melbourne and Henley

For our families

First published in 1984
by Routledge & Kegan Paul plc

14 Leicester Square, London WC2H 7PH, England

9 Park Street, Boston, Mass. 02108, USA

464 St Kilda Road, Melbourne,
Victoria 3004, Australia and

Broadway House, Newtown Road,
Henley-on-Thames, Oxon RG9 1EN, England

Set in Sabon 10/12pt
by Input Typesetting Ltd, London
and printed in Great Britain

© John M. Williams, Eric G. Dunning and Patrick J. Murphy 1984

Library of Congress Cataloguing in Publication Data

Williams, John. (John M.)
Hooligans abroad.
Includes bibliographical references and index.
1. Spectator control. 2. Soccer—Great Britain—Fans.
3. Soccer—Social aspects—Great Britain.
I. Dunning, Eric. II. Murphy, Patrick. III. Title.
GV715.W55 1984   302.3'3   83–26988

British Library CIP data available
ISBN 0–7102–0143–5 (pbk.)

CONTENTS

LIST OF ILLUSTRATIONS

FOREWORD
SIR NORMAN CHESTER

I am very pleased, indeed proud, to be associated with this major contribution to the understanding of association football as the country's major spectator sport. I found it compelling reading even though I was already familiar with its findings. It completely confounds those who believe that sociologists can only write jargon so making it more rather than less difficult to understand the society they are analysing and explaining. Here is a book which can be read with both pleasure and profit not only by all those interested in football but also by those interested in the ways their fellow creatures behave.

The role I played as Deputy Chairman of the Football Trust was to persuade my fellow Trustees that it would be wise and not rash to give money to the Leicester University Department of Sociology to study and report on crowd behaviour. Eric Dunning had already done some excellent pioneer work in this field which impressed some of the doubters by its down-to-earth understanding of the game and its problems. Nevertheless two or three Trustees were frankly sceptical at first but have been completely won over. I think there is now general agreement that academics can help the authorities to deal with hooliganism by studies of those involved, the kind of people they are and what motivates them.

It is not however a case of *tout comprendre, tout pardonner*. Indeed the more one understands about the factors underlying this current social malaise the less easy it is to see the solution, or at least a solution which falls within the law-and-order framework of action. For that is largely concerned with punishment rather than changing attitudes within the family or the behaviour of adolescent groups on large municipal housing estates. No doubt punishment in the form of fines or detention centres may deter many potential hooligans but some of them accept this danger as part of the excitement and fun of the occasion. And, in so far as most are in the 18–24 age group, the faces of the ringleaders change quite rapidly.

Association football, particularly at the professional level, has certain features which encourage hooliganism. First, League football is the spectator sport of 'the masses'. The other major team games, rugby union football and cricket, on the whole draw upon a rather higher social stratum and, in any case, attract comparatively few spectators.

Second, the emphasis in soccer is on competition, which means on winning. The whole structure of the game from village and youth football upward is based on leagues, on gaining promotion and avoiding relegation, and on winning knockout competitions. This is not the case with rugby, save at the County level and is not so pronounced with cricket though the one-day County matches have increased the competitive element. The pronounced emphasis on winning must undoubtedly affect the attitude of players and spectators and reduce the feeling that they are participating in a purely pleasurable activity in which the guiding sentiment is: may the best side win. Spectators who are keyed up to see their side win may well be inclined to express their disappointment in hooliganism when their side loses. The desire to win intensifies the normal emotions.

Third, League football is not only the major spectator sport, it is the only sport which attracts large numbers to travel to away games. This is a comparatively recent phenomenon made possible by the five-day week and the greater ease of travel. In the 1930s and the imediate post-war years most people worked on Saturday morning until 12 or 1 o'clock. Moreover, in the winter months, games would start around 2 p.m. in the absence of floodlighting. The regular fan therefore found he had little choice but to attend his nearest ground – the First team one Saturday, the Reserve team the next Saturday. Now he has plenty of time to travel even quite long distances to see the First team (Reserve teams attract hardly any spectators). The development of motorways and the mass ownership of cars and motor cycles have made it easier to travel. The significance of this social change is, of course, that a great deal of hooliganism occurs in confrontations between home and visiting spectatators. The worst effects can be prevented inside the ground by the segregation of the two opposing factions but this is less easy outside the ground with the result that the worst forms of hooliganism now take place outside. It is also probably the case that fans behave more badly when visiting another town, e.g. by attacking shops, than they do when on their own territory.

This volume by John Williams, Eric Dunning and Patrick Murphy concentrates on the experiences of English soccer fans in Europe. Nevertheless the points I have just made about games in this country are relevant. The emphasis on winning, the greater ease of travel and the sense of freedom to misbehave when not on one's own patch all spill over when the away game is on the continent. These ingredients can be hotted up by national quarrels and attitudes as is so clearly shown by the happenings in Madrid. One feature of the European scene is, however, surprising. Clearly it is more expensive and time-consuming to go from London to Holland or Spain than to go to Birmingham or Leeds. One would have thought, therefore, that this would act as a social censor excluding the lower-working-class element which local studies have shown to provide a high proportion of the hooligans. Yet, as John Williams's participant observer study shows, cost and time were by no means insuperable barriers. Many of the worst English hooligans in Spain could be found at Chelsea, West Ham and other grounds during the season. Many of these, like soldiers in old-time wars, appear to have lived off the country. In most cases the actual game was but a small part of their 'enjoyment'. And alas for the future many no doubt returned to their home towns and terraces as heroes of many battles with many lurid stories to tell.

PREFACE

Hooligans Abroad is the first of two books on football hooliganism based on work we have been carrying out at the University of Leicester since 1979. The research it reports was financed by the *Football Trust*. The second book, *The Social Roots of Football Hooligan Violence*, is based on research funded by the Social Science Research Council and is due for publication towards the end of this year.

Although we have had to touch on a number of complex issues in writing *Hooligans Abroad*, we have tried to write a book which is relatively free of the technical vocabulary of sociology. Hopefully, this will make the book accessible to the general reader, but it means, inevitably, that there are oversimplifications. This is especially the case in the Introduction and the Conclusion where theoretical issues are most directly addressed. We trust that our academic colleagues will bear with us regarding the oversimplifications. Important issues which lack sufficient elaboration here will be discussed at length in *The Social Roots*.

The bulk of *Hooligans Abroad* is devoted to three 'participant observation' studies carried out by John Williams. He is young enough and sufficiently 'street-wise' and interested in football to pass himself off as an 'ordinary' English football fan. To avoid repeating John's name in the text, the book is written as if all three of us went to Spain, Holland and Copenhagen. John also conducted the interviews and drafted the preliminary reports. However, the initial research design and its theoretical underpinning were developed by Eric Dunning and Patrick Murphy. All three of us collaborated in writing up the research, and its various aspects underwent considerable development in the course of our discussions. The book is, therefore, a *collective* product in the truest sense of the term.

In the Conclusion, we look at the part sociological research can play in tackling problems such as football hooliganism. Appendix 4 presents some short-term proposals designed to restrict the prospects for seriously violent and disorderly behaviour by English fans at continental matches. The Conclusion also explains our rationale for putting forward proposals of this kind, and offers some briefly sketched recommendations for broader, longer-term initiatives which aim to address the root causes of hooligan behaviour. In our view, without backing from politicians and administrators for long-term policies of this kind, deep-seated social problems like hooligan behaviour will be with us for a very long time. Sadly, recent governments seem to have little understanding of the sorts of things that are required in this regard. Indeed, some people in government circles at the moment appear to have an almost paranoid suspicion of sociology and the other social sciences, coupled with a compulsive fascination with the use of repressive sanctions as the sole means of dealing with social problems. Perhaps this book will make a contribution to the breaking down of these suspicions and help in the construction of policies which stand a real chance of resolving social problems rather than being irrelevant or to exacerbating them.

We should like to thank the numerous individuals who have helped us with our research. Sir Norman Chester has not only written the foreword, but supported us strongly throughout. Ilya Neustadt, too, has helped with his encouragement and advice. We are grateful to Richard Faulkner, Brian Burnett, Leslie Walker, Steve Stride and Mick Marshall for their expertise and patience. We also offer our thanks to Eve Burns and Val Pheby for typing the manuscript through its various drafts, and to the Central Photographic Unit at Leicester University for their sterling work with the illustrations. Last but not least, we would like to thank all those fans in Spain, Rotterdam and Copenhagen who took time off from their various endeavours to talk to us.

INTRODUCTION

In this book, we report the findings of three studies of the behaviour and control of English football fans whilst they were at and travelling to and away from matches in continental Europe. The matches in question were: the European Cup Final between Aston Villa and Bayern Munich played in Rotterdam in 1982; the European Championship match between Denmark and England which took place in Copenhagen in September the same year; and the matches played by England in the 1982 World Cup Finals. Our principal study is of the behaviour of English fans at the World Cup Finals. Before we embark on a discussion of the findings of these three studies, we shall place them in context by considering some general aspects of football hooliganism as a social phenomenon.

One does not have to be a sociologist to realise that football hooliganism is widely regarded in present-day Britain as one of our most serious causes for concern. We have been told about it often enough by the media and politicians in recent years, usually in tones that bear all the hallmarks of a 'moral panic'.[1]

Although references to football hooliganism can be found in the press much earlier, it was in the mid-1960s that concern about it began to reach present proportions.[2] At first, it was spectator misbehaviour in conjunction with *domestic* matches that was the source of this concern. Since the mid-1970s, however, it is the behaviour of British – especially English – fans *abroad* that has come increasingly to form the principal focus for anxiety.

One of the first widely reported incidents of misbehaviour involving English fans on the continent took place in West Germany in 1965. However, in that case, the Manchester United supporters who fought on the terraces with their West German counterparts during the match between their team and SV Hannover were British soldiers serving in Germany. It was not until 1974, when Spurs fans were reported to have 'gone on the rampage' in Rotterdam, and Manchester United fans were reported to have brawled with local youths in the Ostend city centre, that the football hooliganism by 'civilians' which had already become a regular feature of the game in England began to be exported abroad.

At first, it was fans supporting *club* sides who principally engaged in such behaviour. Then, in Luxembourg in 1977, in Turin in 1980, and in Basle and Oslo in 1981, hooligan behaviour in a continental context began to occur at matches involving the *England* team. It was probably these incidents, particularly their coverage by the mass media, which brought home most clearly to people in this country that Britain's boast of having the most peaceful football spectators in the world could no longer be sustained. The events of 1980 and 1981 also roused severe anxiety about what might happen should the national team qualify for the 1982 World Cup Finals which were to be played in easily reachable Spain.

As a result of this history of disorder and the associated belief that they are usually, if not always, the aggressors, English fans have come to be regarded in continental football circles as by far and away the worst in Europe, if not, indeed, the world. Such is the nature and extent of the threat they are held to pose that the European football authorities have even been led to consider totally prohibiting English sides from playing on the continent. At a time when professional soccer is battling against the effects of a recession which has had severe repercussions at the turnstiles, such a move might well have crippling consequences for the game in this country. But whether it comes to this or not, a ban on playing on the continent would certainly constitute a comment on England and the English in some ways comparable to the one implied by the sporting boycott imposed on South Africa on account of its apartheid policies. It is not without reason, therefore, that many people in this country are worried about the threat to the image of the English held abroad posed by the recurrence of the disruptive behaviour at continental football matches by what is usually only a small minority of English fans.

Despite the perceived urgency of the problem, however, there is at present little real understanding of what has led it to occur. There are, for example, only limited data currently available on the social backgrounds of the fans who travel abroad in support of their favourite club and/or the national side. There are even less on those who are most liable to engage in hooligan behaviour and what their motivations are. There are frequent references in the press to the activities of 'mindless English thugs' and, somewhat less frequently, to provocation by home spectators but there is little reliable evidence available on what one might call the 'dynamics' of football disorders in foreign contexts, that is, on what contributes to their build-up and why they occur on some occasions whilst on others they do not.

Although the general tendency is to condemn football hooligans as entirely 'beyond the pale', there are a number of popular attempts to explain their behaviour. One line of reasoning attributes spectator disorderliness to the types of fans who go, i.e. it assumes that some fans who go abroad are simply hell-bent on fighting and destruction. Another attributes it to match-related causes, assuming, for example, that it is the consequence of the build-up of excitement at a match, of frustration at what are perceived to be the biased decisions of the referee, or of anger at the use of unfair and violent tactics by the players of the opposing teams. A similar line of reasoning sees spectator disorder as a consequence of the elation experienced by fans whose team has won or of dejection by those whose team has lost. Yet another sees football hooliganism simply as a consequence of over-indulgence in alcohol. Apart from sometimes being incompatible with each other, these popular 'theories' tend to treat what is an extremely complex phenomenon as if it were one-dimensional. Our own view, which will emerge as the analysis unfolds, is that there is more than one type of spectator disorder and that they tend to result from a combination of causes rather than from a single cause.

We do not pretend that we have come up with a definitive answer to the question of what the causes of football hooliganism are. Indeed, we may stand accused by some commentators of asking entirely the wrong questions to begin with! We do, however, believe that our analysis will serve as a basis for further research in the area and that it points up courses of action which stand a rather better chance of success in the longer term than the sorts of hit-and-miss, punitive policies that have been introduced to deal with football hooliganism so far. Let us now briefly explore some aspects of the methods we employed in our study of the behaviour of English football fans abroad.

Some methodological issues

The difficulties in studying crowd behaviour are legion. This probably accounts in large measure for the dearth of systematic research in this and related fields. Such difficulties are severe enough as far as a crowd of, say, 25,000–30,000 inside a football stadium is concerned. They are exacerbated considerably when account has to be taken of behaviour *outside* as well, especially when travel over long distances is involved.

A standard survey methodology using questionnaires and/or interviews is, of course, a means of gaining information about the social composition of a crowd.[3] It is also a useful way of obtaining quantitative data about the attitudes and opinions of its members. But, in the context of crowd research, questionnaires are difficult to administer and, in some respects, unreliable. Moreover, the survey method cannot tell one anything in a direct sense about the dynamics of disorderly incidents. For that, direct observation is required. In particular, the presence at such gatherings of a trained *participant observer* is a useful way of providing information of a richer and more reliable kind than that to which we have been accustomed hitherto. Here, too, of course, one encounters problems. How, for example, can one be sure that one's observations are accurate and would not be disputed by another participant observer or by the 'ordinary' participants in an event? How can one guard against the possibility of being at the wrong place at the wrong time? Despite problems of this kind participant observation research into crowd behaviour is far from totally impractical. As far as football hooliganism is concerned, the task is eased considerably by the fact that it is only a minority of fans who regularly engage in disorder. It is eased even further if one has some knowledge and experience of the kinds of contexts and situations in which disorder is liable to occur, and of the sorts of fans who are likely to seek out or be drawn into such situations. That is because, if one has such knowledge, one is more likely to know what to look for and when and where to look for it.

Each of the three studies reported in this book was based on the 'covert' form of participant observation. For the Aston Villa–Bayern Munich match, one of us travelled to Holland as an 'ordinary' Villa supporter, remaining inconspicuous by wearing, in common with large numbers of the fans themselves, an Aston Villa football shirt on the trip. In Spain, he travelled on a cut-price package, this time as an 'ordinary' England fan. He tried to remain similarly inconspicuous on the trip to Copenhagen. On each occasion, his task was not only to observe the behaviour of fans who seem to be most regularly involved in disorder but also to experience events which they themselves experienced. In each case, too, he was concerned not only with observing incidents of fan disorderliness inside and outside stadia, but also with their build-up and the official reactions to them. He also tried, by means of conversations, to obtain as much information as possible on the ages, occupations and political leanings of fans. In addition, he probed the reasons they gave for following football and their memories of previous hooligan encounters, both in a domestic context and abroad.

Besides such direct observational data, information was collected on the wider framework within which the trips occurred, especially on aspects which it seemed might contribute in different ways and degrees to the occurrence or prevention of disorder. More particularly, attention was paid to travelling arrangements, the organisation of matches, the crowd control measures employed and some of the political contingencies that prevailed at the time. As we shall show, the heightening of national sentiment in conjunction with the Falklands War – orchestrated, in large part, by sections of the popular press – played a part of some significance in the spectator misbehaviour which occurred in Copenhagen and in Spain, a country which has long-standing ties with Argentina. Finally, attention was paid to the coverage of matches in both the English and the foreign press. This was done partly in order to gain additional information but more importantly, of course, because press reports are not neutral reflections of what goes on at such events but constitute an active ingredient in their totality.

Before turning to our study of the 1982 World Cup Finals, we shall discuss some general aspects of football hooliganism as a social phenomenon. We shall start with a brief critical examination of some of the myths that have grown up about it. After that, in order to clarify further some of the assumptions which guided our research, we shall sketch in the outlines of a sociological explanation which places the phenomenon of football hooliganism in its social context.

Football hooliganism: a critique of some prevalent myths

As is often the case with social problems, a number of myths have grown up about football hooliganism. More particularly, there appear to be four that are relevant in the present context: that it is purely and simply – or mainly – a British phenomenon; that the problem is worse in this country than abroad; that British fans are always the aggressors and never the victims; and that soccer is the only sport in which hooliganism regularly occurs.[4] Each of these ideas is unfounded. Let us deal with them one by one.

(i) Football hooliganism: a purely British 'disease'?
We have not attempted to ascertain systematically how widespread, internationally, football hooliganism is. Yet, in the course of our researches, we have come across more than 70 reports of crowd disorderliness at football matches in various parts of the world between 1904 and the present day.[5] This figure excludes incidents in which British fans were involved and covers disorders in 30 different countries. Had we undertaken a systematic cross-national survey that was not reliant solely on British newspapers for information, we should undoubtedly have come across many more incidents and in a greater range of countries.

Some of the incidents that have come to our attention occurred at international matches, but most were generated domestically. They are thus indicative of the widespread existence of rivalry between fan groups *within* as well as *between* countries. Italy, with 14 reported incidents, and West Germany, with 12, head the list but it includes countries as diverse as Argentina, Bermuda, China, Colombia, Gabon, India, Peru, Turkey, the USSR, and Yugoslavia, in fact, quite a high proportion of the countries where soccer is currently played. Nor do we deny that hooliganism at British football matches differs in certain respects from that experienced in other parts of the world. Clearly, though, football hooliganism is by no means purely and simply a British phenomenon. Nor is it solely found in Western capitalist societies or in those of the 'developed' world.

(ii) Some examples of football crowd disorderliness abroad
It is not our wish to deny the seriousness of the violence sometimes involved in football hooliganism in this country. However, we have not yet witnessed scenes in Britain to rival those which took place in Lima in 1964 when, in the match between Peru and Argentina, the referee refused to allow a goal to the home side and, in the ensuing riot, 318 people were killed and more than 500 injured. That is by far and away the worst football riot on record, but 74 people died in a riot during a match in Argentina in 1968, 69 after a match in Moscow in 1982, and 29 at a match in Colombia, again in 1982. In these cases, some of the reported deaths resulted from the collapse of terraces and stands. Others were a consequence of suffocation and trampling as the riot intensified and panic took hold.

In the mid-1950s, the Yugoslavs experienced a wave of football disorder which they called 'Zusism'. ('Zus' is a Serbo-Croat acronym for 'slaughter, kill, annihilate'.) Describing a match near Belgrade in 1955, the official Communist Party newspaper, *Borba*, reported how fans 'rushed on the field carrying knives, . . . knocked down the referee and put him out of action for at least 6 months'. *Borba* also reported preparations for a match in a town near Belgrade where spectators were planning to come 'armed with hammers, mallets and metal bars'.[6] In Turkey in 1967, fans of the Kayseri and Sivas clubs fought with pistols, knives and broken bottles for days after the end of a match between the two sides. Before troops restored order, cars were burned out, 600 spectators were injured and 44 killed, 25 by stab-wounds.[7] More recently, in Italy in 1979, a 33-year-old fan died after being hit in the eye by a home-made rocket fired from a flare gun. And, in Holland in 1981, the Feyenoord goalkeeper, Joop Hiele, was injured when a Molotov cocktail was hurled from the crowd during their game with NEC. Clearly, while the English may currently be the *enfants terribles* of Europe as far as spectator misbehaviour is concerned, it is a misconception to regard the more violent forms of football hooliganism as the preserve of any one country. Apart from ethnocentric bias in the reporting of news, especially in the popular press, and in the perception of it by readers, one of the sources of the myth that only British fans are hooligans may be the fact that the majority of continental fans who visit this country appear to be relatively well behaved.[8] However, as our examples clearly show, that fact does not mean there is no domestic hooliganism in continental countries.

(iii) English fans as aggressors and victims
Another widely held belief, generated for the most part by the popular press, is that it is always English fans who are the initiators of aggression. However, writing in 1980 of the highly publicised terrace fights which took place in Turin and Basle in that year, Stuart Weir showed how the provocative actions of local youths had played an important part in producing them.[9] At a pre-season 'friendly' match in Nuremburg in the summer of 1980, even the dreaded Manchester United fans were reported to be under attack from local supporters who were 'clearly looking for trouble'.[10] We have come across reports of 21 incidents since 1965 in which English fans allegedly initiated the proceedings.[11] However, we have also come across reports of 14 incidents in which, allegedly, they or English players were the victims.[12] The ratio expressed in these figures is probably just as much a function of selective reporting by the British press as it is of the fact that, during this period, British football hooligans were coming to achieve the bad reputation which they currently enjoy. The figures probably also mask the frequency with which mutual provocation between rival fan groups plays a part in the build-up of hooligan encounters. In saying this, we are not suggesting that English fans are blameless. Indeed, there seems to be some justification for claiming that England supporters were largely responsible for the violence and destruction which occurred at the international matches in Luxembourg and Norway in 1977 and 1981. What we *are* saying is that the English are often wrongly assumed to be the initiators of *all* hooligan incidents at matches they attend abroad.

(iv) Hooliganism: a problem peculiar to soccer?
Spectator disorderliness is also often talked about as if it were a problem peculiar to soccer. 'It doesn't happen in rugby', we are told but, as Richard Holt has shown, serious spectator violence is a long-standing problem in French Rugby Union, particularly in the South.[13] Similarly, we are sometimes told that, even though the United States is in most respects a more violent country than Britain, its sports spectators are considerably more peaceable than ours. That is yet another myth. In 1975, an American sociologist collated the number of riots at sports events reported in 6 newspapers in the USA in the years 1960–72. He discovered that a total of 312 riots (involving 17 deaths) were reported in that period, an average of 26 per year. The sport-by-sport breakdown was as follows: baseball, 97; American football, 66; basketball, 54; ice hockey, 39; boxing, 19; horse racing, 11; motor cycle and car racing, 10; golf, 4; soccer, 3; wrestling, 3; athletics, 2; tennis, 2; and air sports, 2.[14]
An extract from an article entitled 'War in the Grandstand' which appeared in the St. *Louis Post-Dispatch* in December 1976 will give an idea of the sort of problem with which the Americans are faced in this regard:

At a National Football League game at Foxboro, Mass., between the New York Jets and the New England Patriots, rowdy fans continually ran out on the field, stopping play a dozen times. By the time the game ended, two fans had died of heart attacks, 30 were taken to hospital with cuts or bruises, 49 were arrested, a policeman's jaw broken, and a spectator had been stabbed. In the parking lot a policeman was giving mouth to mouth resuscitation to a heart attack victim when a drunken fan urinated on the officer's back.

Nor have we yet witnessed scenes in Britain comparable to those reported as having taken place in Pittsburgh, Pennsylvania, in what one might call the 'celebratory' riot which occurred following the victory of the Pittsburg Pirates baseball team in the final of the 1971 'World Series':

An extraordinary orgy of destruction, looting and sexual excess took hold of Pittsburgh, Pennsylvania . . . following the unexpected victory of the Pittsburgh Pirates baseball team. . . .

During nearly 10 hours of wild, drunken celebrations around the city, men and women indulged in public love-making and nudity. More than 100 people were injured and about 100 others arrested. Some 30 shops were looted and another 30 damaged. Two incidents of sexual assault occurred in full view of hundreds of celebrating fans who, according to eye-witness reports, cheered the assailants and made no attempt to help the victims. . . . There was scattered gunfire during the rampage and one of those admitted to hospital was a middle aged man suffering from a gunshot wound.[15]

We have now reached a point at which it is necessary, very briefly, to sketch in the sociological explanation of football hooligan violence that has developed out of and guided our research.

The social roots of football hooligan violence

Anyone seeking to understand football hooliganism must, in our opinion, first distance him or herself from certain features that are prominent in the public debate about it. A crucial initial step in this process is to forego the tendency to dismiss football hooliganism as 'meaningless' behaviour and football hooligans as 'mindless morons'. That is because all human behaviour involves at least some degree of rationality and meaning. The tendency to dismiss football hooligans as 'morons' and 'thugs', and to describe their behaviour as 'meaningless' involves the labelling by outsiders of others whose behaviour they fail to understand because it is based on values that are different from their own. Just because it appears 'mindless' and 'meaningless' to them, they seem to assume that it is 'mindless' and 'meaningless' *per se*. Moreover, such a stance rules out by definitional fiat any possibility of understanding the phenomenon.

Paradoxically, adherence to this moralising and dismissive approach is often coupled with a willingness to embrace single-factor explanations. In effect, as we have suggested already, these amount to the assertion of a simple causal link between football hooliganism and such things as the excessive consumption of alcohol or violence on the field of play. A little simple probing would soon reveal the superficiality of this type of explanation. Thus, not all fans who drink heavily are football hooligans. Nor is violence between players invariably followed by hooligan encounters. We do not deny that such factors sometimes play a part in triggering football hooliganism. However, it is a complex phenomenon and they have to be incorporated into an explanatory framework that is simultaneously broader and deeper.

Another issue taken up in the public debate is whether football hooliganism is best understood within the context of the game, or whether its sources lie elsewhere. This is, in some ways, a fruitful line of enquiry, although it is hampered by the fact that no hard and fast definition of 'hooligan' activity is readily to hand. What counts as 'hooliganism' for some is simply 'high spirits' for others. Some football disorders widely described as manifestations of 'hooliganism' appear to be more or less spontaneous expressions of elation, dejection, frustration or anger generated by the ups and downs of a match. Others, however, most notably the vandalism and fighting between rival fan groups that are currently so widespread, appear to be less closely connected with the game *per se*. At least it is difficult to trace them *directly* to incidents and outcomes on the field of play. Rather, they appear to grow out of life-styles which are generated in the wider social structure. The game thus forms a context – though it is by no means the only one – for the expression of some aspects of these life-styles.

A common feature which appears to underlie the behaviour of those fans who take a leading part and/or who engage in the most extreme forms of disorderly behaviour, is that such fans have social standards that are in crucial ways different from those which predominate in society at large. It is the social generation of the standards which guide the behaviour of football hooligans, particularly those who use football as a context for fighting, on which we shall centrally focus in trying to construct an explanation. That is, we shall attempt to show how these standards grow up as a consequence of the social characteristics, internal relations, social locations and social circumstances of particular groups. In fact, the groups who engage most persistently in football hooligan fighting appear to come predominantly from the 'rough' working class, i.e. from the ranks of groups who stand at or near the bottom of the social scale. Accordingly, we shall be concerned in what follows chiefly with explaining how what we take to be the characteristic social standards of the 'rough' working class are produced and reproduced.

Football hooliganism, fighting and the 'rough' working class

In order to illustrate the characteristic values of the youths and young men who typically form the core groups most centrally and persistently involved in fighting at football matches, let us take the case of 'Frank', a 26-year-old lorry driver and self-confessed football hooligan who was interviewed by Paul Harrison at the 1974 Cardiff City–Manchester United game. 'Frank' is reported by Harrison as having said:

> I go to a match for one reason only: the aggro. It's an obsession. I can't give it up. I get so much pleasure when I'm having aggro that I nearly wet my pants. . . . I go all over the country looking for it. . . . (E)very night during the week we go round looking for trouble. Before a match we go round looking respectable. . . ; then if we see someone who looks like the enemy we ask him the time; if he answers in a foreign accent, we do him over, and if he's got any money on him we'll roll him as well.[16]

'Frank' probably exaggerated his involvement in and enjoyment of 'aggro'. Nevertheless, our research suggests that the values he expresses are representative of those held by the small minority of fans who are involved at the sharp end of football-related violence.

Information on the social origins of such fans is currently rather scarce. However, the data available on those convicted of offences related to football confirm our earlier contention, namely that the phenomenon is predominantly the preserve of males from the lower levels of the working class. The Harrington Report, for example, concluded in 1968 that, 'the present evidence suggests that (football hooligans) are mainly from a working class background with the special problems inherent in large industrial cities and ports where violent and delinquent subcultures are known to exist'.[17] Over a decade later, Trivizas reached a similar conclusion, namely that 80.1 per cent of the persons charged with football-related offences were manual workers or unemployed.[18] Harrison's impressionistic account of Cardiff City's 'committed rowdies' in 1974 had them coming from '. . . Canton and Grangetown, rows of terraced houses with few open spaces, and from Llanrumney, a massive council estate with an appalling record of vandalism'.[19] Although Peter Marsh and his colleagues failed to address the issue of class background directly in their study of Oxford United fans, some of their informants did provide relevant comments. For example, one of them said: 'If you live on the Leys (a local housing estate) then you have to fight or else people piss you about and think you're a bit soft or something.'[20]

In fact, over 50 per cent of the Oxford United fans arrested during serious disturbances at their away cup-tie with Coventry City in 1981 came from this, the Blackbird Leys estate.[21] Evidence from Leicester points in the same direction. Thus, of the 428 local persons arrested inside or in the vicinity of the Filbert Street ground between January 1976 and April 1980, 20.3 per cent came from a single lower-working-class council estate.

There is, of course, often a degree of arbitrariness about who is and who is not arrested in a football context. As a result, such figures have to be treated with caution. Nevertheless, the emerging pattern is sufficiently strong and geographically consistent to make it unlikely that the figures distort the social origins of football hooligans to a significant extent. The pattern is also confirmed by the participant observation we have carried out in Leicester.[22] This raises the question of what it is about the structure of lower-working-class communities that leads to the generation of the norms and values that these youths and young men express through fighting, both in a football context and elsewhere. Our view on this complex issue can be briefly summarised as follows.[23]

The social generation of a violent masculine style

There is a tendency, deeply rooted in present-day liberal thinking, to see the relatively high levels and open expression of violence that are characteristic of poorer communities, or at least of specific sections of them, as resulting in a direct sense from the multiple deprivations from which such communities suffer. Our own view is that, while these deprivations play an important part in the production and reproduction of this violence, they do so in ways that are rather more complex than current explanations suggest.

Of more immediate significance in this regard are the social relationships typically generated by the life experiences of people in
communities of this sort. Accordingly it is on these that we shall
concentrate in the discussion which follows. Although we cannot
elaborate on this issue in the present context, these relationships
and the relatively high levels of open violence they engender are
both to some extent caused by, and reciprocally play a part in
maintaining, the poverty of the lower working class. The location
of the lower working class in the wider social structure also plays
a part in maintaining their poverty and violence, as does the fact
that society as it is presently constituted appears to require the
maintenance of an impoverished class at the bottom. However, as
we have suggested, our main task for the moment is to examine
the internal relationships of lower-working-class communities in
order to explore how they typically generate a level of violence
which is higher than that usually found among groups above them
in the social hierarchy.

In addition to sharing the experience of poverty, members of the
'rougher' sections of lower-working-class communities traditionally place strong emphasis on ties of kinship and territory. They
also tend to display hostility towards outsiders, even – in some
ways perhaps especially – towards outsider groups who are placed
similarly to themselves. In addition, they tend to be characterised
by fairly rigid patterns of segregation along the lines of age and
sex. This has a number of important consequences. Rigid age-
group segregation, coupled with a variety of domestic pressures,
means that children are frequently sent to play in the streets, unsupervised by adults, at an early age. There, they tend to develop
dominance hierarchies based on age and physical strength. Rigid
sexual segregation means that, by adolescence, girls tend to be
drawn into the home. Some of them also form relatively aggressive
girls' 'gangs' or simply 'hang around' the groups of boys where they
tend to be regarded as subordinates. However, the development of
strong loyalties to one another and, in particular, the development
of a sense of proprietorship over the local 'turf' are, typically, the
preserve of 'the lads'. That is, adolescent boys in such communities
tend to form what are popularly known as 'streetcorner gangs'. So
strong are the 'in-group' ties of these streetcorner groups and so
strong their hostility towards outsiders, that they come regularly
into conflict with similar groups from adjacent neighbourhoods.

This way of socialising children and the formation of gangs within and between which fighting is frequent are two of the sources for the production and reproduction in lower-working-class communities of standards which tolerate a relatively high level of violence in social relations. Such a pattern is reinforced by the standards characteristic of the dominant adults in communities of this sort. The dominance of men over women and the consequent lack of softening female pressure work in the same direction. Indeed, many women in such communities grow up to be relatively violent themselves and to expect violent behaviour from their men. To the extent that this is so, the violent propensities of the men are reinforced.

A useful way of expressing it would be to say that such sections of lower-working-class communities are characterised by a 'positive feedback cycle' which tends to encourage the resort to aggression in many areas of social life, especially on the part of males. The best fighters are apportioned great respect, and there is a tendency for males from these kinds of areas to see fighting as an important source of meaning and gratification in life. That is, there are males in communities of this sort who tend to be excessively *macho*, to follow the norms of what one might call a 'violent masculine style'. In fact, along with gambling, street 'smartness', an exploitative form of sex, and heavy drinking – the capacity to consume alcohol in large quantities is another highly valued attribute among males from the 'rougher' sections of the lower working class – fighting is one of the few sources of excitement, meaning and status available to males from this section of society and accorded a degree of social toleration. That is because they are typically denied status, meaning and gratification in the educational and occupational spheres, the major sources of identity, meaning and status available to men from the middle classes. This denial comes about as a result of the fact that the majority of lower-working-class males do not themselves have – nor do they typically prize – the attributes and values that make for educational and occupational success or for striving in these fields, and because they are systematically discriminated against in the worlds of school and work.

A feature of the streetcorner gangs that regularly form in lower-working-class communities which is especially interesting for present purposes is the way in which rival gangs, say from a particular working-class estate, often unite in the face of an attack from an outside estate. Robins and Cohen found such a pattern in their study of a working-class estate in north London.[24] We observed it, too, on the Leicester estates that we studied. More significantly for present purposes, Paul Harrison refers to what he calls 'the Bedouin syndrome' in the contemporary football context.[25] What he means is that, just as groups which are otherwise hostile sometimes combine in the event of disputes with gangs from a neighbouring estate, so, at football matches, the estates from the home town stand side by side in the cause of 'home end' solidarity, that is, in opposition to the fans of the visiting team. If the challenge is perceived in regional terms then, again, enemies may join forces. For example, northern fans visiting London often complain about confrontations with combined 'fighting crews' from a number of local clubs. Southerners visiting the north voice similar complaints. Finally, at the international level, club and regional rivalries can be subordinated to national reputation, though, at each of these levels, and particularly if the opposing groups are not present in sufficient strength, lower-level rivalries are apt to re-emerge.[26] It is with the international level of this pattern of unification and division between hostile groups that we are concerned in the present study.

We have now reached a point where we can introduce the findings of our first case study, that of the behaviour of English fans at the 1982 World Cup Finals. As we shall show, those fans who were principally involved in the disorders which occurred in Spain were predominantly from the lower working class and acting in terms of the norms and values of a 'violent masculine style'. Moreover fans who regularly fight each other at matches in England united on this occasion in opposition to the Spanish 'foe'.

One last point needs to be made before we begin this discussion. Our argument is not that youths and young men from the lower working class are the only football hooligans. Nor is it that all adolescent and young adult males from the lower-working-class communities use football as a context for fighting. Others fight elsewhere and some do not fight at all. Our point is rather that youths and young men from the lower working class are the most central and persistent offenders in the more serious forms of football hooliganism. As such, particularly given the intensive coverage of their activities by the media, they may have come to form a reference group for some disaffected youths from 'respectable' working-class and middle-class backgrounds. However, youths from the higher reaches of the social hierarchy who become football hooligans are unlikely to persist so long in their hooligan behaviour. Most of them have other sources of identity, status, meaning and excitement available to them, and are much more likely to come under the influence of dominant standards.

Part I
ENGLISH FANS IN SPAIN

Chapter One
PREPARATIONS FOR SPAIN

At around 8 o'clock on the evening of Wednesday November 18, 1981, Paul Mariner, the England centre-forward, stumbled and diverted a mis-hit shot from mid-fielder Trevor Brooking into the Hungarian net. His goal gave England the victory which sent them into the final stages of the World Cup competition for the first time in twelve years.

While English football fans rejoiced, some no doubt returning home from the match to dig out maps of the continent and plan their summer's footballing adventures, FIFA officials viewed England's qualification for Spain with emotions more nearly approaching alarm. The Spanish civil authorities, despite their not inconsiderable experience in coping with public disorder, probably also cast an anxious glance at the result which emerged from Wembley that night. The reason for all this concern was the fact that, whatever it signified in football terms, England's victory meant that the most vilified fans in Europe would be on the march across the continent again.

The cheers for Mariner's goal had hardly died down when the authorities and the media in this country, too, began worrying at the prospect of British-inspired disorders in Spain. One of the first to express concern was the Conservative MP, John Butcher. Less than 36 hours after England's qualification, he was warning Michael Heseltine, then Secretary of State for the Environment that, unless massive precautions were taken, '... a large international television audience will be treated to scenes of the degrading and humiliating behaviour exhibited by a certain element of British supporters whenever they visit the continent.'[1]

Mr Butcher went on to request that a 'treaty' should be negotiated with the Spanish government for the return to trial in this country of British fans convicted of offences in Spain. He also demanded that the passports of those involved in disturbances at the Finals should be withdrawn. His concern was echoed in a growing number of media comments and official pronouncements in the closing weeks of 1981. It was premised upon what he and many others took to be the certain prospect of bad behaviour by a minority of British, but most probably primarily English, fans in Spain. Underlying this concern was the threat to the national image which they felt such behaviour would imply.

As we noted in the Introduction, a number of England's recent matches in Europe, in particular those in Basle and Turin, had been scarred by terrace disturbances. Significantly, these matches had been televised in several countries but, for Spain, the international viewing audience promised to be even larger. With over 7,000 media personnel due there to cover the tournament and the peak TV audience expected to be somewhere in the region of 1.4 billion, the public's demands for what *The Financial Times* called 'the facts, titbits, excitement and scandal in the world's biggest single-sport jamboree', threatened to focus the eyes of the world squarely on English terrace excesses if and when they should occur.[2] After the scenes in Turin, Prime Minister Thatcher – she was in Venice at the time, attending an EEC 'summit meeting' – made it clear that she was 'severely embarrassed' by the behaviour of the England fans involved. With murmurs growing from EUFA and FIFA about the possibility of a total ban on English sides in Europe, there was clear recognition both in government and football circles in this country that precautions would have to be taken to ensure that England's hooligan following did not 'cut loose' in Spain.

Towards the end of November 1981 the newly installed FA Chairman, Bert Millichip, used the forthcoming Finals and the likelihood of hooliganism there by English fans to preface the outlines of a comprehensive attack on hooliganism by English fans at home and abroad. His ten-point plan ranged from recommendations for the return of corporal punishment in schools, through the prevention of movement at home and abroad of fans whose dress or demeanour was 'offensive', to the reintroduction of the Riot Act to deal with football-related disturbances. With Spain more specifically in mind, Millichip was equally unyielding if decidedly pessimistic. At a conference of the Central Council of Physical Recreation held in Bournemouth on 27 November he is reported to have said:

> With the World Cup almost upon us, the Spaniards, without doubt, are nervously contemplating the arrival of ferocious gangs of moronic louts from this country who find the game of football such a convenient platform from which to launch and display their show of naked and uncontrolled aggression. Nothing can prevent this invasion. Tickets or no tickets, they'll be on the boat to Bilbao, get drunk, wreck the boat and then get drunk in Bilbao and wreck that. They might get shot, but that is their problem.[3]

Millichip's pronouncements may have been somewhat alarmist, yet on past performances he had good reason to expect serious disturbances at the Finals. Indeed, given the length of time English fans were expected to stay in Spain and the reputation of the local police, scenes in excess of those experienced in Basle and Turin could not be ruled out. Nevertheless, the Spanish Basques did not appear to be unduly unnerved at the prospect. Nor did they share the FA Chairman's sense of the inevitable. Indeed, reports from Bilbao later suggested that the locals, perhaps for reasons as much political as based on simple politeness, professed themselves to be 'delighted' at the prospect of hosting England's Phase One matches.[4]

Meanwhile through the agency of the Minister for Sport, Neil Macfarlane, the government pressed ahead with plans aimed at minimising British hooliganism in Spain. A meeting in December with representatives of the home Football Associations produced five main proposals.

(i) that a pamphlet of 'do's and don'ts' should be circulated through supporters' clubs to fans travelling from England, Scotland and Northern Ireland;

(ii) that talks should be held with FIFA to try to ensure the segregation of English fans from opposing supporters inside grounds;

(iii) that plans should be implemented to increase the consular staff in Spain during the World Cup and to create liaison posts, followed by a series of meetings with the relevant Spanish authorities;

(iv) that a close look should be taken at the distribution of tickets and the plans of tour operators;

and (v) that liaison should be established with the Minister's opposite number in Spain.

The most innovative of these proposals, and arguably the most liable to be effective in terms of actually making contact with travelling fans, was the distribution to British spectators of what *The Daily Telegraph* described as a 'good behaviour guide to Spain'.[5] This 'strongly-worded list of do's and don'ts' was in large part drawn up by Stanley Ford, the British consul in Madrid. It later became the central feature of the 'Amigos' campaign, the brainchild of West Nally, a London consultancy and sports-promotion group, and produced by them in conjunction with the government and the Football Associations of England, Scotland and Northern Ireland.

Using the official mascots of the three home countries which had qualified for Spain,[6] together with that of the host nation, badges, stickers and pamphlets were produced in their thousands, carrying a logo which underlined co-operation and friendliness between British fans and their Spanish hosts. The Amigos pamphlets opened out to reveal a message from the captains of the British squads which stressed the distractions for players of 'aggro' on the terraces. This message was backed up, in the case of the English at least, by pleas from players on television and in the press for good behaviour from what *The Sun* described as the 'yob' element of English support.[7] Inside, too, was information on survival in Spain, ranging from the role of the fans as 'ambassadors' for Britain, to the use and abuse of inoculations. Under the heading 'Law', strong warnings were provided about the stiff sentences that were liable to face miscreants in Spain. On the back endpiece of the folding pamphlet one could also find the addresses and telephone numbers of all the British Consulates in Spain. Before turning to an assessment of the Amigos campaign, we shall briefly consider the controversy which surrounded the choice of the English World Cup mascot, 'Bulldog Bobby'.

In December 1981 the Football Associations of England, Scotland and Northern Ireland revealed to the public their official

World Cup mascots, the equivalents of Spain's 'Naranjito', a humanised, football-toting orange. Companies would pay to use these mascots on products ranging from T-shirts and drinks to souvenir mugs and key rings. The Irish chose a decidedly traditional, even old-fashioned, image of the football fan, 'Yer Man', who was clearly already *en route* for Spain, suitcase in hand, armed with a scarf and other favours, and bathed in innocent exuberance. To launch their campaign, the Scots produced an impudent-looking Highland schoolboy who rejoiced in the name 'Wee Sandy'. For their part, the English came up with the more strikingly belligerent figure of 'Bulldog Bobby', a barrel-chested, bare-toothed bull terrier sporting an England shirt and standing imperiously with one foot firmly controlling a football (see Figure 1). It was an image which was not universally acclaimed as one suitable for a country whose fans had, on more than one occasion, been likened by the more imaginative newsdesks and some politicians to 'wild animals'. For example, prior to the departure of the fans and team for Spain, a Conservative MP sought assurances in the House that the Spanish authorities realised what a 'very vicious and unpleasant animal is the British football hooligan'.[8]

David Miller in *The Daily Express* similarly argued that England's World Cup Mascot had 'the unfortunate appearance of one of England's more aggressive supporters . . . complete with bared teeth and beer belly. We have seen him all too often growling around the bars and railway stations of foreign capitals at one in the morning.'[9] Frank McGhee of *The Daily Mirror* also disapproved. The mascot, he argued, had already been 'heavily attacked, even by a Government Minister, for his belligerent, beer-bellied appearance as well as his unfortunate connection with the National Front – something the FA chose to ignore in their response to the criticism.'[10]

The connection with the National Front alluded to here lay in the name of one of the extreme right-wing organisation's newspapers, *Bulldog*. Although the FA undoubtedly had in mind the traditional symbolisation of the British nation through the bulldog and felt that they could not, as they had in 1966, choose the lion as the team's mascot once again, it was a choice that proved prophetic in view of the activities at the Finals of English youths vowing allegiance to groups from the far right.

In the face of what was fast becoming the widespread condem-

Figure 1   The controversial figure of Bulldog Bobby, England's World
Cup Mascot. Beer-bellied or barrel-chested?

nation of the bulldog image, the football authorities rallied to Bobby's defence. FA Chairman Millichip, for example, pointed out – and with justification – that the image of an animal in football strip could hardly be used to account for English fans who might be driven to acts of violence in Spain.[11] Indeed, the Amigos campaign had Bobby, arm around his Spanish equivalent, Naranjito, and grinning amiably while, in the foreground, English and Spanish hands were clasped in friendship.

Ted Croker, the Secretary of the FA had been at pains to indicate at the outset that the advertising and marketing campaign which had Bobby as its focal point, would lay great stress on 'dignity'. To this end, it was explained that the World Cup emblem would not be used to advertise cigarettes or spirits. His remarks seemed to take little account, however, of the fact that, for some time, Ron Greenwood, the England manager, and his squad had been committed to a sponsorship deal with a major brewer. 'Obviously', as *The Daily Express* commented in December, 'there is a moral superiority in being drunk on beer rather than whisky.'[12] In principle, of course, the use of a mascot or logo in a marketing exercise of this sort constitutes a financially attractive proposition which benefits the game as a whole. The Bulldog Bobby campaign was designed to bring in money for the grassroots of football to the tune of £750,000. It was also closely linked to the players' commercial pool. In retrospect, however, the choice of the bulldog logo did prove a little unfortunate although, judging by the number of 'Bobbies' in evidence on the bare arms and chests of English fans in Spain, it helped to keep a number of tattooists in business before the Finals! We wonder whether 'Wee Sandy' and 'Yer Man' were regarded as similarly suitable material for display by brawny Scots and Irishmen. We think probably not. The Spanish press, too, were quick to spot the links between the reputation of English fans and the aggressive, *macho* bulldog image. Fans in Spain were regularly photographed snarling up eager camera lenses and pointing to newly acquired illustrations of Bobby on their tanned features. (See Plate 19.)

There were the inevitable pirate off-shoots, too. The authorities soon found that the 'Bobby' image proved distressingly conducive to what they perceived as nihilistic adaptations. Among the most popular T-shirts worn by young English fans in Spain was one depicting a distorted 'Bobby' rampaging across the continent, bottle in hand and wearing 'bovver boots'. The shirt read, 'Official Hooligan – Spain '82'. Its message was clearly not consistent with extending the hand of friendship to the Spanish hosts.

Assessing the success or otherwise of the Amigos campaign is, of course, an extremely difficult task. One might suppose, for example, that, because levels of hooliganism in Spain did not, in the event, turn out to be as high as some prominent officials had feared, the campaign must have had at least some effect in curbing the enthusiasm of English visitors who had come in search of 'aggro'. At the same time, however, stickers, badges and pamphlets were not conspicuous among young English fans in Spain. This was especially the case among those fans who travelled to the Finals under their own steam. Furthermore, specific advice proffered by the pamphlet, such as the need to carry passports at all times whilst in Spain, was palpably ignored or just not seen. In any case, a match-day 'uniform' of shorts and sports shoes was simply not conducive to the carriage of identification documents. And what if you lost your passport? Who knew then what atrocities the Spanish police might inflict? In fact, information about the activities of the Spanish police did not typically come from Amigos but from personal experience or word of mouth.

Apart from its advice to those who fell ill, perhaps the most useful item in the pamphlet to fans in distress was the addresses and telephone numbers of the British Consulates in Bilbao and Madrid. Soon after the first batch of British supporters arrived, the Consulate in Bilbao was dealing with a flood of passport, ticket and money losses, as well as the usual 'misunderstandings' which occur abroad. They were dealing with a few, more serious incidents as well.

With the wheels of an extensive, government-backed anti-hooligan campaign set in motion towards the end of 1981, still some six months from the start of the Finals, attention turned to the problems inherent in moving an anticipated 20,000 fans, and in accommodating and controlling them once they were there. Three major sources of concern over and above those generally applicable in the context of a tournament of this sort were clearly apparent in the lead up to the Finals. These were, in the order in which they became significant sources of nervousness to the English football authorities:

(i) the activities of Sportsworld Travel;

(ii) the effects of the Falklands crisis on Anglo-Spanish relations and as a possible determinant of British withdrawal from the Finals;

and (iii) the attitude of the Spanish authorities towards English fans.

Let us briefly consider each of these issues. We shall look firstly at the part played by Sportsworld Travel in preparing for the exodus from England.

(i) The rise and decline of Sportsworld Travel

In 'normal' circumstances, ticket arrangements for international football tournaments or for particular matches within them are handled by the relevant Football Associations. The marketing of tickets for the 1982 World Cup Finals, however, took a decidedly 'abnormal' turn when the Spanish organising authority, Mundiespana '82, sold the exclusive rights to sell World Cup tickets in Britain to one travel company, Sportsworld Travel. Sportsworld's franchise was obtained in the spring of 1980 before any of the home countries had qualified for the Finals. Their coup took established British travel agents and the football authorities by surprise.

It was a Mr Geoffrey Phillips, a director of the travel company 'Continental Coach Tours' who, along with two other directors, formed the Sportsworld group in order to bid for the exclusive rights on offer from Mundiespana '82. The rights were eventually obtained for an initial investment of £500,000. 'The major operators weren't prepared to come in because they got their fingers burnt in Moscow', Mr Phillips was reported as saying in *The Observer* on 22 November 1981. He was, of course, referring to the shortfall of British interest in the Olympics following the Russian invasion of Afghanistan and the concern expressed by the British government about allowing a team to go to Moscow. Little did anyone realise at the time, in view of what was about to happen in the South Atlantic, how ironic Mr Phillip's statement was to turn out to be.

There were, from the start, widespread misgivings about Sportsworld's involvement in the World Cup travel and ticket arrangements for British fans. Firstly, the company was not a member of the Association of British Travel Agents, which meant that the usual financial safeguards afforded to the travelling public by ABTA membership were not applicable in this case. By November 1981, Sportsworld's application for ABTA membership had been considered twice but had yet to be accepted. Secondly, Sportsworld was a new company with no experience of running trips of this kind, a factor which perturbed the English FA and no doubt played a part in the decision of an established sports tour operator, David Dryer Sports, to announce in December that, despite Sportsworld's apparent ticket monopoly, they would go ahead with plans for tours to Spain.[13]

Thirdly and finally, Ted Croker, the FA Secretary, professed himself 'worried' by the prospect that Sportsworld's franchise for Spain would mean that it would be impossible to prevent potential hooligan fans from making the trip. His objections were, at first glance at least, a little puzzling. For one thing, FA involvement in ticket distribution in the past had seemed to have little effect. Its 'Travel Club', for example, did not prevent disturbances occurring in Luxembourg, Basle and Turin, although it does seem that members of the Travel Club were not involved in these disorders.[14] This apparent anomaly apart, Stephen Marnham, Sportsworld's General Manager, was keen to allay the FA's worst fears about hooligan fans who would be 'out of their (the FA's) control' as a result of the Sportsworld–Mundiespana deal. 'We are very concerned about the fans', he assured Daily Express readers in November. He continued:

> You can't control them 100%. What has been shown is that those involved with hooliganism are mainly youngsters. We do not accept bookings from large parties of young people and if they're under 21, they must have two adults with them and responsible for them.[15]

Quite where Mr Marnham was getting his data about football hooligans from was not made clear, but clearly, for Sportsworld, age was the critical factor.[16] Later, at a meeting between Sportsworld directors and the English, Scottish and Northern Irish Football Associations, another Sportsworld director, Michael Norris, agreed to let the English FA inspect his list of customers. Mr Norris explained:

> We do not want troublemakers going on our packages any

more than the FA or the Spanish authorities. If the FA tell us
that a certain person would not have got a ticket from them
because of previous hooliganism, we will refund his money
and cancel his trip.[17]

Although, to our knowledge, the FA declined to take up the
Sportsworld offer, the company's travel brochure, World Cup –
Spain '82, did, in a list of terms and conditions for the carriage of
fans to Spain, carry an 'unsuitability' clause. This decreed that
Sportsworld could, at their discretion and without giving reasons,
cancel bookings or decline to take a client any further whilst in
Spain should he or she prove to be an 'unsuitable person' to take
part in a tour/holiday.

If conditions such as these were a source of at least some comfort
to FA officials, then, on one level at least, it might have been
assumed that the cost of Sportsworld's package deals for Spain
would provide further reassurance. At first, trips were costed for
hotel accommodation, internal travel and match tickets. Later,
marginally less-expensive camping packages were added to the
array of deals on offer. With prices ranging from over £200 to
almost £2,000 per package, it was reasoned that the high cost
might dissuade potential miscreants from travelling with Sportsworld, and, with the availability of match tickets a potential
problem, perhaps deter them from travelling to Spain at all. The
Times later commented that the decision to link match tickets to
hotel accommodation was aimed at 'young British supporters
whose unfortunate behaviour abroad has driven organisers into
craftiness'.[18]

Whether they had been arrived at to combat hooliganism by
accident or design, the kinds of arrangements offered at the lower
end of the Sportsworld range did not find universal favour. In
February, for example, there were questions in the House for Neil
Macfarlane, the Minister for Sport, about what the Labour MP for
West Stirlingshire, Dennis Canavan, described as 'the questionable
standards of accommodation being prepared for the World Cup'.
Quoting the case of an advertisement in the Spurs programme
which proposed, in his words, 'herding fans into camps with four
to a tent at £275 each', Mr Canavan condemned these as the
arrangements of 'travel agent sharks'. He further asked the Minister if he thought that 'this kind of exploitation is conducive to

good crowd control and behaviour?' Mr Macfarlane, in reply, pledged that his officials would monitor the situation closely. For good measure, he added that fans travelling to Spain would be well advised to 'make sure they have accommodation and . . . tickets at the outset before they set off'.[19]

As far as meaningful control over travelling fans was concerned, however, the English FA – its cause for concern was greater than that of its Scottish and Irish counterparts – was in no doubt that the high cost of Sportsworld's package tours was, in fact, a double-edged sword. Past experience suggested that, despite Sportsworld's apparent UK monopoly of tickets, there would be large numbers of English fans travelling to Spain without having arranged either accommodation or tickets. This, after all, had been the main source of the FA's difficulties in the past, even when it had had a degree of direct control over ticket sales. Evidence strongly suggested that it is from within groups of spectators who travel casually to matches in this way that the most troublesome factions are liable to emerge. The key to this matter as far as the World Cup Finals were concerned lay in the Spanish Organising Committee's decisions about the precise nature of ticket distribution for matches, and the capacity of Sportsworld Travel and its equivalents in other qualifying countries to offload their costly tours on an increasingly discerning and football-satiated public. Let us briefly consider these two dimensions of the problem as they applied to the situation in England before the Finals.

In terms of the numbers of paying customers who attended, the 1980 European Championships in Italy had been a disaster. Visiting teams played each other in largely empty stadia, while local supporters scrambled for tickets wherever and whenever Italy were scheduled to compete. It was a situation which Raimondo Saporta, President of Mundiespana '82, was determined to avoid. As a result, the Spanish organising consortium decided that tickets for the 1982 World Cup Finals would be distributed in the following proportions:

65% to tourists, travel agents and foreign Football
  Associations;
25% to the Spanish Football Federation;
10% on open sale at World Cup venues.

In this way, and despite loud protests from local fans and Spanish clubs, it was hoped to maximise interest in games in which the home country would not be involved. It was the third category of ticket sources which most concerned FA officials in England. Secretary Croker predicted that, at least in part because of Sportsworld's monopoly of UK tickets, it would be almost impossible to stop hooligan fans from watching England contest their matches in Spain. 'Hordes of people will travel without tickets', he told *The Daily Express* in November. He also warned about possible trouble between rival fan groups because the system of ticket allocation used by Mundiespana did not lend itself to crowd segregation.[20]

Meanwhile, as the Finals neared, Sportsworld was experiencing problems of its own. In February, for example, there was a relax-ation of the company's ticket monopoly, and a consortium was formed with other companies to market match tickets through travel agencies. A 'special deal' on match tickets was negotiated with the Scottish FA's Travel Club in March, though it was stressed that travel bookings would still have to be made through Sports-world.[21] There were strong rumours that Sportsworld's packages were not selling well.

With the Finals less than four months away, *The Times* reported that under 4,000 British fans had signed up for accommodation-linked football holidays in Spain. The sale of such packages had hardly been more successful in other countries. Only 1,500 French supporters had made firm bookings, for example, while in Kuwait, with *per capita* incomes among the highest in the world, there were 5,000 confirmed bookings.[22] These figures have to be considered against the claim that, for the matches in Bilbao alone, Sportsworld had secured from Mundiespana an allocation of 10,000 tickets per game for English fans, with options on 6,000 more.

It would be difficult to argue that this shortfall in demand resulted from the lack of a 'hard-hitting' sales campaign. 'The Spanish wish for strict crowd control and sectoring by nationality in the stadia', was picked out in the Melia Travel/Sportsworld brochure as a major reason why the discerning fan would be well advised to book with the recently formed consortium. In the event, when, partly as a result of inadequate segregation, trouble did briefly flare up during the England–France match in San Mames, Sportsworld clients were far from clear of the trouble spots. As

Figure 2 The Iberian peninsula

Ted Croker had feared, many of them had been allotted tickets for the same terrace as French supporters.

The Melia-Sportsworld brochure also warned the would-be 'casual' traveller of a 'drastic shortage of accommodation' in and around Bilbao. Mundiespana, it was alleged, had reserved 'all the available hotel and hostales accommodation along the west coast to Santander and east as far as San Sebastian' (see Figure 2). 'It is already being made known in Spain', the brochure continued, 'that all the Bilbao matches are sell-outs'. Of course, this could hardly have been the case, since almost 5,000 tickets were earmarked for public sale a few days before the matches were due to start, and since at least the Czechs appeared certain to return a large proportion of their ticket allocation. These ticket reserves were soon to be supplemented by thousands of unsold tickets returned by the Sportsworld consortium prior to the competition's start. English fans who arrived late in Bilbao or who missed out on ticket sales at the gate at San Mames, reported that, before England's matches in the North, match tickets were freely on offer outside railway and coach stations with prices barely above face value. However, as the opening game with France approached, prices and tempers tended to rise.

Neither was accommodation in Bilbao and its surroundings a problem. It was both plentiful and cheap, even for fans who had simply come 'on spec'. Mundiespana had been obliged to make major cancellations of hotel and hostale bookings. In some parts of the Basque country, these were reported to be up to 100 per cent.[23]

In short, then, the Sportsworld/Mundiespana monopoly of tickets and accommodation in Bilbao and its environs, much publicised in the early months of 1982 had, by June, turned out to be little more than an expensive miscalculation. By the eve of the Finals, Mundiespana's prediction that 1,000,000 visitors would flood Spain for the soccer had been scaled down by 75 per cent. Of 200,000 packages for the first phase, it was thought that only 25,000 had been sold. Mundiespana was also awash with match tickets, 'trunkfuls' as one officials said. 'Mundiespana sales policy', concluded *The Financial Times* on 12 June, 'had been little short of disastrous'.

When numbers were at their highest (probably for the French match), there were, at most, some 10–12,000 English supporters in Spain. The Consul General in Bilbao's estimate was lower, more specifically that a constant 7,000 were present, with 1–2,000 short-term visitors for the game with France.[24] Whichever estimate one accepts, probably less than 30 per cent had travelled on Sports-world or similar packages. What had begun as an enterprise which might have restricted the numbers of 'casual' travellers, had, in the event, turned out to be the private traveller's best friend. Of the supporters who had travelled with Sportsworld that we met in Spain, few were satisfied with their arrangements. The reasons given were various, but the chief among them will become clear as our analysis unfolds. Suffice it to say for the moment that one of the most common conversations overheard in Spain during the Finals was one which went: 'How did you get here? Sportsworld? What a rip-off!', followed by nods of agreement all round.

The answer to the question why there was a shortfall of interest in the Sportsworld packages before the Finals is complex. The desire for greater freedom of choice, the threat of hooliganism, and certainly the high prices were probably all significant. However, another probable reason why bookings were low, particularly in the months of April, May and June, was the war that was raging in the South Atlantic. With all its Argentinian connections, Englishmen were not guaranteed to be the most popular figures in Spain over the summer. Let us now briefly attempt an assessment of the influence of the Falklands crisis on national sentiments and attitudes to the participation of British players and spectators in the World Cup prior to the Finals in Spain.

(ii) The Falklands factor

On 2 April 1982 Argentine military forces invaded the Falkland Islands, initiating a brief war in the South Atlantic between Britain and Argentina. As far as British involvement in the World Cup was concerned, there could hardly have been a more untimely development, above all because Argentina were about to compete as World Champions. Should the British play with the enemy while lives were being sacrificed in a distant war? From the beginning of April right up until the home countries' first matches in Spain, a heart-searching debate took place about British involvement in the Finals.[25]

From the outset, both the government and the football authorities remained adamant that the situation could not be properly assessed until the point of departure for Spain. Some English players were reported to be unhappy about the prospect of competing if Britain was still at war. This, despite the non-refundable fees paid to Sportsworld by fans and the financial outlay already undertaken by the Home Associations. The SFA, for example, was reported to have invested somewhere in the region of £500,000 in wages, fares and hotel deposits.[26] Moreover, withdrawal from the world's most prestigious football competition might have untold damaging effects on interest in the sport at a time when the number of paying customers was already in sharp decline. Ian Archer, the Scottish journalist, described any decision on the part of the Home Associations or the government to withdraw as one which could 'bankrupt the game both in a monetary sense and spiritually as well.'[27]

Less than a month before the Finals were due to commence, The Times was still asserting that: 'It is generally accepted that if Britain is at war, British teams will withdraw.'[28] By contrast, The Guardian saw an end to the uncertainty and speculation surrounding British involvement in the Finals in the Sport Minister's comment to the

House that: 'Many millions of people would find it very odd if we, as the non-aggressors, were not to take part in the World Cup.'[29] Later, Mr Macfarlane returned to a more guarded stance. 'I cannot answer hypothetical questions about what might happen over the next seven to ten days,' he said late in May. 'The British Government *at the moment* has no objection to British teams going to the World Cup Finals.'[30]

As they turned out, events confounded most conventional wisdoms on the subject. Britain *was* still at war with the Argentine when the Finals began. Argentina had *not* been expelled from the competition by FIFA as the British had demanded. What is more, the three British teams that had qualified *were* playing in Spain. Instead of vilifying British players for playing football in the same tournament as the enemy while British troops were dying in combat, the nation's involvement in Spain was hailed by the emerging consensus as a source of inspiration to British soldiers. Match results were relayed to the Falklands as a boost to forces' morale and a reminder of the links with home. England manager, Ron Greenwood, spoke emotionally about the connections between the team's 'mission' in Spain and that of the 'Task Force'.[31] And Margaret Thatcher pleaded in the House that fans travelling to Spain 'will be as good representatives of this country as our armed forces have been in the South Atlantic'.[32]

In this new climate of national unity on the issue, the prospects of actually meeting the Argentine on the football field in Spain were thrust firmly to the back of most people's minds. Of more immediate concern, to the authorities at least, was the effect the Falklands affair was liable to have on Anglo-Spanish relations throughout the tournament. Aston Villa fans had already shown their involvement in the Falklands conflict on two continental trips undertaken to watch their team before the Finals began. Moreover, in the first case at least, that of the European Cup semi-final match against Anderlecht, taunting by opposing fans over the Falklands had accompanied the outbreak of terrace disorder.[33] As a result, the affair seemed almost certain to provide dangerous fuel for heightened nationalistic fervour during the Finals with, as *The Daily Mail* put it, 'Spain aligned by blood, language and its school-room history books to the cause of Argentina.'[34]

The groundswell of anti-British sentiment over the Falklands was noticeable throughout most of Spain, the principal exception being the Basque regions of the north. There, opposition to the Spanish Government and a desire for an identity distinct from that of the rest of Spain, had many locals rooting firmly for the English. This proved early on the benefit of playing Phase One matches in the north, but it meant confusion and increased hostility when the teams and fans moved south to Madrid. Here, as in the rest of Spain, local feelings were clear. Indeed, at the opening ceremony of the Finals, shunned by British television because of the Argentinian involvement, the British flag and national anthem were roundly booed. At Argentina's opening match against Belgium, however, Spanish flags proclaimed, '*Malvinas son Argentinas*'. *The Guardian* noted – and not without some trepidation – that some locals 'appeared to want to make the tournament an extension, albeit a peaceful one, of the Falklands issue'.[35] There were traces of this, too, in the British press, with *The Sun*, for one, trading in inter-changeable front and back page headlines of 'Argies Smashed', one a reference to the Falklands, the other to the surprise defeat of Argentina by Belgium.[36]

The shadow of the Falklands also produced some remarkable reactions from English fans in Spain: the complete and respectful silence in San Mames for the Czech national anthem, for example, followed by the lusty delivery of 'God Save the Queen'. This moment stirred a 'purely personal feeling' in Ted Barrett, the British Consul General in Bilbao that, 'the Falklands crisis may have induced a feeling of respect for traditional values which militated against the more extreme manifestations of hooliganism'.[37] More usually, however, the *Malvinas* issue and, increasingly as the Finals progressed, the fate of Gibraltar, proved to be focal points of Anglo-Spanish antagonism, culminating in the well-publicised stabbing incidents in Madrid.

But we are now looking too far ahead. Before Madrid, English fans had a date with the people and, more significantly perhaps, the authorities in Bilbao and the north.

(iii) Policemen, policemen everywhere . . .

The draw for the World Cup Finals had been made in Madrid on the evening of Saturday 16 January amidst an air of confusion which bordered on farce. The draw had the appearance of being fated from the start, with the containers holding the names of the qualifiers wrongly drawn, then wrongly placed, and, finally, containers falling apart inside the wiremesh barrel that was used to give the draw at least an air of unpredictability.

Before the draw was made, six countries had already been seeded by FIFA amidst protests from the French and others. England, for example, a side which had barely scraped into the final stages, was allowed a privileged position in the draw because, so the official explanation went, they were past winners of the tournament. On this basis, West Germany, Argentina, Brazil and Italy were also seeded, along with the host nation, Spain. The grounds for the protests about the seeding of England lay in the fact that the other five seeded sides were fancied to do well, and, had countries been seeded on current form, they, in all probability, would have retained their privileged position. England, undoubtedly, would not. There followed the inevitable murmurs about 'politics' and a variety of factors extraneous to football. Seeding, for example, carried with it the advantage of playing all the First Phase matches at one centre, a prospect no doubt, of considerable interest to the Spanish authorities, faced as they were with the likely problem of controlling the excesses of English and perhaps of other fans. Was it coincidence, too, that the Scots ended up in the extreme south of the country, the opposite pole to the English who were based on the northern coast? And was it accidental that the English were allotted a city which claimed to be the most anglophile in Spain? *The Daily Mirror*, for one, was no believer in coincidences: 'The reasons why the organisers want the England team penned into one place is that they would sooner have our murderously militant fans penned with them instead of wandering all over Spain.'[38]

In short, it seemed an ironic possibility that the reputation of English supporters which had plagued the authorities for so long might now have played a part in presenting the England team with the advantage of a privileged position in the draw of the sport's most prestigious tournament. It was a possibility that few figures in the game wanted to dwell upon.

It was the coastal city of Bilbao in the heart of Spain's Basque region that was faced with the task of staging England's Phase One matches. Described rather uncharitably by one British TV pundit as 'the Middlesborough of Spain', this heavily industrialised seaport has few of the attractions of a holiday resort. Its claim to be the most anglophile city in Spain received confirmation when it was reported that many local residents were delighted when they heard in January that the England team and their followers would be stationed in the north for the first ten days of the tournament. Local lore even now is that English coalminers and sailors working in and around Bilbao were responsible for the introduction of the game to the Basque country – a fact which purportedly accounts for the English-sounding name of the local football club, 'Athletic Bilbao'.[39]

The Bilbaons' almost unqualified welcome for the English in the early months of 1982 served to generate the uneasy suspicion, at least among English journalists and government officials, that the Basques held an image of the English football fan that was a great deal more flattering than the one held by the authorities in this country and recently reinforced by the disorders in Luxembourg, Basle and Turin. An *Observer* report in May, for example, noted that recent discussions between a Foreign Office official, local organisers, World Cup officials and senior Bilbao policemen, had not done much to allay English fears that the Basques had little idea of what to expect from the forthcoming English invasion.[40] Ted Barrett, the British Consul General, was afraid that:

> The people here don't know what's going to hit them. They will be horrified to see drunken England supporters stripped to the waist and cavorting around town. Heaven knows what they will think of us when it is all over.[41]

There was danger, too, as the Finals approached, that some sections of the British press might be stoking the fires of confrontation in English bellies even before the departure for Spain. In June, both *The Daily Mail* and *The Daily Telegraph* wrote in derision of a report in an unnamed British paper which had labelled Bilbao a 'City of Hate' following a minor incident in a bar. 'Mercifully', commented Ian Wooldridge from Bilbao, 'no local newspaper has chosen to reprint the words which cruelly libel a city whose sympathies have been strongly pro-British since trade links were established in 1890.'[42]

At first it was the Bilbao police who were least impressed by arguments about the need for 'special measures' to cope with the English fans. This position was slightly modified after a Spanish official had attended the League match between Tottenham Hotspur and Leeds United in January. He is reported to have returned to Spain 'shocked' by what he had seen and to have been determined to 'rethink' Spanish plans for crowd control in Bilbao.[43] Of greater concern to Spanish authorities in the north, however, were the prospects of politically motivated attacks and demonstrations during the English stay in Bilbao by ETA, the Basque separatist movement.

Wherever they are held, major international sporting events are nowadays always political targets for extremist groups who have an eye to obtaining world-wide publicity for their cause. Host nations, keen to impress that *their* security arrangements are watertight against the threat of violent intrusions, have tended to adopt policies of 'saturation policing' at such events, both to ensure the safety of their guests and to reassure and retain the good favour of their sporting partners. All such efforts have, perforce, increased since the deaths in Munich in 1972 of Israeli Olympic competitors at the hands of Arab activists.[44]

In Spain in the summer of 1982, the ever-present threat of ETA demonstrations and the potential for spectator disorder, especially, it was felt, by English fans, made security perhaps an even greater problem for the authorities than ever before. Accordingly, it was decided that a special force of 31,500 security men was to be on duty during the Finals in an operation codenamed 'Orange'. Most of the force were to be in civilian dress so that, according to the Spanish authorities, 'people will not have the feeling that they are being watched'.[45] Police sources in Madrid confirmed that the force would include 22,000 policemen, 6,000 paramilitary civil guards and 3,500 inspectors. These personnel were to be equipped with guns, and also with helicopters and radios so that they could reach the scene of any 'emergency' in minutes.

In recent years, and despite extensive security precautions, ETA had chosen to attack the televised Pamplona Festival in order to draw attention to its cause. What better stage, then, than the World Cup Finals – guaranteed a huge, worldwide audience – to state the Basque case and the commitment of the region to independence? In January, *The Daily Star* reported on a plan, allegedly formulated by ETA, which had the England football squad as 'prime targets' of terrorist attacks during the Finals. Commenting on the extent of the law and order problem in Spain, a Bilbao police spokesman went so far as to describe the region as 'Spain's Ulster'.[46] More generally, however, ETA had given assurances that the Finals were *not* in danger of disruption and that they wanted the Basque people to enjoy them without interruption. The authorities remained sceptical, reasoning that the consequent publicity afforded to what the police called 'ETA manifestations' in Bilbao would prove irresistible to the separatists.[47] They pledged massive protection for the England squad during their stay in the north, and extreme vigilance throughout the Finals.

It was a combination of their experience in the face of the constant threat of separatist attacks and the still strong traces in the Spanish state's 'law and order' forces of an only recently relinquished forty years of fascist rule, which suggested that the police in the country hosting the 1982 World Cup Finals were more than ready for the problems a few violent football fans might pose. In Scotland some well-informed investigative journalism ensured that many of the Scots fans travelling to Spain would be aware of the uncompromising practices likely to be adopted by the various Spanish police forces.[48] For the English, however, some practical demonstrations were provided before the summer departure.

In March, for example, an England XI were due to play Athletic Bilbao as part of a pre-tournament public relations exercise. Large numbers of Spanish police, described by *The Daily Star* as 'commandos', were put on the alert for this 'World Cup Warmup Operation', and a police spokesman warned English fans that, 'those who come to make trouble will wish they had never left England. We will have no mercy on those who bring violence.'[49]

Just over a month later, a British Consulate official described the use of 600 police to contain a handful of Tottenham supporters, in Barcelona for a European Cup Winners' Cup match, as 'overkill'. Complaints had been made to the Consulate following a baton charge on 20 Tottenham fans who were reported to have been 'singing and chanting' in a main square. Brian Glanville of *The Sunday Times* reported that Spurs fans were 'clobbered with truncheons simply, it seemed, for crossing the street'.[50] The Spanish police were unrepentant, denying that they had been unduly harsh with fans. A police spokesman noted 'that English fans had a reputation for violence.' More to the point, however, it was reported that 'the Barcelona authorities said the police operation was a trial run for the World Cup this summer.'[51]

It was made clear from the outset, then, that English fans would be given an uncompromising and, to them, unfamiliar welcome by the *Guardia Civil* and the *Policia Nacional.* Shortly before the Finals, and under the headline, 'Soccercop '82', *The Sunday Mirror* provided fearsome pictorial evidence of the Spanish approach, with police armed with rubber bullet guns, gas canister launchers, and electric clubs (see Plate 2). Described by *The Daily Mail* as 'the most riot-hardened police in Europe', the *Policia Nacional* made it clear that they did not favour the more relaxed and less threatening style of crowd control usually practised at football matches in England.[52] Instead, equipped with sophisticated and potentially lethal anti-riot weaponry, the Spanish forces were prepared to meet disturbances with an uncomplicated resort to their own brand of intimidation. As Trevor Grove warned readers of *The Observer*: 'Over-reaction is the authorities' automatic response.'[53] The Secretary General of Police in Bilbao made the Spanish position clear:

Now it has been spelled out to us how much of a problem your hooligans can be, we have alerted Madrid with regard to reinforcements. It will be up to me to deploy those forces throughout our city, from the stadium to the airport and the docks. In the hotels and restaurants on the streets.

It is not our policy to use our guns except in extreme circumstances. We prefer to use methods of rubber bullets, water cannon, tear gas, the baton and swift arrest.[54]

Penalties for fans convicted of offences against Spanish law would be severe, too. Drunkenness, for example, not unknown among English supporters, would mean jail until freed by the court, while 'disrespect' for the Spanish flag or any national anthem could lead to a jail sentence or at least a heavy fine. Damage to property, too, promised a stay in jail until a fine was paid or suitable reparations made. Penalties for assault were to be severe as well and linked to the seriousness of the injuries inflicted. For example, an assault victim whose injuries required 30 days' hospital treatment could mean a jail sentence of up to 12 years for his or her attacker. Special mention was reserved in the British press for the so-called 'black hole of Bilbao', an 8 ft by 6 ft steel cage located beneath the San Mames stadium and designed to hold 80 'vicious' hooligan fans.[55] One thing was certain, namely that, as *The Sunday Post* had put it in March: '. . . anyone arrested for causing trouble in Spain can forget about seeing the rest of the World Cup.'[56]

Chapter Two

ENGLISH FANS IN NORTHERN SPAIN

Travelling to Spain

There was uncertainty about the participation of England and the other British teams in the 1982 World Cup Finals right up to the eleventh hour. Since our brief was to study only the behaviour of English fans in Spain and not to examine crowd behaviour in that context generally, this meant there was also uncertainty about this aspect of our research.[1]

About three weeks before the tournament was due to begin, even though the Falklands war was still in progress and the participation of England in the Finals remained in doubt, we decided that a provisional booking could be delayed no longer. A place on a Sportsworld campsite was reserved by means of a £100 deposit, the balance of £235 to be paid before departure. This was the cheapest Sportsworld holiday on offer. The price included coach travel to and from Spain, tickets for England's matches in Bilbao, and camping accommodation for eleven nights. A campsite booking was chosen because we felt a campsite would provide an ideal location at which to mix with English fans travelling at the lower end of the organised tour price range. It would also provide a useful base from which to make contact with fans who had travelled to Spain by other means.

About ten days after the £100 deposit had been despatched to the Melia/Sportsworld office, a telephone call was received requesting payment of the balance. This was sent by the next post. We then waited. By Thursday 10 June, we had still received no word from Sportsworld. The departure for Spain was on Monday 14th, so we decided to telephone. Calls to London proved abortive for most of the day. The person dealing with the matter was said to be *inter alia*, 'out to lunch', 'not here at the moment', 'just gone off to . . .', etc., etc. Finally, at 4.30 p.m., the excuses ran out. A voice at the other end said we had been 'very lucky'. Anyone told this by a travel agent at such a stage suspects there must have been a botch-up. There had, a complication in the campsite booking arrangements. 'Is there any particular reason why you have made a campsite booking', we were asked. 'Well actually, yes,' we replied. 'We are planning to do some discreet research on English fans.' 'Oh!', came the reply, followed by hurried consultations with seniors off the phone. 'Well,' the voice returned, 'at this late stage we're prepared to offer you a place on a flight to Spain on Tuesday, with a booking in a one star hotel at no extra cost!' We were unimpressed. 'Is there no chance, then, of a campsite booking?' 'No, I'm afraid not. This is a much better holiday, over £200 more expensive than your original one.' We took it. We were promised tickets and departure information the next morning. In fact, they arrived by registered post on Monday morning, a day before we were due to set off.

Although this development meant potential problems for the research at an early stage, we soon found we were among Sportsworld's luckier clients. On the flight to Spain, we met a number of customers whose experiences had been similar. *All* had been forced to contact Sportsworld rather than the other way round. In one case, Sportsworld had even claimed that a couple's cheque had bounced and that their holiday was null and void. This was despite the fact that Sportsworld had cashed the cheque some months before. In another, a teenage fan from Manchester had been forced to travel to the Sportsworld offices in London to pick up his flight tickets. 'Tel', an 18-year-old pipelayer from Blackburn and a Leeds United fan, had received his tickets only on the morning of the departure. None of these were late bookings. In each case, moreover, the Sportsworld error resulted in the fans having to pay an extra £85–£100 towards the cost of the more expensive holiday none of them had booked for. 'Tel' had had to borrow the cash from his grandma. It seems that our telephone manner and mention of 'research' resulted in the decision to offer the more expensive holiday at no extra cost. Less-firm and less-influential customers were pressured into covering at least part of the cost themselves. This was the first of a number of Sportsworld/Mundiespana 'mistakes' which had their victims seething. As a result, a favourite pre-match song *en route* to Bilbao for the First Phase matches was, 'We hate Sportsworld, and we hate Sportsworld! We are the Sportsworld haters.'

Although a blow to our earlier research plans, the new arrangements were not without their advantages. For a start, note-taking would be easier in an hotel. Contact could still be made with campsite users and 'casual' travellers along the northern coast. The village of Cestona, where we were now due to spend the first eleven nights, was located between Bilbao and the main campsites at San Sebastian. It was also within striking distance of Zarauz, another important camping base for English fans. (See Figure 2.) In addition, the new arrangements provided a useful opportunity which we had not anticipated at the outset. Some fans at Cestona had paid almost £1,000 to stay in Spain for the entire tournament. Thus, in addition to examining the activities of fans who had travelled to Spain on a shoestring, we would now be in a position to speak with some authority about the kinds of people who were willing and able to pay between £450 and £1,000 for the privilege of watching England's progress in Spain. As we shall show, some of them were rather different from what one might initially have expected.

On the morning of the departure of the Sportsworld flights to Spain, news in the English press was of a situation already 'hotting up' in the country hosting the Finals. In the north, West Ham and Chelsea fans were reported to have joined forces to fight French fans. The latter were accused of buying batches of tickets for the England–France match, due to be played next day, and then selling them to ticket touts. Police wielding electric batons had moved in to break up the fighting.[2] On the same day, it was reported that, with touts selling French tickets to English fans, segregation plans for the match appeared to be in disarray.[3] Meanwhile, a few miles up the coast in Pasajes, a paramilitary police sentry had been shot dead. It was the nineteenth politically motivated killing of the year in the Basque region. It bore all the hallmarks of an ETA attack and increased police fears about World Cup security.

In the south, too, the authorities scarcely had cause to relax.

Two coaches which had brought fans from Edinburgh for the Finals were destroyed by fire in the Mediterranean resort of Torremolinos, near Malaga, where the Scottish team were due to play their first World Cup match. The Spanish right-wing organisations, 'General Belgrano' and 'Gibraltar Espanol', were suspected of sabotage. Both were reported to be fiercely 'pro-Argentina'.[4]

At Gatwick on the night of 15 June, the airport's temporary TV room was jammed with English fans bedecked in hats, scarves and flags, willing New Zealand on to defeat Scotland. A few 'celebrities' were in their midst. Two lads in their late teens from Leigh had booked for Spain with a travel firm which had then 'gone bust'. At the last minute, they had re-booked with Sportsworld. Photographers had captured their plight for the local papers but unsurprisingly they had done nothing towards off-setting the cost of their second package, for which each had gone heavily into debt.

On the flight to Bilbao, the first-time flyers fidgeted endlessly with their ears, while the veterans tucked into the food and duty-frees. A Barclaycard investigator, a fanatical Burnley fan in his late twenties was replete with stories about how he had 'helped home' various Burnley FC personnel after 'heavy' nights on the town. He also told of an occasion when a seat in the directors' box at Blackburn had saved him from the excesses of Chelsea fans. To see Burnley's arch-rivals under siege in this way evidently gave him satisfaction.

Towards the rear of the plane, some Queens' Park Rangers supporters, West Londoners mostly in their teens, were working their way through duty-free bottles of vodka and boasting to the rest about the club's recent Wembley appearance. A larger, older, Newcastle United fan, known to his mates as 'Big Geordie Stan', reminded them of the score. Stan was unemployed and had come out 'on his redundancy' for the Finals. He seemed generally unimpressed with 'loudmouths' from south of the Watford Gap, especially when they were well on their way to being drunk.

On their arrival at Bilbao airport, somewhere close to 2.30 a.m. Spanish time, the planeload were met by a group of unsmiling, heavily armed policemen. This was the fans' first glimpse of the brown uniform, heavy army boots, dark glasses (even at night), firearms and truncheons which were the hallmark of officers of the Policia Nacional. Their mode of dress gave them a distinct military air. To complete their general aura of *macho* aggressiveness, some had cigarettes drooping limply from their mouths.

Papers were examined in stern silence at passport control. The young QPR fans, by now quite drunk and hauling half-empty vodka bottles behind them, were detained for 'questioning'. They had stopped singing. In the reception lounge, passengers who had made it through the checking area were met by nervous Mundiespana couriers in their garish turquoise uniforms. Fans were required to form themselves into groups by hotel or hostale. However, because of their poor English, some of the couriers had difficulty conveying this information to their charges.

The coach travelling to the hotel for which we had booked, we were told, would cater for two other hotels as well. Each group was to be dropped off in turn. A drive of at most half an hour was anticipated. The courier said that the first stop would be at the Hotel Arteche in under two hours. What is more, the coach was actually moving *away* from Bilbao. Two London cabbies, perhaps in their early forties, almost came to blows in the first hours of their 'holiday of a lifetime'. They had brought their wives and two young children with them – virtually the only children we saw with British fans until some Northern Ireland supporters were encountered in Madrid – and were worrying at this coach journey away from where all 'the action' was to be. While one complained, the other warned that he was liable to 'bollocks the whole holiday' if he continued to moan. Their wives remained silent.

Mention was made earlier of 'Tel' (Terry), an 18-year-old pipe-layer from Blackburn who supported Leeds United. He had missed only two Leeds games, home and away, during the 1981/82 season (one of their poorest), and this was his first trip abroad. He wore his hair short, but not in 'skinhead' style, and sported combat trousers and a Union Jack T-shirt. He had been at West Bromwich when Leeds fans had rioted there in March. 'You can't blame the fans', he reasoned, 'for liking Leeds so much.' 'Tel' had tried to smuggle two older lads on to the coach. They had booked a Sportsworld flight without accommodation, and were now left stranded at the airport with the Policia Nacional for company. 'Tel' agreed that he could have them 'dossing' on his floor for the night 'till they got themselves sorted out', but this was of academic interest now. The courier had nabbed them.

After just under two hours, with the clock now showing close to 4.30 a.m., the group arrived in Cestona at the Hotel Arteche. Five minutes hard banging on the door and the owner was up, signing in eight bleary-eyed new guests. In just over 12 hours time, England and France were due to kick off in the San Mames stadium.

Later, it was learned that some other journeys to Spain had been rather more eventful. A number of fans independently retold the tale of the drunken Spurs fan who had 'gone overboard' from the ferry on the Southampton–Santander crossing. A small boat was sent back to pick him up. There were stories, too, of misbehaviour by English fans travelling across France by rail. French police had already intervened on a number of occasions, it seems, before a Manchester United fan, the worse for drink, was reported to have climbed on to the roof of a slow-moving train before being arrested.

The English fans at Cestona

Cestona, a village of 4,500 inhabitants situated in the Urola valley 10 kilometres from the Cantabrian coast, was an unusual place to find 60 energetic English football fans. (The group found, when they awoke, that fellow supporters had arrived before them.) Perhaps the qualities of the village, with its quiet, sleepy, traditional atmosphere, would have been appreciated more by a maturer tourist group with a 'better' balance between the sexes and different age groups. It cut little ice, however, with young Arsenal, Chelsea and Nottingham Forest fans in search of excitement between World Cup matches. Frank, a 24-year-old Nottingham miner, sent a post-card to his mates at home after a few days. It read: 'Weather OK, food crap, nothing to fucking do!' The Sportsworld and Mundiespana organisations can be excused, perhaps, for supposing that their more expensive packages for English fans might have attracted an older, more 'up-market' clientele, perhaps with a large number of male-female couples. In fact, of the 60 or so guests at the Hotel Arteche, there were just two couples, both pairs in their early twenties. Impressionistic evidence suggests that this proportion of female spectators was unrepresentative, and that female fans probably constituted less than 2 per cent of the total English support in Bilbao. In Madrid, indeed, there were fewer female English supporters still.

Despite the high cost of this Sportsworld package, it was not limited to older people or persons from the upper reaches of the social scale. It was possible to gain occupational data from observation of and conversations with forty-five of the Cestona party. Accurate information on the ages of some of its members was also obtained. In other cases, a well-informed guess was possible on the latter score. These data are reported in Tables 1, 2 and 3. Table 1 lists the occupations of the Cestona group. Table 2 groups them by social class using the Registrar General's Classification of Occupations.[5] Table 3 reports their ages. As can be seen, our Cestona 'sample' was skewed heavily towards classes III, IV and V, with class V providing the single largest number. Moreover, the overwhelming majority were under 30, and most fell into the 21–25 age group.

Table 1   *The occupations of English fans in Cestona*

apprentice pipelayer	postman
schoolteacher (overseas)	engineer
fruit and vegetable roundsman	apprentice turner and fitter
printer	assistant newspaper photographer
7 labourers	clerk (DHSS)
video shop proprietor	quality control clerk (United Biscuits)
3 army personnel	2 apprentice weavers
(one corporal, two privates)	miner
2 air force personnel	3 insurance clerks
(trainee helicopter pilots)	2 students
hotel proprietor	apprentice engineer
used car salesman	director of a small business
2 galley workers	railway line worker
(cross channel ferries)	housewife
croupier	2 unemployed (one female. Previous
computer operator	occupations not known)
apprentice butcher	bank clerk

It must be stressed that these figures are not representative of the overall social class and age-group distributions of the English fans who attended the World Cup Finals. Indeed, observation of English fans not based in Cestona suggested that the average age of the fans who travelled to Spain was younger. The Spanish newspapers and authorities concurred with this impression. They depicted the majority of English fans as between 18 and 20 years of age. Like their Cestona counterparts, moreover, the majority of

Table 2 *Social class membership of the England fans in Cestona*

Class	Number	
I	0	
II	5	13 non-manual
III (non-manual)	8	
III (manual)	9	
IV	3	23 manual
V	11	
Total	36*	

* Total excludes the 2 unemployed persons, the 2 students and the army and air force personnel.

Table 3 *The ages of England fans in Cestona*

Age	Number
16–20	10
21–25	16
26–30	14
31–35	2
36–40	0
over 40	3
Total	45

English fans based elsewhere whom we met were engaged in occupations which, measured by the Registrar General's classifications, stand at or near the bottom of the social scale. We shall return to these issues later.

We noted earlier that a small number of the Cestona group had originally booked Sportsworld's cheaper, camping packages. Three persons whose occupations are listed in Table 1 – the apprentice pipelayer, the apprentice engineer, and the housewife – come into this category. A further seven had travelled to Spain using their own transport and had paid £275 for the package. These were the three army personnel, the used car salesman, the hotel proprietor, and the two galley workers. The remaining thirty-five fans, including all the unskilled manual workers, had each paid a minimum of £455. Five of this group – the croupier, the DHSS clerk, the computer operator, and the two students – had paid almost £1,000 each to stay for the whole tournament. The Cestona group provides an occupational mix which might not have been expected on a package of this price and type. For some, even those with a fairly high level of readily disposable income, saving for the trip had been painful. 'Mick', a massive labourer in his late teens from North London and an Arsenal supporter, still lived with his parents. He had saved since February for the trip and in no week since then had he drunk more than four pints of beer. 'Tel' the apprentice pipelayer was earning £46 a week before tax, and he related how he had started saving as soon as England qualified. In many other cases, the stories were the same. Later, in Bilbao and Madrid, we were to learn the complex art of really doing the World Cup Finals on the cheap.

The point we are trying to make is that, even at this higher end of the World Cup holiday price range, one could still find 'hard' lads engaged in manual occupations who showed a keen interest in 'trouble' at matches at home and abroad. They were anxious to maintain the reputations of their respective 'home ends', and that of England's travelling support. To take an example, 'Kel', one of the Arsenal lads on the trip, was a builder's labourer. In addition to being an avid supporter of the Highbury club, he was a fan of Alan Minter, the London middleweight boxer. The shows of nationalism at Minter fights, he said, reminded him of England matches abroad. Kel had been an amateur fighter himself and, throughout his time in Spain, he wore his boxing shorts and boots. He was a veteran of Turin and Basle where he thought the England fans had 'given a good account of themselves'. His holidays abroad consisted entirely of football trips. He had been to Winterslag in Belgium to see Arsenal play and had spent a night in a Belgian jail for fighting with local youths. For Kel, and for some of the other Cestona-based England fans, 'trouble' at matches abroad was something which added spice to the trips. One evening in a Cestona bar, he said:

'What makes me laugh is when the missus [his girlfriend] says, "You must be football mad, you, going all over the place to watch the Arsenal and England." But they don't understand, do they? It's not just the football, is it? It's all the other. The boozing and the fighting and the good laughs you have when you're away. They don't know anything about all that. They just think it's the football.'

Most of the Cestona-based England fans were, unsurprisingly, avid football supporters and followed the fortunes of their clubs on a regular basis. For some, however, this was impossible. The servicemen and the Canadian students, for example, found it difficult for obvious reasons to attend the matches of their favourite English clubs. There was also in Cestona a preponderance of fans from the London area and the south of England. This is in keeping with impressionistic evidence from Bilbao and Madrid that it is primarily southern fans who provide the core of England's travelling support. Fans from the provinces arrived in Spain in small groups and were more keen to advertise their attendance at matches by a flag – the more obscure or unfashionable the location or the team, the more indispensable and larger the flags seemed to become. Tel, for example, arrived with a huge 'Hello Blackburn' sheet, much to the amusement of the more experienced, southern contingent.

Explaining the fact that England's support is preponderantly from the south is a complex matter. In the first place, there are simple geographical considerations to take into account, as well as the relative affluence of the south east compared with the more northerly locations. A lack of Midlands players in the England squad might account for the apparently marked absence of large groups of fans from the Birmingham area. However, the same argument could not be applied, for example, to the Manchester region. The fact that all England's home games are played at Wembley might lessen provincial support for the national team, as might also the threat posed by some London 'fighting crews' to fans from the provinces. Finally, with the notable exception of Liverpool and Manchester United fans, supporters of the London teams simply have longer traditions of continental travel and thus more experience of manoeuvres on the continent. Some of these reasons might help to account for the presence in Bilbao of large numbers of West Ham and Chelsea followers although the last-named club had spent some time out of Europe in recent years. However, there also seemed to be a disproportionately large number of Portsmouth fans there, a fact which might not be unconnected with the location of the sailing points from England to Santander in northern Spain.

Again on an impressionistic level, there seemed to be fewer supporters of the major north London clubs present in Spain. In fact, Mick and Kel, our two Arsenal fans in Cestona, claimed they had travelled to Spain with Sportsworld because of the lack of interest among 'Tick-tock' (Clock End) regulars in the trip. They suggested that one of the reasons for this was the 'aggravation' aimed at Arsenal fans by West Ham and Chelsea supporters who were members of, or sympathisers with, the National Front. The north London club had recently introduced a couple of black players into its first team. In addition, because of the real or alleged Jewish connections of their clubs, Arsenal fans and, to a greater extent, the followers of Spurs, are simply 'yids' to some members of the goal-end factions at Chelsea and West Ham. 'You get a lot of (National) Front supporters at England matches,' Mick commented early in the holiday. The Cestona-based Chelsea fans, clearly proud both of the large Chelsea following for the national side abroad and of their National Front connections, nodded their agreement. Two of their number were, in fact, paid-up members of the right-wing organisation.

Table 4 provides a rough guide to the regional origins of the English fans in Cestona:

Table 4   *Regional origins of the English fans in Cestona*

Region	Number
North east	1
North	13
Midlands	4
West Country	3
London and the south east	20
Total	41*

* This figure excludes the two Canadians, a South African and one female fan who defied our best efforts to gain clues about her regional origins.

To sum up our demographic data about the Cestona-based English fans: they were overwhelmingly male; primarily aged between 21 and 30 with a large smattering of younger fans; mainly engaged in manual occupations; and about half of them came from the London area.

Let us now move on to a brief discussion of our findings about crowd control and crowd behaviour at England's matches in Bilbao. In many ways, it was England's match against France which proved to be the most eventful and interesting as far as crowd contingencies were concerned. As a result, our observations will often centre on that game.

Crowd control and crowd behaviour at England's matches in Bilbao

English fans on the organised trips to Spain were located at hotels, hostales and campsites right along the Cantabrian coast. On match-days, they were ferried into Bilbao by coach. This, presumably, was a satisfactory arrangement for the Spanish police, who already had the task of coping with the early morning influx of other English fans into Bilbao, some in search of tickets, most in search of cheap bars with an English atmosphere.

For the Cestona group, the arrangement was fairly simple. We were scheduled to leave for Bilbao on match-days at around 2.15 p.m. – there was almost universal dismay at this late departure time – and to arrive in Bilbao around 3.45 thus leaving about 1½ hours to soak up the atmosphere and, of course, some of the local brews. Not that the late start from Cestona interrupted pre-match preparations. An 'English' bar had already been established in the village and, for some, pre-match drinking began at 10 a.m., continued through lunch with beers and wine, to be completed on the coach to the game with more wine and the occasional resort to neat gin – a snip in the local supermarket at less than £2 a bottle. For later matches, lunch was omitted altogether in favour of an extended session in the Cayote bar. Judging from pre-match appearances in Bilbao, the majority of England fans in Spain followed roughly the same kinds of preparation for matches. Throughout our stay in Spain, the alcohol-doused Englishman was one of the images most commonly favoured by the Spanish press to characterise England supporters. Admittedly, subjects were not difficult to find.

Most days in Spain – at least before the excesses of the local

police were fully discovered – English fans felt undressed without
an England favour – a hat, a T-shirt, an England football shirt,
etc. Match-days, however, were occasions for dressing up *par
excellence*. Flags, hats, home-made favours, bugles, scarves, shirts,
even trousers, carried the England colours or a Union Jack. The
Cross of St George on its own was less common as part of a match-
day outfit.

On the coach to Bilbao, 'the lads' – the groups of younger fans,
largely from the south, some of whom had already had the benefit
of an extra afternoon to get to know each other – monopolised
the prized seats at the rear. Bottles of red wine passed freely among
them. On the trip to Bilbao for the match against France, Stevie,
one of the British Army privates who was serving in Berlin, was
in a particularly bad way and had to spend the whole of the
following day in bed. Others were not far behind him. Older fans
who stationed themselves at the front of the coach tended to be
more reserved, inviting derision from those at the back. Songs and
chants were almost continuous during the journey to Bilbao for
the French game, though they tended to wane as the tournament
wore on. They fell into two main categories: those which rallied
support for the England team and those in support of the National
Front.

In the first category, the most frequent were songs made popular
by the England players, such as 'Fly the Flag' and 'This Time', ably
supported by versions of, 'We're on the March with Greenwood's
Army'. In category two, the basic themes were general statements
about Britain's racial mix and particular comments about the racial
and ethnic characteristics of individual teams and players. Here,
the most popular songs and chants were devoted to the forced
repatriation of British citizens of 'New Commonwealth' origin,
e.g., 'There ain't no black in the Union Jack, send the bastards
back', and, 'If you're white, you're alright. If you're black, send
'em back', through to, 'You're just a Scottish Jew, Archibald,
Archibald', (a reference to the fact that one of Scotland's World
Cup squad played for Tottenham, a club maligned by the Front
for its alleged Jewish connections), and 'You're just a bunch of
yids, Arsenal, Arsenal', etc.

The impetus for these racial taunts was twofold. The Chelsea
fans had transported their local prejudices to the international
setting. In fact, at least two of the Chelsea fans in Cestona were

members of the Croydon branch of the National Front which, they claimed, catered for a lot of Chelsea and England support, and was the hub of much of the terrace disorder which followed England across Europe. They expressed themselves proud that Chelsea were the only 'all-white' team left in London. Some even believed that a clause had been written into manager John Neal's contract, prohibiting him from signing black players. The signing of 'coons' argued 'Butley', one of the Chelsea lads, would alienate a large proportion of the Chelsea 'faithful'.[6]

The Chelsea lads were backed up in their commitment to National Front slogans by the presence of the chairman of the NF branch of a northern seaside town. In his mid-thirties and describing himself as 'involved in selling cars – business like that', 'F', as he was known to the group, had made the trip with a friend, a hotel proprietor from the same resort. His hotel was used to 'entertain' prominent Front members during weekend retreats in the north to discuss NF strategies, the planning of marches, etc. 'F' was vociferous in his support of the NF and the degradation, in particular, of blacks. 'NF – White Power' stickers were soon in evidence on arms and foreheads, and later, all around the Cestona hotel. 'F' and his companion, Fran, had brought two 'official' NF Union Jacks to Spain. Their distinctiveness, they explained, lay in the fact that each flagpole had a metal point at the end, used to attack opponents during marches and demonstrations. Needless to say, both flags were confiscated by the Spanish police as the Front contingent was entering the San Mames stadium for the game with the French.

Many young fans, not yet committed to the cause of the Front, joined in the racist chanting 'for a laugh'. For others, the meeting with Front members resulted in recruitment. Stevie, for example, promised to enrol as a member and was already making plans for some Berlin-based friends to come to England when a large march was in the offing. There was particular excitement for the Front members here because Stevie promised to return with 'real Nazis', i.e. Germans who sympathised with Hitler's National Socialism and commitment to the 'final solution'. The most repeated song on the trip to Bilbao, in fact, was a revamped version of the official Spurs Wembley song. The new version expressed the following sentiments:

Spurs are on the way to Auschwitz.
Hitler's gonna gas 'em again.
You can't stop 'em,
The yids from Tottenham,
The yids from White Hart Lane.

We shall return later to the role of far-right sympathisers and activists in football-related disturbances abroad.

Around Bilbao, scenes by now familiar to followers of England's matches abroad could be observed. The streets were flooded with young English fans, aged for the most part between 18 and 25. On the afternoon of the French match, the heat was oppressive even for Spain, with temperatures around the 100°F mark. This meant that many of the English were naked from the waist up, some already showing signs of a lack of protection to skin not used to these scorching temperatures. Some took refuge in the ornate fountains which seemed to dominate every square. Nor was it only the upper half of the body which was sometimes revealed. 'Mooning' (pulling down one's trousers) was an occasional pre-match gambit, too, though it invariably failed to draw approval either from local girls or the police.

Around the ground, bars claimed as English territory were filled to overflowing. Supporters spilled on to nearby roads and pavements or simply slumped inside and outside shop doorways. Few England fans were actually staying in Bilbao. For those who had arrived early to claim tickets for the game, the format had been to stay in the town for one evening and then to retreat to the coast to camp or stay in cheap accommodation. Hostel accommodation in Bilbao and the nearby coastal areas could generally be obtained for between 400 pesetas (£2) and 1,000 pesetas (£5) per night, but even these low costs could be further reduced by the prudent traveller. A group of twelve teenage Liverpool fans, for example, were all 'dossing down' in Bilbao in an 800 pesetas per night double room near the railway station. Theirs was a story which became more and more common as the trip wore on. Some of the group were unemployed and all had arrived in Spain with little money. They were committed to living largely on what they could steal from bars and supermarkets, and many were using the experience gained from a number of years of following Liverpool across Europe. They had not found survival difficult in Spain so far. 'They're all soft here', said one of them. 'You go in and they don't ask you for nothing, so you can have what you like and then fuck off.' In Spanish bars, the bill for food and drinks is paid at the end and not between rounds as in England. It was simply 'common sense' for many of the English lads, short on ready cash, to leave bars without paying when the barman's attention was distracted, a ploy widely regarded as evidence of the 'smartness' of the English and the inherent stupidity of the Spaniards.

Rather than become embroiled in the complications of accommodation, some English fans simply slept in vans hired or purchased for the trip. Others slept in streets and parks, wrapped in their flags, waiting for the bars to open the following day. For some of these fans, who risked the far-from-gentle attentions of the Spanish police when sleeping rough, 'baggage' was limited to the clothes on their backs. By the time of the match against Kuwait, there were quite a few dishevelled English supporters around.

Since the beginning of the week, Bilbao had been losing its attraction for many of the fans in cheap hostel accommodation or sleeping rough. They began to stream out of the city to the northern coastal resorts in their hundreds. A Newcastle United fan, who had just left the city himself, warned us not to stay in Bilbao overnight because 'the Spanish coppers are crazy. They just wade into bars, on the English.' He balanced this account by admitting there had been fights in town between English fans and local youths. French supporters, by contrast, appeared more mature and urbane. Most arrived on the day of the match by car, and they tended, on the whole, to be older than the English fans, better dressed and more cosmopolitan in their behaviour. They also appeared to be doing far less drinking, at least in the immediate vicinity of the San Mames stadium. For example, no bars around the ground had obviously been claimed by the French. There must have been at least twenty, however, overflowing with English fans in various stages of inebriation.

The Spanish press were keen to chart the difference between the English and French contingents. Describing the Finals as an occasion for 'days of wine and goals', the newspaper, *Egin*, commented on 17 June that:

. . . wine was running freely down English throats on Tuesday evening. The English fans are very young one would say by looking at their almost child-like faces. They were drinking heavily, straight from the bottle and one could also see many beer bottles around. Neither the wine nor the beer was of a particularly good quality, either. Drunkenness, then, had already started to show on the eve of the match and a lot of English visitors lay asleep in the most unlikely places, stealing places in hidden shop corners or newstand shelters from the many tramps who live in Bilbao.

The French seemed more serious and were better dressed. They only left their cars briefly to go into cafés and bars. They carried small banners and flags saying '*Allez France*', and they wore typical little hats of three colours, in contrast to the naked and tattooed bodies of the rival (English) fans . . .[7]

El Diario Vasco rhetorically asked its readers: 'What was the behaviour of the Englishmen like?' and provided the answer itself:

. . . before the match it was usual to see them gathered in groups of five or so, walking across the full width of the pavement or entering foodshops and helping themselves freely out of the fruit baskets which were displayed there, as well as carrying wine and beer bottles in their hands.[8]

Tribuna Vasca, describing the debilitating effects of the heat, particularly on the English, noted that:

Tourists in general, but especially English tourists, were searching for some relief from the heat, refreshing themselves in the town fountains built in some bank buildings or in the main streets down town, where they tried to soak themselves or brush their teeth. Visitors were either in shorts or in swimming trunks, and some had simply wrapped themselves in flags. They were wearing funny hats, sports caps, badges and other typical fan items in support of their teams. Britons were more notorious than others, but maybe that's just because there seemed to be many more of them. Crowds of youngsters wearing clean-shaven scalps, funny haircuts and tattooed arms consistently shouted for their favourite players while they carried beer cans and wine bottles in both hands.[9]

There was lack of consensus regarding the numbers of English and French fans in Bilbao for the match. According to figures registered at one tourist office set up by the Basque government, there were 15,000 English and 8,000 French supporters in Bilbao, although this was clearly an underestimate of the numbers of Frenchmen present. The newspaper *Deia* agreed with *Tribuna Vasca*, that 'the English fans were unquestionably making a lot of noise in support of their team', but went on to explain that,

> according to official data, there is no doubt that there were more French spectators than English present. There were three French visitors for each English one. French fans were also supporting their team, although their behaviour was better than that of the English.[10]

Officers of the Policia Nacional were in evidence in large numbers around the San Mames stadium for all of England's matches in Bilbao. They moved in groups of five or six, some carrying rubber bullet guns, some tear gas guns. All carried truncheons and revolvers. For the French match, 65 police vans, 5 police 'microcoaches', 4 armoured cars and numerous motor cycles and police horses stationed around the end designated for English fans were evidence of the enormous security operation which had been launched. At least one reason why the police may have been especially sensitive towards the behaviour of the English is that twenty Englishmen had already been arrested in San Sebastian and Bilbao. Conversations with some lads from the campsite suggested that West Ham fans had caused damage estimated at 100,000 pesetas (£500) at the *La Perla* discotheque on the seafront. According to our source, the police, armed with a description of the characters involved – they were alleged to have been 'fair haired, with tattoos' – had picked up eleven innocent fans and jailed them, pending a court appearance and a fine. There was, however, some embarrassment for the officers concerned because two persons selected as having been involved in the incident were Mundiespana couriers. According to our campsite connections, two teenagers from the West Country – one sporting the 'official hooligan' T-shirt, the sentiments of which he regarded as 'just a joke' – the fans actually involved in the disturbance were not even booked in at the campsite. As far as they were aware, no complaint had been made on behalf of the innocent, arrested parties, but there was talk of organising a collection on site in order to hasten their release.

On Tuesday evening in central Bilbao, there had been a serious incident in Arriago's cafeteria, following which a fan from Somerset was held by the police, accused of stabbing a local man. (The fan was later released because of lack of evidence.) Nine English fans in all were arrested in Bilbao on Tuesday evening as a result of street disturbances. Three more were recommended for hospital treatment as a result of what were described as 'rows among foreign visitors', although, significantly, two of them refused to go to hospital.[11] About the affair at Arriago's, *El Diario Vasco* commented:

> To be fair, we must admit that they (the arrested English fans) had good reason to be angry when they found out that football tickets were reselling in the cafeteria at up to 15,000 pesetas (about £75).[12]

Tickets for England's matches against Kuwait and Czechoslovakia were fairly easily obtainable at face value. Tickets for the match against the French were a little more difficult to come by. Fans who had missed the official ticket sales at San Mames at the beginning of the week were forced into the black market. A couple of days before the match, tickets which at face value cost 700 pesetas (£3.50), were selling, depending on the state of the market, for between 2,000 and 3,000 pesetas (£10–£15). Even at official agencies, tickets for the game returned by the Kuwaitis were reselling at three times their normal price. Tickets for other matches in Bilbao were selling at the Ecuador Agency for 1,000 pesetas (£5). It was reported by *El Diario Vasco* that the Ecuador Agency had been given permission by Mundiespana to increase prices by 20 per cent. Another agency, Wagon Lits, which had resold tickets with only the 20 per cent increase, was reported to have sold out of tickets.[13] *Egin* roundly condemned the activities of Mundiespana in this regard:

> The focal point of the violent reactions of half a dozen (English) supporters turned out to be the appalling black market ticket prices which obviously stemmed from highly placed officials attached to the Mundial organisation. The excuses given by Mundiespana organisers such as, 'Sorry, that was a mistake', make no sense because we all know that crooks wearing nice ties and smart suits are involved here.[14]

Deia commented in a front-page report of the same day that:

The World Cup Championship has been badly organised by Madrid's central planning officers – services were too expensive, and there was not enough planning. Football tickets were initially priced at Ptas 700 but are known to have been resold at up to Ptas 10,000 (about £50). Also, the number of tickets returned, unsold, at the beginning of the World Cup clearly demonstrates how poor the overall planning has been.[15]

According to *Deia*, 6,000 pesetas (about £30) was a common price to pay for a match ticket on the black market, although around the ground there was evidence of cheaper transactions. Also, tickets changed hands between English fans for considerably less. For example, the British servicemen in the Cestona group sold spare tickets outside the ground at face value. Two of their friends had been called up to serve in the Falklands prior to the tournament, and Sportsworld had refused to refund the cost of their holiday.

Before the French game, tickets were a source of consternation to English fans without them right up to the kick-off time, although, in the end, very few remained ticketless and outside the stadium. Some resolved to 'turn over' (rob) touts who were asking the most outrageous prices. After a number of incidents in nearby bars, the more prudent sellers conducted their business closer to the ranks of the Policia Nacional.

A further source of trouble in bars around the ground was beer prices. Those fans who did stay to consider their drinks bill were rudely surprised at the cost. Away from the centre and on the coast, draught beer could be bought for as little as 25 pesetas (12p) a glass. In some of the 'English' bars around San Mames, the asking price was anything up to 150 pesetas (75p) a bottle. It was generally agreed that the operations around the stadium could justifiably be described as 'time to rip-off the English'. One fight developed in the 'Winston Churchill', a rather plush establishment which, because of its name, had attracted the custom of many English fans. A group of northern fans in their early twenties refused to pick up their check because of their belief that they were 'being done'. Before they could leave, the police moved in flailing at bystanders left and right. The bill was reluctantly settled – in full.

As the police moved outside, English fans who had witnessed

the incident began to 'screw' them (i.e. to try to stare them down). At this point the police decided that a show of strength was in order. English fans outside the bar, who by now numbered about 100, were pushed back off a slip road onto the pavement. Some sauntered back towards the kerb, keen not to lose face even before such a spectacularly armed force. The police interpreted this as a sign of resistance. Truncheons were drawn and fans beaten back the final few yards. Phil, one of our Chelsea crew of six, carried an 18-inch truncheon wound across his chest for about a week before it disappeared. There were murmurs now among the English of 'revenge' and what might happen to the Spanish police if they were 'men enough' to shed some of their weaponry. Before these sentiments could develop, however, more police arrived to disperse the hostile crowd.

There were other problems, too, outside San Mames before the French match. A group of Basque labourers from '*Union Correcera*', a local brewery, had set up a wooden stall at which they were selling souvenirs and distributing pro-Basque leaflets. They were 'demonstrating for their rights', as the northern Spanish press described activities of this sort. The Policia Nacional, this time with full riot gear, moved in to disperse the gathering group of demonstrators who, by this stage, had been 'reinforced' by some interested English bystanders sporting Basque flags. The Basques were favoured, one English flag-bearer informed us, 'because they hate the Spanish and the coppers'. English fans and Basque demonstrators were dispersed by a baton charge down a street which ran at right angles to the side of the stadium. Chants from the English of '*Malvinas Inglaterra*' aimed obliquely to support the Basques, did little to improve the humour of the police, who then began to charge small groups of 'demonstrating' English fans. Significantly, this phrase was probably the only Spanish the majority of English fans picked up during their entire stay in Spain. The 'Malvinas' references did not amuse the Spanish press, either. The day after the match, *El Diario Vasco*, carried a picture of an English supporter standing outside a Bilbao bar, flaunting a T-shirt which proclaimed, 'The Falklands are British'. The picture was captioned. 'Los "supporters" se dejaron notar con sus habituales malos modos. (English supporters were showing their usual bad manners.)'[16] The following day, an editorial in *Tribuna Vasca* spoke disparagingly of the English attitude towards the Argentinians which had served to 'drag up a colonial war as we near the 21st century'. 'The English', the editorial continued, 'were facing the most stupid war ever known.'[17]

Outside the stadium before each of England's matches there were some unusual sights for the continental eye. For example, a group of four teenage Leeds United skinheads were trying desperately to swap their seat tickets for standing ones. Three were on the dole, and they were all camping with someone they knew on the official site in San Sebastian free of charge. They had caught the ferry to Santander and claimed to have 'jumped' the San Sebastian train to Bilbao. They also recommended pub food because it was 'free'. As the tournament progressed, these were the two lessons that emerged most clearly from English lads in Spain: you never paid in bars, and only mugs paid on trains. It was possible to survive quite comfortably on only little money if you kept out of the way of the police and were not averse to stealing and, occasionally, running. If the police could be baited, too, and the locals fancied their chances in a fight, then 'laughs' could be thrown in as well. One of the Leeds 'skins' at the French match already showed signs of battle – a plaster over one eye gained from 'a fight wi' me mate when I was pissed up'. A Spanish photographer approached him for a close-up and the fighter duly obliged, fist raised in the air. We asked why he had not asked for payment. 'Fuck it,' he said, 'I'm a star!' His condition deteriorated as the week wore on. Behind us, two lads from Manchester in 'Vice Squad' T-shirts were trying to find ways into the terraced sections. They had made the trip 'on the cheap' with a northern holiday firm who were ferrying them by coach daily across the border with France. Tickets were picked up outside the stadium on the day, but they were always for the unwanted, seated sections, which necessitated these manoeuvres.

A large group of London skins, predominantly followers of West Ham and Chelsea and pledging allegiance to the National Front, contented themselves with greeting all foreigners with Nazi salutes and 'Sieg Heils'. Later, *The Observer* captured some of the group on film (see Plate 3). Some of these were 'vanning it' around the northern coast and had already been active in fights in Santander. Copies of *National Front News* were on sale outside the San Mames stadium before the French match, peddled by three southern fans with the Cross of St George painted on their faces.

Perhaps the most fearsome of all the English fans who had made the trip to Spain, at least as far as appearance was concerned, was a huge, completely bald 'skinhead' from Peterborough who looked to be in his early twenties and spoke in monosyllabic support of the British Movement, an ultra-right-wing spin-off from the National Front. His allegiance to West Ham was tattooed across both arms, and a Viking ship sailed silently across his bare chest. Braces, jeans, black Doc Marten boots and a black Basque beret completed his uniform. His mate, also from Peterborough, was smaller and a painter and decorator by trade. He did most of the talking. They were dossing in Bilbao and had already had some trouble with the locals in a fight in a Bilbao bar. They had already met some of the West Ham ICF who were stationed, so they thought, at San Sebastian. (The Inter City Firm, or ICF, are a West Ham 'fighting crew', who obtained their name from the fact that they travel to matches by service train to avoid the attentions of the police.) Later, the ICF Union Jack of the West Ham crew was clearly visible inside the stadium. The Peterborough pair were talking to some young French skinheads and punks, one of whom sported a Mohican hairstyle and extolled the virtues of 'Sham '69', a London punk band recently disbanded because their concerts were increasingly being dominated by NF and BM supporters. 'These Frenchies are good kids', Tony the decorator informed us, 'they wanna break the fuckin' gates down!' This new Anglo-French group were ticketless but confident that something would turn up before they were forced into demolition.

In summary, one can say the following about England's supporters in northern Spain: they were predominantly young, and a large number were drawn from what can be described as First Division 'home end' support. There was a lack of the younger kids of 14 and 15 who tend to 'hang around' the 'hard' lads at matches. There was, however, evidence of a regular 'hard core' of support for England, especially among southern fans and, for some fans at least, the prospect of 'trouble' at England's matches in Spain was an attractive proposition rather than a potential problem.

As has already been noted, while there were a considerable number of fans from the north of England at the matches in Spain, they seemed to be outnumbered by fans from in and around London. The southern fans also appeared to move around in larger groups than their northern counterparts. Writing of a camp site outside Bilbao, a reporter for *Deia* commented:

About 200 young lads were only half-dressed, revealing their blue tattoos mixed with red, sunburned shoulders. Low prices at the campsite allowed the English fans to extend their stay. Most of them were from crowded working class areas around London.[18]

At all three matches in Bilbao, Spanish police carefully frisked English fans as they entered the San Mames stadium. Flag poles, sufficiently sturdy to constitute weapons, were confiscated at the turnstiles. There was no alcohol on sale inside the ground, which was probably a prudent step on the part of the authorities considering the consumption which had gone on outside. English fans were also searched for alcohol before entering the stadium although, at the match against Czechoslovakia, a number managed to gain entry with litre bottles of red wine.

For the French match, the south terrace at San Mames was reserved solely for English fans, with the north terrace split between the English and the French. French fans took most of the north stand, while to the south, the seated sections catered for both French and English support. Local fans tended to be located in the main stand and in the seated sections which ran alongside the pitch. For the Kuwait and Czechoslovakia matches, the opposition brought little terrace support, so both the north and south ends of the stadium could be used exclusively by the English.

It is interesting to note that, at the French game, the unsegregated terraces to the north contained Sportsworld clients as well as fans who had bought their tickets in Spain. Some Sportsworld clients were given their match tickets literally as they arrived at the ground. Many were later dismayed to find themselves on terraces alongside French spectators. Sportsworld Operations Director, Geoffrey Phillips, blamed the complication on Mundiespana, claiming that Sportsworld's ticket allocation for the tournament was handed over in two unnumbered blocks just four days before the competition started. He and his staff had had to work for 60 hours in a vault to sort them out before they could be handed to clients. To add to the confusion, many seats turned out not to exist, a result of the new numbering system at the revamped stadium. There were fewer problems in this regard for the two later matches in Bilbao. For one thing, at the later games the stadium was somewhat below capacity. For another, as has already been said, there were no Czech or Kuwaiti terrace supporters.

Although English and French fans shared the same stretch of terracing for the first game in Bilbao, there was no attempt by the English to move into the favoured sections directly behind the goal which were occupied by the French. Union Jacks, however, were stretched along the front of *both* sets of supporters. Their slogans read like a northern road map – Halifax, Blackpool, Stockport, etc. One group of fans had no illusions about their means of survival in Spain. A large white banner at the far end of the ground read, 'Wigan Thieves'. Another, with tongue-in-cheek humour catering for the home market, announced, 'There's no hooliganism here, Mum!' Yet another, with reference to the Falklands, spoke of 'Ron Greenwood's Task Force'.

Among the flags carried by English fans in Bilbao, although outnumbered by Union Jacks, the Cross of St George seemed more popular than is usually the case on expeditions of this sort. This was due at least in part to the sale of them outside San Mames at the expense of the Union Jack. The flag of the Basque Nationalist Party, the Ikurina, was also conspicuous at the English end.

Of all England's First Phase matches, the game against France was the most tense and exciting. A win would mean almost certain qualification for Madrid. The match also got off to a rousing start with a goal for England in the first minute. The games against Czechoslovakia and Kuwait paled by comparison. There were also many more English fans at the French game than at any other in Spain. A sizeable proportion had taken advantage of one-match package trips and an early start to the weekend. We also met a number of fans who had 'gone on the sick' to make the trip. A young apprentice coachbuilder from York even returned home after the Czech match to report to work for three days only to return to Spain for the matches in Madrid. Others had simply taken days off without warning, not knowing if their jobs would still be available when they returned home. Others still claimed to have simply given up their jobs in order to come. 'It was boring anyway', claimed a teenage apprentice joiner from the Stockport area. 'All my mates were coming and they (his employers) wouldn't give me time off. I didn't say owt. I just came out here. They can stuff their job.'

Pride of place in this department was reserved for a West Ham fan from Manchester whom we met in Madrid. He had been refused time off work (he was a painter) to watch the England-France match on TV, but had taken time off in any case and reported for work on Saturday morning instead. When his employers threatened to sack him, he had packed his bags and set off for Spain, leaving behind a wife of nine weeks and a note. He was in the Madrid embassy because of a phone call from his wife threatening immediate divorce if he did not return. He had no money and was hoping to make enough by selling his story to a Sunday newspaper to pay his air fare home.

The matches against Czechoslovakia and Kuwait generated little in the way of atmosphere largely because of the lack of terrace opposition. It was true that the locals got behind the Kuwaiti underdogs for the last match in Bilbao but, by then, the England team had already qualified for Madrid. In any case, despite the appearance of a number of Basque players in its ranks, the local people were certainly not avid supporters of the Spanish national side. Hence, even when they expressed it, they were hardly fanatical in their opposition to the English.

The nationalistic fervour among the English generated by the Falklands conflict, later to be supplemented by increasing concern over the Gibraltar issue, resulted in some unexpectedly respectful receptions for the national anthems of their opponents. At the Czechoslovakia game, for example, there was almost stony silence for that country's national anthem, followed by a lusty delivery of 'God Save the Queen'. Both at that and other matches, choruses of 'Malvinas Inglaterra' were also sung but 'Rule Britannia', with its references more directly applicable to the efforts of the task force in the South Atlantic, was more popular still.

The Policia Nacional maintained a high profile inside San Mames, with officers in full riot gear stationed with dogs at the front of the terraced sections. More riot police gathered at the rear of both the standing and the seated areas. That disorder inside the stadium was kept to a minimum throughout each of the three matches in Bilbao was probably due to four main factors:

(i) the general lack of provocation from the non-English spectators;
(ii) the favourable results obtained by the England side;
(iii) the deterrent effects of the Spanish police;

and (iv) the lack of 'controversial' incidents on the field of play.

The only major incident of disorder inside San Mames during England's Phase One matches occurred on the north terrace 16 minutes into the second half of the match against France. Significantly, the disturbances began immediately after the French equalising goal which was scored on the half hour, the only goal the English conceded throughout the tournament. The 'niggle' which developed at the meeting point of the English and French contingents was at that stage still relatively minor but easily detectable to those with an eye for preventive policing. The Spanish police failed to take action, however, and the problem simmered for 30 or 40 minutes until a stretcher was called for. A French fan had been injured in a fight, although, clearly, only a few persons were involved in the incident.

With a sensible and timely response from the authorities, this minor incident could have been handled without undue fuss. There was certainly at no stage a 'running battle' between rival fans as *The Guardian* later suggested.[19] When the Spanish police did intervene, it seemed at first that they were simply clearing a space for the stretcher-bearers to perform their task. Instead, they drove into the ranks of the English who, by this stage, had become more subdued. The effect of this baton charge, not surprisingly, was to panic the English into a hasty retreat which resulted in the demolition of a fence at the north west corner of the San Mames as they fled to cover.

It was an extremely dangerous and unnecessary manoeuvre on the part of the police. Only good fortune dictated that no spectators were seriously injured. One English fan was arrested. After the match, some English fans claimed that it was a Spanish spectator who had been involved in the original incident. Others said the affair began after an English spectator had his T-shirt stolen by a French fan. According to the English, the French fan pictured in a heap on the terraces was not badly injured at all and soon after the photograph had been taken was up on his feet again, fighting.

This was not the only occasion during the First Phase matches on which the Spanish police over-reacted with violence to minor crowd disturbances. With West Germany and Austria playing out a half-hearted contest, the result of which – a draw – would ensure the qualification of both teams for Phase Two at the expense of Algeria, an angry Algerian fan climbed on to a fence near the pitch to protest. Photographs in the Spanish newspaper *Egin* showed the Algerian being brutally beaten by the Policia Nacional. The Spanish press were not uncritical of the actions of their police at the England–France match. Under the headline, 'Minor Trouble At The World Cup', *Deia*, for example, devoted front-page coverage to what the paper regarded as 'excessive security control at the game'. The story continued inside, this time under the headline, 'Police Intrude On The Terraces Destroying The Happy Atmosphere of San Mames'.[20] *El Pais* commented that

After 17 minutes of the second half, and due to a minor incident between English and French fans, police took action against anyone standing on the northern terrace.[21]

Tribuna Vasca reported that there had been some 'minor fights between the two sides, but nothing serious until police arrived on the spot.'[22] Referring to the treatment of spectators and demonstrators outside the stadium before the match, *Egin* commented that:

It was rather unpleasant when police quickly pushed away people around the stadium, telling them to go away if they were not about to enter to see the match inside. . . .

A traffic policeman also seemed to enjoy the new wave of beating people and, at the end of the match, he started to be nasty to a group of fans – Englishmen included – who, carelessly, were crossing against a red light. The other pedestrians looked at him in such a strange way that he soon felt bad and realised how people were laughing at his stupid, violent manners.[23]

After each of England's games in the north, there ensued mass celebrations by the English, particularly inside San Mames. This was the time for relieving opposing fans of favours and flags. Some of the Cestona lads 'strong-armed' French fans out of a huge flag they had brought to the stadium. The song, 'You'll Never Walk Alone', complete with the waving of banners and scarves, was a regular feature on the San Mames terraces for up to half an hour at the end of each match. Later, to the undisguised alarm of the riot police and the delight of local spectators, mass 'congas' up and down the terrace steps took over. Outside, spectators generally dispersed quickly from the stadium environs. The police did not encourage large groups of fans to hang around and, likewise, English fans were keen to move away from the threatening presence of the local force.

After the French game, there were a number of minor incidents involving rival fans which police motor-cyclists broke up before van-loads of well-equipped riot police moved into the vacuum created by the arrival of their colleagues. Although there were no incidents of crowd disorder apparent immediately following the games against Kuwait and the Czechs, there was, after the latter, an impromptu gathering of National Front sympathisers outside a bar at the north west corner of the stadium. Again, a few northerners were involved but a large majority of the 50 or so present were young Chelsea fans. In a recent court case, Chelsea fans were described as the country's premier focus for football-based NF activity.[24]

Notable in this present context was the appearance in Bilbao of 'Kellerway', a railway ticket collector from Battersea, then approaching his forties and one of Chelsea's long-standing chant leaders and brawlers. His face shows clear signs of numerous 'disagreements' with opponents, both inside and outside a football context. Together with others like him and despite his recent retirement from the forefront of major 'rucking' at Chelsea matches, Kellerway persists in attracting young crews from Battersea and the surrounding areas for both domestic and continental football journeys. Throughout the match against the Czechs and using his 'Zigger, Zagger' routine from the stands, Kellerway conducted groups of followers on the terraces below. After the game, in typical fashion, he was touring Mundiespana coaches, making a 'collection' for a fictitious female fan alleged to have been robbed by local thugs. Lads 'in the know' realised the collection was destined for purposes rather closer to his own heart. At least this affair was conducted with more subtlety than similar 'collections' on Chelsea away trips in England. These are reputed to be taken *without* a story, but *with* menaces.

The Kellerway crew's place at the forefront of the racist and violent section of Chelsea's following has now been challenged by groups like the one led by 'Mardiner', a fan from the unlikely base of Tunbridge Wells. Just as the performance of English fans abroad has served to attract the attention and attendance of 'hard' lads from around the country, so, too, has Chelsea's domestic reputation had a wide appeal. A Mardiner-led mob is held in high regard by some of the Chelsea home end largely on account of the part they played in an ambush of the hated Newcastle United fans who were, at the time, well out of London and *en route* to the North East.

The latest English goal-end alliance in the offing, and discussed in Spain, was that of Chelsea and West Ham 'hard' lads for a trip to a Chelsea 'friendly' match in Glasgow against Rangers. The meeting, if it went ahead, was regarded as an ideal opportunity to 'pay back the Jocks' for their scant regard for the home turf on trips to Wembley for the England–Scotland match.

The attitudes and beliefs which underlie the stance taken by extreme right-wing groups towards what they regard as alien races are similar in many ways to those which play a large part in generating disturbances between geographically distinct groups of white lower-working-class youths at football matches. As Nigel Fielding has argued:

> . . . for the NF, the drawing together of 'British stock' embodies the idea of menace and safety, the small group of those in the know. The nationalistic enterprise is *essentially an exercise in defining in-groups and out-groups.* . . . The NF use the idea of race as a means of crystallising the distinction between 'Britishness' and 'foreignness'. . . . In the discussion of NF racial theory . . . the complexity of the various grounds for rejection (e.g. alien habits, competition) must be seen as subordinate to the *overwhelming simplicity of the general relations of stranger to in-group.* It is this latter aspect which fuels the character-attitude which rejects all alien intruders, not just blacks. . . . It is particularly significant that East Enders who eventually provided the anti-alien British Brothers' League with a membership of 45,000 were at first suspicious of its founder who was a West Ender, and who was therefore an outsider.[25]

The heightened sense of suspicion of aliens and 'outsiders' which tends to be characteristic of lower-working-class youths even when no racial and few cultural differences are involved, served, in the unfamiliar territories of Spain, to generate an intense concern for intra-group solidarity and a co-relative disregard, even hatred, for Spanish culture and the local people. Such feelings were most generally articulated in pejorative descriptions of the physical and cultural characteristics of the Spanish people, but occasionally they found expression in violence. Because the experiences of lower-working-class youths tend to be relatively restricted and their horizons relatively narrow, and because most of their relations are with people of similar background to themselves, outsiders tend to be perceived as being similarly undifferentiated. Thus, just as 'all blacks look alike', so all Spanish persons were regarded by English fans from this kind of background as 'greasy', 'smelly' and so on.

In the case of international football matches abroad when the visiting fans' sense of cultural distinctiveness is heightened and, in the contest, it is *national* identities which are stressed, then (to use the term coined by Émile Durkheim)[26] the 'bonds of similitude' which unite geographically distinct and conflicting groups of the same nationality are similarly emphasised, overriding the differences between them. Thus, domestic disputes between rival fan-groups are generally subordinated to the national cause when England fans travel abroad. Occasionally, old rivalries still erupt, however, especially when domestic foes are perceived to be gathering in threatening numbers. For example, John Williams was warned by Chelsea fans that, as a 'Scouser', he was lucky to be alone. Large groups of Liverpool fans were perceived by Chelsea lads as 'liable to be looking for trouble', even in Spain. In the circumstances, it was important to get the first strike in. Indeed, as we noted in the Introduction, there is some evidence to suggest that, at England's matches abroad, rival groups of English fans occasionally fight among themselves.[27]

Spanish press coverage of the behaviour of English fans at the matches in northern Spain

The behaviour of English fans in Bilbao before, during and after matches was, on the whole, reported graciously by the northern Spanish press. It showed itself to be refreshingly level-headed and impartial in its appraisal of the 'strange tribes' which had descended on Spain. For example, while *El Diario Vasco* and *Egin* both reported on trouble involving English fans during celebrations following the game against France, the latter was at pains to point out that 'the few British youths involved were no doubt highly provoked by the many Bilbaoners who were running on the streets with them'.[28] *Egin* was also fully aware of the consequences of the fact that the reputation of the English had preceded them to Bilbao. Under the headline, 'Quarrels, But Not Too Many', *Egin* continued:

> Mass media reporters had arrived in Bilbao and were alert to report any possible trouble or quarrel which was morbidly almost expected from the World Cup supporters. 'The Englishmen are coming, the Englishmen are coming', some news editors were happily saying, greedily rubbing their hands and gloating over the idea of fans making trouble. When, later on, these Englishmen finally started to appear, hardly any trouble occurred and reporters had to rely on their own wits to create some news. There were some minor problems . . . and some trouble of little consequence.[29]

Tribuna Vasca, however, was of the opinion that 'Some are too aggressive' and to substantiate its argument, reported that:

> Some English supporters, not contented with getting into trouble and beating around with sticks and throwing bottles, were enquiring where to buy pistols. Just too much like Europeans. . . .[30]

Deia decided that the reputation which preceded English supporters required what they called an 'In Depth Look At The Football Fan'. It was published following the French match and is worth quoting in full:

In Depth Look At The Football Fan

The feared British supporters have arrived and gone. They might come back but now they will be no surprise to anyone anymore. Before they came we heard lots of warnings. It was almost as if Attila was coming into town. However, we must admit that so far – touch wood – nothing terrible has happened.

Certain common denominators apply to all British fans, English as well as Scottish supporters. For instance they all have a sense of unity. They move in groups of at least five or six. They are all young, shy, colourful and are primarily from lower (class) neighbourhoods. They are heavy drinkers, uninhibited, quarrelsome and exhibitionist. Fair enough, all these types of behaviour depend upon the context. Therefore, even if some of these adjectives appear contradictory, they can apply to the same individual in different circumstances.

Most of them were young, average age between 18 and 20 years. On their own, they seemed shy. If questioned by any journalist, they would not know what to say. They normally live on the outskirts of big towns such as London, Manchester and Birmingham. They had little money and their manners were not too good. However, they tried hard to make friends with local people. They would end any attempt at conversation with *'gracias amigo'*.

It did not make sense, this inborn shyness, and yet their freedom to wear shabby and outlandish clothes. It was not unusual to see people around wearing shorts made out of a flag, or someone carrying an enormous flag.

The Bottle, The Constant Companion

The words, 'heavy drinkers', have been used to describe our British visitors. In fact, it was unusual to find them without a wine bottle or beer can in their hands. They were capable of drinking plenty, and wine – our national drink – was very cheap for them. This fact, plus the habit of carrying a glass, meant that they were at saturation level at all times and they were quarrelsome, defiant and ready to pick a fight at any moment. The two lads we interviewed said, 'We are very happy in Bilbao where the people are very friendly and kind. Not at all like the people in Santander where we were attacked for no reason. The problem comes when we start to drink a bit and we can become nasty.' His friend added, 'Yeah, we drink a lot and can be very nasty!' 'Exhibitionists' was also a good way of describing them, when, because of their dress they would be stopped by newspaper photographers. Then they would display all their tattoos and put on a special pose.

That is a brief description of our little friends from England.

Not quite like saints, but neither are they the feared devils some wanted to make us believe.[31]

The reference here to the mixture of shyness and exhibitionism of the English fans is perceptive. As *Deia* notes, it was the context in which the English found themselves which tended to determine their reactions. Alone or in small groups in unfamiliar territory, they could be withdrawn. In larger groups, they were more liable to be exhibitionist and to behave in a hostile and threatening manner towards locals and opposing fans.

By the time of the Czechoslovakia game on June 21st, there was also some evidence in the press that the people of Bilbao were beginning to come to terms with the influx of English fans whose arrival had threatened such dreadful carnage. Under the headline, 'The Intermittent Invasion', *Egin* reported on June 22nd that:

The people of Bilbao are losing their fear of English fans. Little by little they are convincing themselves that these fans are only here to enjoy themselves, even though one or two of them are a little on the bad side. On Sunday morning, the people took to the streets and a young mother said, 'Oh well, we have come to see the English. After having heard so much about them, we want to see them face to face.'

This story ended with *Egin's* judgment that the English performances on the field against the French and the Czechs had been

a sporting triumph, and a triumph for the thousands of youths who, to many had been a pain but who, in the majority, were found to be very nice lads.[32]

In Chapter 3, we shall discuss the behaviour and control of English fans in northern Spain *outside* the football context.

Chapter Three

THE BEHAVIOUR OF ENGLISH FANS IN NORTHERN SPAIN IN NON-FOOTBALL CONTEXTS

Although the authorities in Britain were perhaps most concerned with the prospects of disorder in San Mames where the television eyes of the world were poised to portray any repeats of the scenes in Turin and Basle, there remained, for the Spanish authorities, the problems of coping with English fans *between* matches.

As we have already said, accommodation for the large numbers of English fans who travelled to Spain without prior bookings proved to be a minor problem. Hostel and camping accommodation were extremely cheap in the north, and a combination of high temperatures and cheap food and drink – free until some bars began to post 'Pay Now' notices for the English – meant that sleeping rough with very little money did not turn out to be such an unattractive proposition as might otherwise have been anticipated. It was advisable to sleep well away from the attentions of the local police, of course, because of their habit of waking unsuspecting park dwellers with a truncheon rather than an early morning call.

The English fans who had travelled to Spain on a shoestring budget had done so, according to *El Diario Vasco*, despite a campaign in England stressing the difficulty of living cheaply in Spain. Talking with English campers at Zarauz, the newspaper noted that:

It was thought that, in England, someone had started a campaign on a grand scale, designed to tell of how expensive everything is in this country. But here there is no proof. The people responsible should be sought out by the experts from Mundiespana.[1]

The most popular locations for English fans, whether on organised packages or private ventures, stretched along the coast of northern Spain and over the border into France. There were large contingents in Bilbao and its environs. Others stayed in Santander, San Sebastian, and in and around Zarauz. In addition, there were groups in Biarritz and St Jean de Luz in France (see Figure 2). Problems emerged at some of these locations at a very early stage, although the decision by Mundiespana to spread English package tour punters across a wide area probably helped to ensure that disturbances remained fairly localised.

Santander and Bilbao were the focal points of early confrontations, although problems in these locations progressively eased as the English sought more attractive venues along the coast. In Santander, judging from conversations with fans at England's early matches, it seemed that English rowdyism had stirred local youths into violent retribution. *Deia*, too, reported that 'some English who spent the night in Santander had even been attacked by local thugs.'[2] However, the next day the same newspaper carried a headline which read: 'English Fans Visiting Santander Were As Feared As Attila.'[3]

Nor was it a question simply of Spaniards countering the expected (and to some extent actual) hooliganism of their English guests by paying them in kind. During the first few days of the tournament, the British Consulate in Bilbao was kept just as busy with cases of English fans who had been robbed or mugged as they were by those who had been arrested. One had even been coshed and robbed by French supporters, proof for *The Sunday Times*, at least, 'that it is not just Britain that exports thugs'.[4]

'Celebrations' after the French match accounted for a number of the early arrests in the north. They were concentrated in San Sebastian and Bilbao, and were probably given further fuel by the failure of the Spanish side to account for little Honduras in the televised evening match. Vandalism in and around bars was the most usual complaint. A Spanish journalist, reporting from San Sebastian on the evening of the French game, wrote that:

At the time I am writing this article – 9 o'clock at night – the

British supporters, the feared English fans are still behaving very badly in the old and central streets of the town.[5]

Celebrations after England's matches began immediately on return from Bilbao. In Cestona, exhausted though many of the young fans must have been, a group of at least twenty invariably made their way to the village after matches. Flags, favours and chants were always in evidence on these outings, designed to show the locals how the English went about 'having a good time'.

As at other venues, an 'English' bar was soon established in the village, i.e. a location where virtually all the English group went drinking of an evening. Such bars were usually chosen on account of specific attractions – because they sold English beer, or at least served the local brew in pint mugs; because they served the ever-popular chips rather than the rich, spicy bar snacks favoured by the locals; or because someone connected with the bar had British credentials. Finally a bar TV was favoured by those who wanted to keep track of the evening World Cup fixtures. In the case of the Cayote Bar in Cestona, the main attraction was the favour it had found with some expatriate Scottish females and their Spanish families. The bar was also sited in the village square which allowed the English to spill outside when the numbers inside became unmanageable, a not uncommon occurrence when drinking parties regularly exceeded twenty persons.

On the first couple of evenings in Cestona, the antics of the English resulted in police 'escorts' back to the hotel on two occasions; a personal appeal from the mayor for the English to temper their behaviour; and a near brawl with a group of local youths which resulted in fines of 10,000 pesetas (£50) for three of the party.

The last-named incident occurred after a particularly heavy drinking session which began at the Cayote, continuing later at the 'dungeon' across the road from the hotel which passed as the local disco. (Here, Spanish lads of around 10 and 11 regularly amused the English with their smoking and penchant for 'acting hard'. Their monopolisation of this night spot added fuel to the fear that all the eligible females had been moved out of the village before the arrival of the English.) Problems began when the two Arsenal labourers and a young apprentice turner and fitter, Jimmy, became embroiled in an argument with a couple of local youths. As the

Spaniards left the Cayote in their car, to quote what one of the Arsenal lads said later, 'bottles just came out of nowhere', smashing on the vehicle as it pulled away. In fact, the Arsenal crew had decided to provide their Spanish drinking partners with a memento of the occasion.

Within minutes, a deputation of 12–15 young Spaniards, armed with bottles and sticks, was down at the hotel in search of the culprits. The latter, however, had returned inside the Cayote. The half-dozen English lads who later emerged from the bar, found all exits from the square blocked by armed Spanish youths. In spite of the disadvantages of the visitors in terms of numbers and weapons, there was talk of an attempt to smash through the Spanish ranks to fetch reinforcements from the Arteche. In the end, after about 20 minutes of stare and counter-stare, the village policeman managed to calm the locals sufficiently to ensure the group safe passage back to the hotel. Next morning, the fines were implemented and paid without fuss. For the rest of the week, the English and the local youths eyed each other with even more suspicion than before.

Generally speaking, English fans in Spain tended not to go out of their way to familiarise themselves with local people or customs. Some managed to survive with no knowledge whatsoever of the local tongue. Even to order beer in Spanish was resolutely resisted by many. They would simply persist with their English and point to what was wanted, muttering about the 'stupidity' of the locals. The attitude in this respect of many of the English in Cestona was illustrated by Frank, the Nottingham miner, when he remarked of the locals, 'Well, we've been here three days now, and if they haven't learned English yet, that's their problem.'

Contact with the people of Cestona, apart from a few drunken exchanges in the Cayote, was limited to pidgin-English sessions with groups of local children who were always keen to give the 'thumbs up' to *Inglaterra* and the 'thumbs down' to *Espana*. Evidence of separatist influences in the village was apparent all around, with new ETA slogans appearing on walls almost every day. The slogans were often written in stilted English. This convinced some English fans, fast developing a persecution complex because of the reactions of the Spanish police and others, that they would be blamed for the slogans. Such feelings, however, did not prevent a few from returning from San Sebastian with

Ikurinas to fly from hotel windows, alongside the Union Jack and above slogans like: 'Stop Basque Genocide'; 'Stop Spanish Police Torture'; and 'Peace Cannot Be So, Until There is Amnesty'. The nationalistic feelings of the English were never far from the surface. On another Cestona occasion, a drunken expedition of around ten fans set off at 3 a.m. to scale a steep hill which overlooked the village. A British flag was staked at the summit and cries of, 'England! England!', interspersed with National Front slogans, were probably audible for miles around. An unidentified torch-carrier who had followed the group was presumed to be the village policeman. He was sent on his way with an avalanche of stones and rocks but, despite threats to the contrary, the matter was taken no further.

Few village jaunts were concluded before 3 or 4 a.m. After the first few days, the long-suffering hotel doorkeeper became resigned to such late finishes, though not to the damage which occasionally resulted from over-indulgence at the Cayote. Intentionally or otherwise, doors and windows were the usual sufferers in this regard. 'Spike', a printer in his late twenties, was a Queen's Park Rangers fan. He was also the group's champion drinker, his sessions regularly resulting in collapse in the village square and an escort home by the police. Spike crowned his holiday performances by exposing himself in the square, urinating in the Cayote, and smashing a number of windows and doors in the Arteche before his departure. It was generally agreed among the rest that some damage was always liable to occur after heavy sessions, but also that Spike was out of order because of the regularity and uncontrollable nature of his displays. Indeed, Spike left for Bilbao airport at the end of the First Phase in such a state of alcohol-induced distress that it is difficult to imagine how he fared in customs.

Conversations, at least among the younger element of English support in Cestona, tended regularly to involve discussions about the reputations of respective home ends and comparisons of English and Spanish culture. In conversations on the latter subject, it often seemed that the only cloud on the English horizon was the influence of other, and what they took to be lesser, cultures at home. In both subject areas, the London lads, and particularly the Chelsea faction, were central contributors. Often, discussions of past confrontations between opposing fan groups revealed that companions thrown together in Spain had been terrace opponents at the same incident. Invariably, there were differing interpretations of the outcome of particular domestic terrace disputes. A terrace 'victory' at QPR for the Arsenal lads was regarded by Spike as a 'rout' of the Arsenal 'end'. Conversations like this were common among young England supporters throughout the trip. However, contacts in Spain which cut across club and regional affiliations bore out little hope for an end to disputes at home. 'I suppose next season we'll be kicking fuck out of each other again,' Kel concluded cheerily after one of these interludes.

The Chelsea boys, in their, 'You Can't Ban a Chelsea Fan' T-shirts, were almost patronising in their praise of opposing 'home ends'. 'Yeah, you did all right there', Phil, one of the galley workers, told a Hull City fan later in Madrid. 'Mind you, you always get the other fans getting everyone out for Chelsea – giving a good show. Everyone wants to take the Chelsea reputation, don't they?' Kev, a £120-a-week building labourer in his late twenties still lived with his parents in Battersea. He was proud of the reputation Chelsea had for providing England followers and also of their 'patriotism' which occasionally spilled necessarily over into violence. 'I tell you this', he said in the Cayote one evening, 'you come down to the Swan in the Fulham Road with all the Chelsea and just say you follow England away and no one will touch you.' Kev was neither condemning nor approving of Chelsea's violent following. The violence was 'just something that happened. They (Chelsea fans) get the reputation and everyone wants to have a go'. He went on:

'Sometimes at Chelsea (matches) away it's bad 'cos there's so many Old Bill around now waiting. Derby was great, 'cos everything was happening there after the match. You don't notice the violence after a bit. Watching Chelsea, you just get immune to it. Butley and Phil and Stevie and them: they're not interested in football. They just want the aggravation. That's what it is with a lot of the Front lads at Chelsea.'

Kev went on to outline the reception given by Chelsea fans to Canoville, the club's young black winger, when he made his debut at Crystal Palace at the end of the 1981–82 season, coming on as substitute. 'Y'know, all the Chelsea were booing and it was, Ooh! Ooh! Ooh!, an' all that, like a gorilla.' Phil claimed that the club's

NF support would ensure that there was no future for black players at Stamford Bridge.

Conversations with the NF lads, including the older, northern official, revealed predictable responses about the nature of their objections to non-whites in Britain. Unemployment, loss of cultural identity, and the high levels of crime among ethnic minority groups, were high on their list of complaints. However, their reactions to the Spanish made nonsense of their claim that it was not 'non-white' people *per se* that were objectionable but rather their presence in Britain.

Whenever these conversations took place in a group setting, other fans felt compelled to chip in with their own observations about how the 'Pakis' or the 'Wogs' were 'taking over'. From this kind of statement, it was only a small step before the 'cultural inferiority' of the blacks and the Spaniards were fused, cemented by a general disdain for Spanish food and drink and the other cultural 'idiosyncrasies' of the locals. Films like *Midnight Express*, which charts the horrific experiences of British captives in a Turkish jail, were used as a rule of thumb guide to the generally 'uncivilised' nature of the Spanish people. The Spanish were simply linked to the Turks in this case by their swarthy *foreignness*.

As time went by, stories and rumours from English fans in Zarauz, San Sebastian and Bilbao served to confirm in the eyes of the Cestona group the attitudes generated and sustained in these group discussions. The English were always portrayed in such accounts as the victims of unprovoked attacks by numerically superior forces: more evidence of the inherent 'cowardice' of foreigners. The reality of the situation was often rather different. When English fans did admit to 'sorting out' a few locals, they were regarded affectionately by the rest as 'good lads' or 'crazy bastards' and so on. Stories of attacks on English fans seldom failed to draw the group together and give rise to 'tribalistic' desires to reinforce the ranks of the beleaguered English whenever and wherever they were in trouble.

The overall effect of this structured flow of information and the way in which it was interpreted was to insulate the English even further from their Spanish hosts. In fact, at the end of the First Phase, there were not many of the young English at Cestona who regretted their departure, despite the fact that they had been treated, on the whole, very tolerantly by the local people, especially the hotel staff.

With its beaches, late-night discotheques and brothels, San Sebastian is in many ways the antithesis of Bilbao and Cestona (though, of course, Bilbao is also noted for the last named). On a hill to the west of San Sebastian bay, Sportsworld had established a campsite for about 600 English customers, almost all of them males below the age of 25. Since their arrival, there had been discontent among them. The camping equipment was often poor and the expertise and advice promised by Sportsworld were not forthcoming. Also, sites on the camp were available to private campers for fees lower than those which Sportsworld were said to be charging. What is more, there had been 'trouble' in town, particularly after England matches. 'Celebrations' by the English fans had generally continued long into the night in a town which was still very much alive at 3 a.m. Sometimes, the reported incidents were amusing – like the West Ham supporters who took a donkey into a local nightspot. Others were more serious. On 24 June, the Chief of Police of the Guipuzcoa Province commented on English fans in San Sebastian that: 'Some of them have taken advantage of our traditional hospitality and have committed all kinds of violence and destruction.' He confirmed that he had asked the San Sebastian police 'to maintain strictness' in this matter and that 'anyone suffering acts of violence, vandalism, threats or abuse due to these people' should report them to the police or the Police Chief personally.[6] According to lads on the Sportsworld campsite, at least one consequence of this 'strict' régime was the sight of Spanish policemen disrupting tent sites during early morning raids.

Although San Sebastian was coping with considerably more English fans than most other places, the English supporters in the town were probably typical of those encamped along the northern coast. There were the same stories, too, of non-payment at bars and restaurants, and of free travel on Spanish trains. A group of young Liverpool fans, experienced football travellers across Europe, had altered the written destination from 'Paris' to 'Sevilla' on their Transalpino cheap rail tickets. By this means, they had made the journey to Spain for not much more than £20 apiece. 'Works every time', they assured us as they left for one of the English bars in town, adding incidentally that some of the 'Huyton Baddies' had made the trip over for the Finals.[7]

The Hollywood bar in San Sebastian was popular with the visitors for its English music, less than exorbitant prices and TV set. It had also become known as a spot where the English assembled of an evening. English lads who did not even known the name of the bar knew where to find it, and the trip there was made nightly by many in search of good times.

In San Sebastian, the English again stressed the imperative of 'sticking together', a strategy designed to counter the presumed threat of local youths and the predatory raids of the police who, according to lads from the campsite, had already jailed ten innocent fans. What was made less clear, of course, was the predatory character of many of the English groups themselves, and the likelihood of them provoking the police and local youths into hasty actions. As often happens in these sorts of situations, the groups involved failed to recognise the degree of mutuality involved in the production of tension between them.

Inside and outside the Hollywood bar, faces familiar from San Mames were becoming more identifiable; the young Leeds fan whose plastered eye had given way to further facial injuries; some of Kellerway's Chelsea mob; two 'skins' from 'Donny' (Doncaster) who were drinking Pernod neat from the bottle, pledging that Leeds were 'meaner bastards' than Chelsea and would prove it in the Second Division; a teenage apprentice 'bricky' from Reading who had arrived with six friends of whom four had gone home because there was 'too much aggro'; and two coachpainters from York, who planned to go home after the Czech match and return to Spain for the games in Madrid.

It was, in many ways, an incongruous sight: the well-heeled, well-groomed Spanish disco-set on holiday, set against the shirtless tattooed English, many of whom were pretty drunk. Outside the bar there were songs, too. 'We're On The March With Greenwood's Army . . .' and the inevitable, '*Malvinas Inglaterra*' with lunges at locals who dared to come too close.

Soon, bottles were being thrown across the street, at nothing in particular, and residents in upstairs apartments were pouring cold water on English heads to get them off the street. Bottles went in that direction too, smashing a couple of street lamps. Soon, as the disturbance threatened to escalate, the sound of police sirens dispersed the English and the Spaniards in the area, or at least those who were sober enough to make their escape. It was, so we were told, a fairly normal night in San Sebastian. Back at the Cestona coach, a combined Arsenal-north country contingent were reliving their experiences in a local brothel for the benefit of the rest. Some of the older members of the party who had come for the sights had decided to take a taxi home at 10 p.m.

The next evening, John Williams returned to San Sebastian by service bus with two of the more reserved among the Cestona set, Phil, a school teacher from Angola in his late twenties, and a young South African trainee photographer nicknamed Yaapi. At the plush 'Basque' bar on San Sebastian Bay, the group met an English party travelling at the top end of the price range. A carpet buyer from the Manchester area was entertaining clients on a four-day luxury package. It included accommodation at a 4-star hotel in Bilbao at which two additional English guests were the footballing Charlton brothers. The carpet group were going across the French border for a slap-up meal, and the invitation was extended to, and reluctantly declined by, the three visitors from Cestona. A few hours later, the decision would be regretted.

Having watched the evening's televised game in the 'Basque' bar, the Cestona group set off for a stroll along the sea front. The time was 11.15 p.m. None wore English colours. None was drunk or singing or drawing attention to himself in any way. Neither were there any large groups of English fans in evidence in the vicinity at the time. As they walked along the sea front, a police officer in the blue uniform of the Policia Municipal approached them and asked, in Spanish, if they were English. They replied, 'Yes', and were immediately handcuffed together with two pairs of 'cuffs'. John Williams began to ask why they were being arrested but, before the first word of his question was completed, he was struck a heavy blow across the shoulders with a truncheon. Phil received similar treatment, this time across the back. The group were motioned to remain silent and sit on the pavement while the officer sought out some more unsuspecting victims.

A small crowd of holidaymakers gathered, by now probably used to the scene being enacted before them. After a few minutes had passed, a Policia Nacional van arrived, siren blaring, lights flashing, and the group were handed over and bundled into the back, still handcuffed. After a short drive, the van pulled into a San Sebastian police station, at which point the group were dragged out and pushed into a reception area. Here, about twenty English fans were already being held. Judging by their expressions and from brief conversations with some of them it was clear that they, too, had simply been picked up at random. Most were from the Sportsworld camp and they were very frightened and bemused.

From here, the whole group were hustled into more police vans. The Cestona trio were simply thrown across those already seated. A teenager from somewhere in the north west sat in the front section of the van behind the driver and nearest the window. As the van prepared to leave, a policeman barked something in Spanish about 'Malvinas' at him, and then, in quick succession spat on the English fan and slapped him sharply across the face.

In the back of the van, the English comforted each other throughout the trip with assurances that the police were merely taking them back to the campsite. After a 20 minute drive, however, they were strong-armed into another police station. Here, the Cestona group were finally relieved of their cuffs and, along with about twenty other Englishmen, forced into a long, thin, brightly lit corridor. They were 'positioned' against the wall. At first, they were required to lean on fully stretched arms with legs wide apart. To ensure the latter, a Spanish policeman painfully kicked everyone's legs apart to their limits. None of the prisoners was permitted to speak. They were forced to stay in this position for about 20 minutes while, behind them, officers of the Policia Nacional joked about the '*hinches ingleses*' (English supporters).

About three times every hour the position was changed to one in which the English lay with their faces against the marble wall, first looking left, then right. It was possible to see beads of sweat from the prisoner's faces trickling down the wall. Changes of position were 'encouraged' by an officer who walked down the line giving each supporter a sharp blow across the kidneys with his truncheon. Occasionally, a Spanish officer would place his face against the wall directly opposite an English one and deliver some edict about the 'Malvinas', accompanied by sharp truncheon blows to the ribs. If the tone of his remarks suggested a question, the stock answer was, 'Non comprend, signor', which produced further cackles from behind and more punishment below.

This routine was supplemented by the periodic disappearance of Englishmen from the top end of the line, presumably taken for interrogation elsewhere. After about 90 minutes, however, the fear began, in some cases, gradually to be supplanted by muted anger.

A young fan from the Manchester area began whispering that the police were 'taking the piss' and started quietly humming and singing 'Rule Britannia', in an attempt to alleviate the collective humiliation of the English. His reward was more attention from a Spanish Officer who viciously kicked the lad's legs so wide apart that it was impossible for him to stay upright. As he began to fall, he was struck with a truncheon in the groin and collapsed in pain, only to be dragged to his feet again, groaning.

After more than 2½ hours of this sort of treatment, during which time the English prisoners were not allowed to speak, questioned by senior officers or charged, a nervous Mundiespana courier arrived from the Sportsworld camp. She told the group later that, by chance, she had witnessed the arrest of five 'quiet' lads from the site, and had come to try and find out why they had been apprehended. When she saw the large number of English fans being held, she realised that the police had been arresting young fans indiscriminately. For the first time, the English were informed of their probable fate. In halting, quivering English, she told the group, who were still standing, POW style, against the wall:

'There has been some damage in San Sebastian tonight which you are supposed to have committed. The police are going to put you in jail and you will come up before the judge tomorrow. Like last time, you will have to pay for the damage.'

The phrase, 'like last time', was a reference to the ten fans still held in San Sebastian who had been similarly selected by the local police to pay for English damage earlier in the week. Nevertheless, the announcement induced some relief in the corridor. At least it meant an end was in sight to the strain on arms and legs which was now becoming unbearable. It also meant a rest from the attentions of some sadistic Spanish policemen.

About 10 minutes later, the courier returned, this time with a different message. She told the detainees:

'Listen, you have been very lucky. You are going to be released. But, *please*, you must be polite to everybody here. Say, "Thank you" and "Goodnight" to everybody, and the Inspector says that you must be nice here and no more fighting now. You must not cause any more damage. Please, don't say

anything as we leave. Just walk out with me. I will be
responsible for you.'

As the group were allowed to troop out, anger slowly began to
replace fear and humiliation. Had the arrival of the courier swayed
the police in their decision not to press charges? Or was this simply
an exercise in intimidation of the English? The courier herself was
certainly too afraid to be involved in a conspiracy. The more likely
explanation was that the English were being returned to their bases
with a clear message: if there is disorder in San Sebastian, then
any Englishman is liable to be arrested and charged. Ironically,
such tactics are reminiscent of the 'tribalism' of hooligan fans
themselves because, for them, an attack by an opposing fan is
repayable by an assault on *any* of his number. In this case, the
police were trying to force an evening curfew on English fans. *El
Diario Vasco* reported that:

> Around 10 o'clock at night, several groups of English youths,
> in a drunken state according to witnesses, attacked and
> vandalised street signs and traffic lights in the streets of San
> Martin and Blas de Leso, causing considerable damage.
>   Once the police were notified, they proceeded to arrest
> approximately 30 of these youths. In the last few hours, some
> of these youths have been released but no other information
> has been offered.[8]

The immediate effects of this incident on the San Sebastian
group, and its effects when relayed to English fans in Cestona,
were to make the English more wary still of the Spanish police. It
also served to confirm the *Midnight Express* images discussed
earlier, increasing the English intolerance of the Spanish generally,
in particular giving rise to a deep hatred of the authorities. Next
day, members of the Cestona party made the short journey across
the border to Biarritz. Two bottles of red wine each – sometimes
more – were the standard order in a Biarritz bar that evening.
More wine was consumed on the return journey. The Spanish
police officer who boarded the coach at the border was confronted
by a hostile, drunken group of Englishmen, still inflamed by the
previous evening's events. It was only the brave efforts of another
Mundiespana courier which ensured that the coach was allowed
to clear the border.

As far as we know, no formal complaint about the San Sebastian affair or other incidents on the northern coast were lodged by the English. The general feeling in the streets on the release of the English captives was that formal channels of complaint would provide little satisfaction. There were, it was agreed, 'better' ways of repaying the Spanish.

While there were problems in San Sebastian, the worst instance of group violence during the English stay in the north probably occurred in Zarauz, the small seaside resort about 10 kilometres from Cestona. Further north, at Igneldo, 300 English fans had gathered early at a cheap site to make daily trips to Bilbao to hunt out match tickets. It was the smaller, Zarauz site, however, which catered for about sixty English fans, where the most serious incidents were centred.

From the earliest days of the tournament, the English had made their presence felt in Zarauz. On 18 June, *The Daily Telegraph* reported that:

> Holidaymakers and the citizens of small towns like Zarauz were awakened throughout the night by drunken mobs screaming obscenities, blasphemies and chanting, 'England, England, England, England'.
>
> One of the common inane chants outside most hotels was: 'Wake up, you bloody foreign bastards . . . England, England, England'.[9]

English fans at Zarauz freely admitted that there had been 'trouble' with the locals which resulted in chairs and bottles being thrown. However, this was nothing compared to the scenes reported to have occurred in the early hours of June 23rd. From conversations later with English fans who had been involved, many of them with heads and arms swathed in bandages as a result of bottle and knife wounds, it seemed that a disagreement in a basement disco-pub, 'Fany', had resulted in a young Spaniard drawing a knife. The English fans went upstairs to the 'Baraeche', the 'English' bar, to recruit reinforcements and then there ensued a vicious and bloody fight with the locals. In the furore, a Spanish policeman trying to secure order shot himself through the leg. Another fired shots 'in the air' which neatly holed one of the walls of the Bar Baraeche at about head height! After the incident, both bar and campsite were given an armed police guard and the

Baraeche was closed in the evenings. Rather than move out of the area, most of the English fans involved decided to remain in the Zarauz region to see the campaign through. Later, at a match at San Mames, a Spanish cameraman captured on film one of the less seriously injured of the English contingent.

In Cestona, news of the Zarauz battle angered the English who interpreted the event as another example of unprovoked Spanish hostility and bloodletting. Talk was of getting 'tooled up' and moving in to aid the beleaguered English. However, the heavy police commitment in Zarauz and, on the part of some at least, fear, finally dissuaded more English fans from moving into the area.

For the Spanish, of course, there was another version of the Zarauz affair in circulation. We enlisted the help of a young Basque, Inigo, who served in 'The Dungeon' and was friendly towards the English, to find out from his friends in Zarauz how the fight had begun. He returned with the news that he had never seen the people of Zarauz so angry. The English, he was told, had been throwing bottles indiscriminately from the balcony of the Baraeche Bar, one of which had seriously injured a young girl. Moreover, throughout their stay, the English had tried to provoke trouble. Inigo was concerned for the English in Madrid. 'In Madrid, it is not like here,' he said. 'There are many boys there who . . .' At this point, he made a jabbing forward movement with his left hand, indicating the stabbing motion of a knife.

These serious incidents at Zarauz were the exception rather than the rule during the English stay in the north. Indeed, contrary to the gloomy prognostications before the arrival of the English in Spain, incidents of serious disorder in the Bilbao region were relatively rare. The final arrest count in the north was: 28 England supporters arrested and detained for more than 24 hours. Seven of the arrests were in Bilbao, 19 in San Sebastian, and 2 in Santander. A further 100 or so English fans were detained and released within 24 hours. At the end of the tournament, 2 English fans were still in custody in the north, held on charges of arson.

The English stay in the north was summed up by *Tribuna Vasca* in the following words:

> Even though the arrival of the British was not the tropical cyclone that was feared, the capacity that the British have for

drinking their beer, and the way we are in the Basque region when our honour is at stake, has given rise to more than one incident.[10]

Chapter Four
ENGLISH FANS IN MADRID

Introduction

Most fans who had booked only for the First Phase matches returned home once they were completed, but a substantial number stayed on for Madrid. The passage of many of them was eased once more by free train travel: for every fan who paid for the journey, there was at least one more who successfully avoided payment. The pattern continued in Madrid itself. When sleeping out in the capital became too dangerous, hundreds jumped on night express trains, travelling as far as the Costa Brava and surviving there on money purloined from passengers and the fruits of shoplifting ventures to local supermarkets. A London holiday-maker, a passenger on one of the express runs, described the trip as 'a nightmare'. She continued:

> 'These bare-chested youths, covered with tattoos and wearing only Union Jacks frightened us to death. They admitted that several had sold their clothes having spent their money in Bilbao watching England in the first round.[1]

In Madrid, we met an Arsenal supporter, a quiet, unassuming London youth who was unemployed. In a matter of fact way, and supported by friends he had teamed up with in Spain, he confided that he had arrived in the country with only £1.50 and had survived since then in the way many others had – by stealing and not paying rail fares. He had dossed down in friends' hostel rooms and had only seen one match, the one against Kuwait when, outside the ground, tickets were literally given away. He was not hopeful of seeing the matches in Madrid, a fact he accepted philosophically. He had come for the 'atmosphere' of the trip and the 'laughs'. At least it made a change from 'signing on' in Islington. As there had been in the north, there were many English fans like him in Madrid.

Along with two of the Chelsea lads from Cestona who had decided to stay on in Spain, we bought a passage on a Sportsworld bus to the capital. The journey was not a pleasant one. 'Birkenhead', one of the older members of the Cestona group, had been over-indulgent the previous evening, spurred on by the younger lads. Now, to their amusement, he was vomiting regularly throughout the trip and thoroughly miserable. The coach also catered for a Kuwaiti family, a fact which did not please the Chelsea lads and some mates of theirs sitting at the back. A war film on the coach TV, which featured concentration camps, improved their tempers and led to loud cheers. At one stage it seemed that the Arab family would be getting off at the common destination, the Hotel Monaco, a prospect which had Phil railing violently, physically wracked with hatred for them. An unpleasant and inconclusive slanging match ensued between him and the FA 'observer' assigned to the trip, before it was made clear that the Kuwaitis were destined for a 4-star hotel. A final point of interest for the English fans on the coach was the inordinate number of brown, Policia Nacional vans which were heading, in convoy, towards Madrid. 'Looks like they're expecting us,' an English voice chirped up from the back.

At the Hotel Monaco, sited in the centre of the town among sleazy backstreets, English fans without bookings or match tickets were offered a room for the night at around 2,000 pesetas (£10) each. Rooms for three persons turned out to be double rooms with a mattress laid on the floor, yet another case for 'the Great World Cup Rip-Off File'. The English hit back in typical fashion, with the Chelsea boys staying unofficially in the hotel without payment for the rest of the week. Similarly a group of teenagers from the Manchester area, having already been ejected from one hostel by the police who had discovered eight English fans in a double room, had now moved into another, even cheaper location with a similar arrangement. The group were collectively paying just 350 pesetas per night (about £2) for the room, and to their delight, the landlady turned out to be 'as good as gold', unwittingly agreeing to take in eight sets of dirty clothes from just two paying customers!

Apart from general complaints about the attempts of some hotels to cash in on the World Cup, there were more criticisms from Sportsworld clients about their accommodation in Madrid. One couple we met in the Spanish capital had paid for 1-star accommodation, only to find themselves in a dirty university dormitory which had been upgraded by Mundiespana. There were reports of married couples being asked to share rooms with other fans, and of disgruntled Sportsworld clients claiming back as much as £100 from the Sportsworld consortium because of the poor quality of the facilities they were being offered.

There was more trouble when Sportsworld's ticket allocation for the remainder of the tournament was delivered by Mundiespana. English fans who had paid up to £1,000 for the trip were to receive only standing tickets for the remaining matches. Mundiespana was accused of corruption by Sportsworld representatives. 'There has been some massive fraud somewhere along the line', remarked Sportsworld's Operations Director, Geoffrey Phillips, 'and it's the ordinary fans who have saved for years to come here who have suffered.'[2] Some of these 'ordinary fans' were also beginning to mutter darkly about the cost of the coach transfers in Madrid which had been included as part of the Sportsworld packages. An amateur statistician had estimated that the consortium were charging somewhere in the region of £50 for transfers to six Madrid matches which, at Madrid Metro prices, were costing the non-Sportsworld spectator a total of 300 pesetas (£1.50).

Sportsworld clients from the north who had booked for the entire tournament were supplemented by about 4,000 Second Phase package customers, making in all somewhere between 4,000 and 6,000 Sportsworld clients stationed in Madrid. Their numbers were bolstered by an estimated 2,000–3,000 English fans who had travelled south without accommodation or tickets.[3] About 1,000 of these had moved directly on arrival to the Bernabeu stadium to queue for tickets for the matches against West Germany and Spain. Soon, flags and sun-tanned, sun-burned, tattooed bodies stretched around the perimeter of the stadium, dwarfing the handful of Spanish and German spectators also in attendance.

The attractions of an extended stay around the Bernabeu were fairly clear. At least English fans sleeping rough had a reason for being there and were not, therefore, liable to be arrested by the police on vagrancy charges. The stadium gathering, too, offered safety in numbers. There was already evidence, however, of the activities of groups of Spanish youths who were seeking out English fans in order to attack them. The appearance of the occasional Basque flag within the English ranks and the prominence given in their chants and conversations to the recent victory in the Falklands were not designed to endear the English to the Spanish police or the members of nationalist movements in the south. Indeed, as the ticket office at the Bernabeu prepared to open, a group of Spanish youths, some wearing headbands and dark glasses, assailed the English with chants of, '*Malvinas, Malvinas*' which was sufficient provocation for some English supporters to attack the local gang. Officers of the Policia Nacional moved in with truncheons to quell the fighting, and the Spanish pro-nationalist group were ushered away from the stadium, still chanting. The English later heard the name of the neo-fascist group, Fuerza Nueva (New Force) applied to their attackers.

English fans who decided not to queue at Bernabeu found little difficulty in obtaining tickets from the stadium later in the week. Accommodation, too, was quite easy to come by in and around Madrid. A guide to cheap hostel accommodation was available at the city's railway and bus stations. In addition, the British Embassy provided English enquirers with a list of hostels which operated on tariffs of less than 500 pesetas (£2.50) per night. Most of these could be found in the centre of the city's main retail district which also contained many 'rough house' bars and street pimps who paraded their charges throughout the early evening and again in the early hours as the bars began to close.

In the early days in Madrid, match tickets could be obtained in town at officially appointed ticket agencies at prices not much above face value. News of this development soon attracted English campsite dwellers into the central district, but after one day's hard selling, the source dried up. Typical of the campers were a group of lads in their early twenties from Chichester. In England, they were employed as apprentice joiners and bricklayers; one was a self-employed plumber, and so on. Two of the group did not know whether their jobs would still be waiting on their return to England because they were supposed to have left Spain after the First Phase. They had risked staying, however, to see the Germany match.

None had paid for any of the train journeys they had undertaken. They talked at length about their dislike of the southern Spaniards – the Bilbaons, they maintained, had at least been friendly; the locals around Madrid were hostile and cold. Compared with the locals, too, the Germans they had met were judged to be 'good lads'. Indeed, during the stay in Madrid, there were few reports of trouble between English and German fans, a trend which carried over even to the match between the two teams at Bernabeu. Conversations later with campers involved in a brawl which resulted in nine Englishmen and eleven Germans being expelled from Spain, suggested, in fact, that the two groups had joined forces in opposition to Spanish youths. Two Frenchmen and an Iranian were also asked to leave Spain as a result of this incident.[4]

It was noticeable that it was typically only the English who were attracted to the cheapest hostel and campsite accommodation in and around Madrid. There were few German, French, Austrian or even Irish supporters in evidence near the central district, although the Germans and the French, at least, were not short of a following in Madrid. It is perhaps significant in this regard that the only German spectator interviewed by the Spanish press turned out to be an insurance agent,[5] and that *The Guardian* commented on the manner in which the majority of English fans in Spain 'provided a colourful if slightly grubby contrast to those Germans who arrived yesterday in their luxury air-conditioned coaches.'[6]

It was again clear, as it had been in Bilbao, that many young English fans came from rather different social backgrounds than the vast majority of other groups of supporters. They were also received in the capital with more publicity than the Germans, the Austrians, the French or the Irish. On 27 June, *Marca* wrote:

> The English players and their mad supporters have arrived in Madrid. The former have come to give a performance on the pitch at the Bernabeu stadium, and the latter, although they are not conscious of it, will also give their performance in the streets of the capital.[7]

Later, on 29 June, *Marca* noted that 'the directors of Real Madrid have worried faces because the terrible (English) supporters are already in the capital and the surrounding areas of Chamartin' (a district of Madrid which includes within its boundaries the Bernabeu stadium). At least one of the probable reasons why the

Madrid directors were anxious was the envious way queuing English fans were eyeing the club's outdoor pool at the rear of the stadium. To have allowed it to be used by the English might have cooled some temperatures later, but the gates remained resolutely closed.

The crowds at Vicente Calderon

At Vicente Calderon to the east of the city, meanwhile (see Figure 3), the Irish, the Austrians and the French were playing for a semi-final place. About 700–800 Irish fans had stayed to support their country in the Second Phase. On the whole, they were older than the English. They tended to live in Northern Ireland, supporting teams like Glentoran, Ards and Bangor. Many proudly wore Irish football shirts, and they even sang the official Irish World Cup song, the laborious, 'I'm Yer Man'. A few of the Irish had brought young sons to the tournament, and the Irish supporters reported little trouble with the locals in Valencia, even though the Irish side had defeated the Spaniards. Significant here may have been the fact that chants about the Falklands and the National Front were not part of the Irish supporters' football repertoire in Spain.

At the match between the Irish and the Austrians, we counted a total of eight Austrian supporters, a reflection of the low level of attendances in the Austrian League, and perhaps also of the feelings of Austrian fans after the accusations levelled at their team in the previous phase which suggested collusion with the Germans in order to ensure the elimination of Algeria.

The French, in their thousands, were noisy and exuberant, but they were well-heeled and charming, too. Again, there was a lack of large groups of teenage supporters and, with few exceptions, match-day uniforms were rather more sober than those favoured by the English. The French flag was in evidence in large numbers at Vicente Calderon, but it was noticeable that, here, local identities did not appear to be cherished as strongly as they were by the English. The tricolour remained untainted by references to French clubs or cities, for example. On an impressionistic level, there also seemed to be more females among the French support, certainly more than the English could muster. There was no doubt too that, like the Brazilians, the French appeared to enjoy music with their

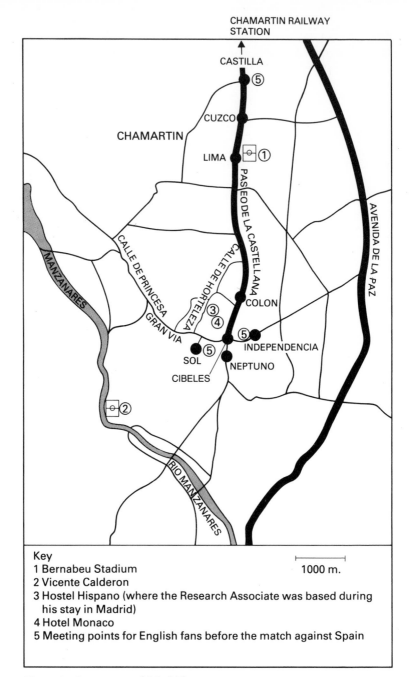

CHAMARTIN RAILWAY
STATION

CASTILLA

⑤

CUZCO

CHAMARTIN

LIMA ⊡ ①

PASEO DE LA CASTELLANA

AVENIDA DE LA PAZ

MANZANARES

CALLE DE PRINCESA

CALLE DE HORTELEZA

CALLE DE HORTELEZA

COLON

③
④

⑤

GRAN VIA

⑤

INDEPENDENCIA

SOL

NEPTUNO

CIBELES

⊡ ②

RIO MANZANARES

Key
1 Bernabeu Stadium
2 Vicente Calderon
3 Hostel Hispano (where the Research Associate was based during
   his stay in Madrid)
4 Hotel Monaco
5 Meeting points for English fans before the match against Spain

1000 m.

Figure 3 Street map of Madrid

football. A brass ensemble of French musicians serenaded their side throughout their matches at Vicente Calderon, finishing each game with an identifiable version of the *Marseillaise*.

While it is difficult to estimate with any precision the number of English fans who attended matches at Vicente Calderon, perhaps somewhere approaching 3,000, most of them probably on Sportsworld packages, attended World Cup matches there. As they had by now come to expect from the manoeuvring of Mundiespana, the English were allotted tickets in the unfavoured upper tiers of the open, all-seated, stone stadium. With temperatures over 100°F, it soon became clear that the official World Cup cushions were selling, not because the seats in Calderon were hard, but because they were unbearably hot.

At none of the matches at Vicente Calderon was there any serious disturbance, although officers of the Policia Nacional continued to oversee the proceedings in vast numbers at all the Second Phase matches staged there. Because Spain, who had been expected to beat the Irish but lost, were favoured to play their Second Phase matches at Calderon, touts found themselves outside the stadium with handfuls of unsold tickets, and senior local police officers seemed to spend most of their time among them negotiating the price in free tickets for allowing the touts to ply their trade unmolested.

Finally, during each match at Calderon, 'Manolo', the Spanish drummer, carried his huge drum around the lower levels of the arena, stirring calls of 'Espana! Espana' from the local contingent who had turned up to enjoy the game. It was the first time the English had experienced support of any substance for the Spanish side. In Bilbao, Spanish fans had remained noticeably reserved in their support for their team. Here in Madrid the situation was very different.

Crowd behaviour and crowd control at the Second Phase matches in the Bernabeu stadium

England had been drawn to meet Germany on 29 June in the first of the Second Phase matches at Bernabeu. The losing team or, in the event of a draw, the Germans, would then play Spain on 2 July, with the final game scheduled for Monday 5 July.

On the morning of the England–Germany match, officers of the Policia Nacional were soon in action, regularly halting groups of English youths in the city centre and demanding proof of identity. A large number were forced to return to their hostel accommodation for their passports. Spanish flags were prominent in the streets of Madrid for most of the day, and groups of Spanish youths in cars paraded up and down the Paseo de la Castellana (see Figure 3) waving flags, shouting slogans and regaling English fans with taunts about the Malvinas and Gibraltar. The English often responded in kind. Nearer the stadium, groups of Spanish youths in open jeeps were engaging in similar activities. Later, they were identified by *The Guardian* as members of Fuerza Nueva, the pro-Franco group which had been involved in earlier disturbances with English fans outside the Bernabeu.[8]

Sited in a plush residential-cum-business district dominated by banks and 4-star hotels, the location of the Bernabeu stadium shares few things in common with its counterparts in England. The only bars within easy reach are situated immediately outside the stadium walls, continuing down a wide but secluded thoroughfare which runs at right angles to the Bernabeu. From about 4 p.m., with the kick-off still some five hours away, English supporters began to monopolise these bars and to take up residence outside them. Several slept on flags, bodies strewn across the pavements. More, however, were concerned with building up their alcohol reserves. Bacardi, wine, vodka and beer seemed to be the most popular orders in the bars of Chamartin and on the pavements around the Bernabeu in the hours before the match.

Some of the English, veterans of the First Phase in Bilbao, were beginning to show signs of wear and tear as a result of their long hours on the road. Washing, for example, had proved to be a problem for those consistently sleeping rough. Others bore marks from fights with Spanish youths and confrontations with the police. Stories abounded about individual adventures. It was interesting to note the way in which accounts of past incidents seemed almost to take on an existence of their own after repeated tellings. For example, Zarauz, unpleasant though it had been, had by this stage come to resemble the annihilation of a small group of defenceless Englishmen. In similar fashion, John Williams heard an embroidered account of his experiences in San Sebastian end with a description of how he had been badly beaten by the Spanish police after his release. While some accounts of incidents were no doubt faithfully retold by their perpetrators and victims, there was also evidence of a considerable amount of poetic licence on the part of some narrators.

In addition to the scars of battle, the appearance of a number of young English fans betrayed an unfamiliarity with the Spanish climate. A Manchester group of about ten City and United supporters who had been jumping trains to and from the coast during their stay, were dubbed 'Emergency Ward 10' outside the Bernabeu. At least five were bandaged around necks, arms and ankles, the result of hospital treatment after severe sunburn. None had been abroad before. One of them was trying to sell a bottle of 'Champagne', stolen from a bar around the corner, for 75 pesetas (about 40p). Three of the group claimed to have no money whatsoever, having spent their last peseta on a ticket for the Germany game.

To compare the characteristics of the English fans in Bilbao and Madrid is not an easy task. There were new recruits, of course, many easily identifiable by the unspoiled nature of their match-day 'kits', and the fact that they tended to be older and better equipped than the majority of the Bilbao contingent. Of those that remained from the north, there was little sign now of the younger, London-centred skinhead following, although remnants of the Chelsea NF brigade remained, as did members of West Ham's 'Inter-City Firm'. This small 'élite' seemed to have been bolstered by some provincial 'hard cases' who, during their stay in the south, appeared to have graduated into the ranks of this travelling corps. Fan groups in Madrid were smaller and, again on an impressionistic level, the London-weighting evident in Bilbao was less apparent here.

The English hard core was bolstered by the presence of three German skinheads who pledged allegiance to SV Hamburg, but who argued in broken English that German support was 'no good'. We had already met these lads in a bar near Sol and, by the end of the evening, the two Chelsea NF lads from Croydon had been exchanging 'Sieg Heils!' in the bar with their new friends. 'English fans are the best', explained the tallest of the three Germans, all of whom seemed to be in their early twenties 'because they fight.' Hamburg skins, the English group learned, hate Cologne skins because, they argued, the Cologne end 'runs away too much'. The London lads chipped into this discussion about hard ends across Europe with recollections from Newcastle to Turin. By this time, the Germans had revealed part of their armoury: a hand machete and a pistol. 'Is it real?' we asked. 'It is real', claimed the Germans. It was impossible to tell if it was, but it was 'real' enough for the police to arrest its carrier in Madrid the following day.

The two remaining Germans moved with the English to Bernabeu. It had to be admitted that they did not fit in easily with the rest of the German supporters who were rather older and more conservative in both their dress and actions. There appeared to be little conflict between German and English fans either inside or outside Bernabeu that evening. 'The German fans and the English fans must stick together,' enthused one of the Hamburg skins. 'They must fight against the Spaniards.'

The first hint of serious disorder outside the Bernabeu before the German match came some three hours before kick-off. Spanish supporters waving flags and shouting support had been arriving, without incident, for about 30 minutes when a nationalist 'demonstration' involving about fifty Spaniards, several of them women, paraded before the English. The locals chanted slogans about the *Malvinas* and Gibraltar, and the English, by now fluent in the Spanish needed for this sort of debate, responded with, '*Malvinas, Malvinas, Inglaterra*'.

Officers of both the Policia Nacional and the Policia Municipal moved in to separate the two groups and to try to calm the Spanish demonstrators. The English, meanwhile, continued to sing on the pavements and later moved into a nearby bar which faced the stadium. Although the English were not prevented from entering, they learned later that the bar was a favourite haunt for pro-Franco Spanish nationalists.

The British fans who remained on the pavement continued to sing as the police dealt with the demonstration. It was made up of what the Spanish press later confirmed to be members of Fuerza Nueva. 'Rule Britannia' and 'You'll Never Take Gibraltar' were favourite renditions by the English at this point. The police decided it was time to move in their mounted officers. About forty mounted policemen of the Policia Nacional had been parading in front of the Bernabeu since 5 p.m. A dozen moved to quieten the English, seemingly interpreting them as about to turn into a dangerously over-excited mob. The methods used to disperse the English fans were rather different from the gentle persuasion used in an attempt to control the Spanish demonstrators. Next day, *El Alcazar* described the scene in the following way:

> Yesterday, with the meeting of the teams from England and Germany, the sons of Great Britain performed all kinds of vandalism and show-off antics in the vicinity of the 'Santiago Bernabeu'. The Policia Nacional had to intervene to stop the embarrassing spectacle by some of the undesirable tourists who, probably due to good Spanish wine, had lost their sense of civic reserve.[9]

The mounted policemen were clearly determined to disperse the English, grouped about a hundred and fifty strong on the pavement in front of the groundside bar. They did so simply by riding into them without warning. All the English scattered save for two who remained lying on their flag, too drunk to make an immediate getaway. As the English regrouped, the next charge came along the pavement, pinning spectators to the wall and forcing about twenty fans to take refuge inside the bar. From the comparative safety of the bar, the singing and celebrations began again until a mounted policemen rode right up to the door. With the head of his horse practically inside, the English were ordered out.

More Spanish demonstrations began, amidst applause from locals for the actions of the police in scattering the English. Undismayed, the English regrouped again behind some police fences that had been hastily erected on the street running at right angles to the stadium. This time, the singing was conducted from English car bonnets in apparent disregard of the efforts of the Spanish police. From this point on, with police sirens wailing as cars hurled along the crowded streets, all semblance of police organisation and restraint seemed to disappear. Instead, there was a kind of legitimised free-for-all in which the Policia Municipal joined with the Policia Nacional in indiscriminate attacks on English fans. Baton charges down adjoining streets had the English scattering. Any fan in the way was in danger of being struck by a police truncheon. A number of arrests were made, including one of the German skinheads, allegedly for throwing a bottle. A young girl was dragged off and beaten for remonstrating with Spanish demonstrators. In this last incident, an English reporter who had photographed the affair had his film confiscated by the police. Local photographers moved in, sensing a story, and the English regrouped for photographs, some of them aiming 'Sieg Heils!' at the Spanish extremists. Finally, at around 8 o'clock, there emerged out of this confusion an uneasy peace. The police, apparently satisfied with their evening's work, shelved their truncheons, and spectators streamed towards the gates of the stadium.

Inside the Bernabeu, the English were confined almost exclusively to the standing sections which, unusually, were found at the highest point of the arena. By contrast, the Germans were seated below in the best vantage points. The match itself was disappointing, resulting in a sterile goalless draw. Throughout, there was provocation and counter-provocation, and occasional skirmishes between English and Spanish fans, the bulk of the latter stationed on terraced areas immediately below their English counterparts. From time to time, officers of the Policia Nacional moved in to subdue the English with truncheon attacks. Later, there were justifiable complaints that the locals were not admonished for *their* behaviour. When Spanish supporters close to the English contingent began singing, usually in response to Manolo and his drum or, more rarely, to a piece of enterprising play by the Germans, they were discreetly kicked by Butley and company. That these skirmishes remained localised and sporadic was probably due as much to the stalemate on the field as anything else. Given the atmosphere that existed in Bernabeu that night, Spanish celebrations of a German goal, for example, might have resulted in disturbances rather more serious than those which did occur.

Outside the stadium, more Spanish provocation was quickly taken up by the English. It was difficult to tell whether the locals outside had actually been to the game. They were performing with their pro-Argentina chants for a Spanish TV crew, the television lights illuminating their display and providing a focal point for attack. In the street behind them, a Union Jack was draped across the road for cars to run over and then ritually spat upon and set ablaze. As groups of English supporters set off in pursuit of the *provocateurs*, the Spaniards scattered, leaving an unfortunate passing motorist and his car to bear the brunt of the English punches and kicks. To the disappointment of some of the English, the Spaniards appeared to adopt a policy of provocation and running for police protection. A Southampton fan, with 'Saints' and Bulldog Bobby tattoos showing above a Union Jack worn around the waist, complained: 'Soon as you get into them, they want the Old Bill in. They see the Old Bill, and they're off like a fuckin' shot!'

Up ahead, on the Paseo de la Castellana, the sounds of police sirens and the appearance of an ambulance suggested that a more serious confrontation was taking place. In fact, an England fan had been stabbed in a scuffle near the entrance to one of the groundside tube stations (see Plate 4). Eyewitness reports suggested that at least one of the group of English supporters who were attacked was carrying a Basque flag. Mark Buckley, an 18-year-old printer from Derbyshire, had evidently been stabbed near the heart by one of a group of Spanish extremists who were chanting, 'Gibraltar, Espanol' (Gibraltar is Spanish) and 'Muerte a los Ingleses' (Death to the English). Later that same evening, gangs of Spanish youths wearing the uniform of New Force beat up and stabbed a further three English supporters who were sleeping in a park near the Bernabeu stadium. All three were seriously injured. Two of them are pictured on Plate 5.

Following the incidents before and after the match against the Germans, the influential Spanish newspaper, El Pais, published an editorial concerning 'The English Fans'. It is worth quoting at length:

The English Fans

The incidents provoked by the English fans and the incidents that they have been victims of; their physical and verbal aggression together with the attacks that they have been responsible for, threaten to degenerate into degrading and even larger confrontations. In this case, it isn't only the emotions about football and the tribal factor that have fed this competition with rivalry.

On the one hand, the enraged nationalism that the war in the Malvinas has stimulated is mixed with the support of a team bearing the colours of one's country, representing one's nation in the World Cup. On the other hand, is the well-known stupidness of the Welsh, Scots or English who live for football, and feeling inspired more by their uncontrolled drunkenness than by their passion for the game.

With the presence of the boastful, shirtless English always obvious in Madrid, some groups of extreme rightwingers from Spain are inclined to resolve their political disputes with the message of the Force. They want to take revenge for Gibraltar *via* football, and they comfort themselves by going on crusades against English supporters. The date, Monday, 5th July, when England and Spain meet, could be an unfortunate time for violence unless someone does something to prevent it.[10]

Up until this time, English newspapers had tended to search avidly for and roundly condemn hooligan incidents involving English fans. Now, however, they were enraged by the attacks by Spanish youths and the police, above all by the stabbings. Here is a selection of headlines which appeared in the English press on 1 July: 'Death to the English' (*The Daily Mail*); 'Nazi Thugs Knife The English Fans' (*The Sun*); 'Victims Of The Fascist Mobs' (*The Daily Star*); and 'Mobs *And* Police Attack The English Supporters' (*The Daily Mirror*). In fact, *The Daily Mirror* described the Spanish extremists in the shorthand used so often to describe football's National Front supporters in Britain – 'short-haired NF youths.'[11] *The Daily Star* noted that:

> The thugs seem to be immune from arrest by the Spanish police who are more interested in beating up the English fans and keeping the fact secret. . . . English authorities in Madrid fear that there will be a blood bath when England play Spain in Madrid on Monday.[12]

English newspapers were a major source of information for English fans in Madrid. After the German match, there was much confusion among them as to what exactly had happened. Rumours abounded, ranging from incomplete information about the number and seriousness of the stabbings, to a fictitious attack by two hundred armed Spanish youths on an English campsite immediately after the match. Many English fans were very frightened by the new developments, interpreting them as only the most violent expressions of a general anti-British feeling in the city. Other English fans were angry and disdainful of the Spanish. The latter sentiments are, perhaps, best exemplified by an incident which took place in the early hours of 1 July when four English fans were arrested on the balcony of a hostel in the Barbara de Braganza, completely nude and cleaning their genitals with a Spanish flag. The next day, police arrived to tear down any English flags still flying from hostel windows in the central district. The fact that the circumstances of their arrest and the order for deportation of the English youths involved were later reported in the Spanish press, probably did much to dissipate whatever sympathies the locals still retained for their English guests.

After the stabbing incidents in Madrid became more widely known to the English, hundreds more joined the daily exodus to the south coast, some probably never to return. The more hardy, together, perhaps, with those in search of revenge, remained in and around the city but they stressed the imperative of remaining in large groups for defensive purposes. For some young England fans, the image of the English 'under siege' was an heroic one. To survive to tell of the very real dangers of refusing to discard one's England shirt for the game against Spain, for example, would stand the teller in good stead at home and on future ventures. Comparisons were already being made by England veterans with the situation in Turin when the visiting English had been similarly threatened by local youths.

For other English fans, the disturbances and local hostility proved to be more than even the World Cup was worth. We met a number of fans in Madrid who, fearing further attacks by the Spaniards, opted to watch the England–Spain game on TV. Later, *The Daily Mirror* reported that at least 2,000 English fans had left their campsites after the German match in order to avoid the attentions of what were described as 'knife-happy fascists'.[13] The newspaper also quoted England's Kevin Keegan urging troubled English fans to 'stay away if you sense danger'. It is certainly the case that many of the English departed from Spain at this point because of increasing difficulties in the capital. A large number left, however, because they had jobs and families to return to, or simply because their funds had run out. The German game was a bonus they had promised themselves should England succeed in the north.

The tension that existed in Madrid between some local youths and the English who remained grew more pronounced as the week wore on. The bar in Sol where the German skinheads were first encountered was now minus a door and most of its fixtures after what the barman described as 'a fight with bottles' between English and Spanish youths. The atmosphere building up prior to the meeting between the two countries was punctured a little, however, by the mid-week defeat of the Spanish side by the Germans. The result meant that the host nation was eliminated from the tournament, and that their best efforts on Monday could only prevent the English from reaching the semi-finals.

The Spain and West Germany affair produced an entirely different atmosphere from that at either of the matches involving England. The bars near the stadium were little used and, despite fanatical Spanish support, the defeat of the host nation produced little discernible trouble outside the ground. This was probably due, in some measure at least, to the continued anonymity of most of the German contingent. There were no English fans wearing colours present at the match.

An article published after the Spain–West Germany game in the newspaper, *Diario 16*, captures the nationalistic fever exhibited by Spanish supporters around this time. It also draws connections between the forthcoming meeting of the English and Spanish teams, the fractious relationship that existed between sections of the English and Spanish support, and the omnipresent shadow of the Falklands. The article reads:

> As usually happens with pretenders, the fall has been harder than expected. If, instead of using and abusing drums and trumpets they had put things into perspective, the upset on Friday would have been a lot less painful. But no, they (Spanish fans) were going to the Bernabeu as if to the crusades, loaded with flags and symbols of patriotism. The amazing multitude had headed for the streets – linked spiritually with millions of TV viewers – as if in the Castellana they found their Malvinas or Gibraltar and had to conquer them at all costs, that is by kicks.
> *That Is Not Football.*
>
> Fortunately, there was no Galtieri there, neither planes nor ships, but warriors of the microphone and the pen almost moved us from the Plaza de Mayo, confusing the White House with the Rosada. Thank God that the opponent was Germany, and that on Monday it will not be important that the British recover Chamartin as the new Falklands, after the disturbed heads we have seen waiting for the arrival of tickets for these last eight days.[14]

By 4 July, a total of 42 foreign football fans had been arrested in and around Madrid on charges ranging from disturbing the peace and resisting arrest to insulting symbols of Spanish nationality. Of these, 29 – 16 Englishmen, 10 Germans, 2 Frenchmen, and one other – had already been expelled from the country. All the Germans were expelled as a result of the campsite brawl and vandalism engaged in in tandem with English fans. The 16 English were found guilty of a variety of offences in different locations in the city.

The Policia Nacional aimed to restrict the opportunities of the English for further disruption by offering 'special measures' to ensure their 'protection' at the match against Spain. More specifically, they planned that:

(i) English fans should not be allowed to purchase tickets on the day of the match. Nor would ticketless fans be allowed within the vicinity of Bernabeu;

(ii) the English, regardless of their tickets, should be directed to 'special zones' inside the ground and isolated from Spanish fans;

(iii) no fans considered drunk would be allowed into the Bernabeu. Drunken fans would be arrested;

and (iv) any fan loitering or sleeping near the Bernabeu outside the hours of the match would be arrested.

As usual, word of the new proposals reached English fans in the capital by rumour and via the English press. Astonishingly, there seemed to be few supporters who failed to take heed, and so it must be presumed that the majority heard of the new measures in some way or another. This was of particular importance with regard to items (iii) and (iv). No doubt the actions of the police at the match against West Germany also had their effects but, whatever the reasons, in the hours between 3 p.m. and 7 p.m. before the Spanish game the bars near the Bernabeu remained almost empty.

Word of mouth dictated that, for the sake of protection, young English fans who were planning to wear their colours to the match should meet at 7 p.m. at one of three prearranged venues, the Plaza de Castilla in the north, the Plaza de Sol in the south, and outside the Sportsman's Bar on Independence Plaza to the east. The Sportsman's was a favourite English haunt because it was managed by an Englishman and the bar served beer in pint pots. Occasionally, too, the manager allowed 'homeless' English fans to sleep in the corner of the bar during the afternoon.

The large groups of English supporters who left the pre-arranged

meeting points were shadowed *en route* to the stadium by vans
containing officers of the Policia Nacional. There was the now
usual baiting of the English by groups of Spanish youths, but the
Sportsman's and Sol groups, which numbered about a couple of
hundred fans, managed to reach Bernabeu without serious incident.
During the long march, we re-established links with two Hull City
fans we had first met before the Northern Ireland–Austria match.
They were in their twenties and one, at least, was on the dole. His
mate was a Hull Kingston Rovers fan, and he bemoaned the fact
that most Hull City 'hard cases' were fans of the Hull Rugby
League club. He talked about how Rugby League was 'coming on',
citing a recent 'battle' at the Hull Rugby League 'derby' match.
The lad on the dole, his friend explained, had just 'done' three
months for being stopped on the motorway on the Hull coach
travelling to Chelsea. An arms cache had been found on board![15]
This followed a six months' stretch for burglary, some of the fruits
of which, he claimed, had helped to pay for the World Cup trip.
This means of finance differed from that of five Geordies we also
met *en route* to the stadium. Two years ago they had been part of
a group of 15 lads who were 'interested' in the venture. However,
for various reasons, 10 had fallen by the wayside. Paid over two
years, the five claimed not to notice the cost of the trip (over £700
each). There was a pipelayer, an insulation worker and a window
cleaner in their ranks, and after the match they were off to Malaga
to doss around for two days, before moving on to the semi-final
in Seville.

The English gathered at around 7.15 p.m. at a groundside bar,
the Cachirulo, as hundreds of flag-waving Spaniards marched up
and down the length of the Bernabeu, singing songs in praise of
the host nation. English fans were, on the whole, more restrained
than on their previous visit, and there was little of the uncontrolled
drunkenness so evident before the match with the Germans. Occasionally, nevertheless, small groups would gather in front of the
Cachirulo for choruses of, 'Rule Britannia' and 'England! England!'
(see Plate 6). The Spanish police, sensing further trouble between
the English and the locals, launched into the offensive. Fans were
forced into the bar and the doors were closed. In conversation
later, fans who had been trapped inside spoke of fights with local
extremists and truncheon-wielding by the blue-shirted Policia
Municipal. When the doors were finally opened, English fans faced

an avenue of truncheons from officers of both the Policia Municipal and the Policia Nacional (see Plate 7). We saw the Hull Kingston Rovers fan being led away by the Red Cross for three stitches to an eye wound. His case was later featured in *The Times*.[16] There were indiscriminate attacks on English fans standing nearby who had played no part in the preceding incidents. Baton charges continued down side streets (see Plate 8). It seemed that any identifiable English fan was liable to be attacked. A Chelsea supporter who had been talking to us was pinned against a wall by a mounted policeman and beaten until he replaced his shirt. The police seemed determined to gain full recompense for the indignities they perceived themselves as having suffered at the West Germany game and throughout the English stay in Madrid. Their work was heartily applauded by local youths, who then picked out English fans for the attention of mounted policemen. Fans thus selected scattered, with policemen in pursuit. After the English had been 'taught their lesson' by the local force, those that remained, unable or unwilling to shed their identifying favours, were, not surprisingly, wary of the Spanish police. The police carried out their work before approving Spanish eyes (see Plate 9). In all, the 'open season' on the English had lasted for about 30 minutes. It gave some credence to warnings like the one issued before the match by *The Sunday Times*:

> For the English fans, tomorrow's prospect is fearful. Some, here and there, have disgraced themselves with silly, drunken behaviour, but by and large they are more sinned against than sinning. What sort of protection will they get from the police if toughs attack them again?[17]

Diario 16 and *El Alcazar* blamed the pre-match violence on the heavy drinking and 'bad manners' of the English fans.[18] Later, however, José Barrioneuvo, the head of the Policia Municipal in Madrid, expressed himself ashamed of his officers for some of their 'uncalled for interventions'. An additional source of embarrassment for senior local police officers was the fact that a local male arrested in the incident inside the Cachirulo Bar was immediately released when it was discovered that he was an off-duty member of the police!

Later, *Diario 16* considered that the scenes outside the Bernabeu merited an article under the title, 'Xenophobia':

I saw a policeman kicking an English fan, and another
policeman clubbing the friends with him. He had not done
anything, just waved an English flag, exactly what many others
were doing. Near him, some Spaniards were also waving flags.

The English fans have a reputation for being very hard and
maybe this reputation needs preventive treatment. But,
frankly, the remedy was worse than the problem. The Spanish
police turned out to be harder than the English fans.

At the end of the game, the police did not intervene when,
on various occasions, groups of Spaniards attacked groups of
English supporters . . . It is good to support one's team, even
if they play badly, but this Xenophobia, a miserable
manifestation of patriotism condoned by the authorities, is pure
barbarity.[19]

The British press, by now apparently willing to forgive English
fans most things after their intimidation by the Spaniards, was
unanimous in its condemnation of the Spanish authorities. Pride
of place in this department went to *The Daily Star* with its astonishingly indignant full-page headline of 6 July, 'Police Brutes Beat Up
Our Fans'. Questions followed in the House of Commons, with
recommendations from some Labour MPs that holidaymakers
bound for Spain should be warned about the excesses of the
Spanish police, and that Spain's application to join the EEC should
be blocked because of the 'brutality and force' used by the Spanish
police in controlling English fans.

Inside the Bernabeu, the situation for English supporters was
hardly less intimidating than it had been outside. Despite the
segregation plans of the police, we found ourselves in a small seated
section at the north end of the stadium along with about fifty other
English fans. Behind were Spanish terrace supporters and, further
back still, the diminished ranks of the main body of England
supporters, apparently hemmed in by a wall of Union Jacks stretched across the front of the terrace fencing. Effectively segregated
from Spanish fans and surrounded by policemen whose instructions
about how to deal with the English had been made clear outside,
the main body of England supporters remained somewhat cowed
throughout the match. The game ended in a 0–0 draw, thus
ensuring the elimination of the England team.

Down below, the small mixed bag of English fans were treated to missiles, including stones, and constant verbal provocation. When a fan turned to remonstrate with the Spanish supporters behind, he was immediately taken away by officers of the Policia Nacional. Spanish fans reacted to the result of the match as if it meant that the host nation had won the World Cup. For them, it seemed more than enough on the night simply to ensure that the English did not qualify for the later stages of the tournament.

Outside the ground there were fights between the English and Spanish supporters but these were quelled, all too soon argued some of the English later, by the enormous number of policemen on duty. There were also reports from the English fans later that a Spanish supporter had been stabbed in the cheek. To our knowledge, it was not reported in either the English or the Spanish press.

Back at the Sportsman's Bar after the game, some of the English fans who had arrived late to take up their positions in the ground were surprised at the reports of excessive intimidation by the Spanish police and spectators. They had experienced little of this kind of treatment. The secret of staying out of trouble had been to travel to the ground in small groups, unmarked by England favours, and to remain silent in the face of provocative chants by home supporters. 'What kind of support is that?' asked a young Crystal Palace fan in full match-day uniform of England shirt and flag. 'That's how wankers watch football!'

Later, upstairs in the Sportsman's small restaurant which served modest English delicacies such as shepherd's pie and steak and kidney pie, there was a surprising late guest, Bobby Robson, the England manager-elect. 'How do they feel, Bobby?'; 'What went wrong?'; 'Will you come and manage our club, Bobby?', were just a few of the questions aimed at Robson, clearly drained by the evening's events. News of his arrival soon reached England fans downstairs. Two Manchester United fans sought Robson's assistance. Both were big and heavily-tattooed working-class lads, one aged about 25, the other younger. The elder of the two was puzzled by something:

'Listen, Mr Robson, what I can't understand is this. We come out here, we live for weeks on nothing. There's lads losing their jobs; we're being battered all the time by the police and getting locked up, and after all that, England players can't even wave to the fans to say, 'Thanks lads', before they walk off the pitch.'

Robson muttered something about players 'feeling sick' and 'not thinking'. The younger lad chipped in then. He was unemployed and had spent five days in a San Sebastian jail. 'Yeah, Mr Robson. It was terrible the way we were treated by the Spanish. It was the police, you see. The Spanish fans, they were nothing. If it hadn't been for the police, we'd've fuckin' murdered 'em'.' With an air of quiet resignation, Robson got up from his seat, made his apologies and left.

On 8 July the Spanish government announced that it was to hold an enquiry into the incidents outside the Bernabeu. The Deputy Mayor of Madrid agreed to conduct the investigation himself, reiterating that what he had seen that evening had made him 'ashamed to be Spanish'.[20] While the English were under attack in Madrid, however, 24 English fans had been arrested in Benidorm after being thrown out of the capital by the Policia Nacional for sleeping rough on park benches. They were said to have 'damaged cars, thrown stones at passers by, wrecked a bar, and attacked a policeman'.[21] At Chamartin railway station in Madrid, meanwhile, large groups of tired, unshaven, tattooed men and youths were bypassing the long queues at the international ticket desk. The English had another train to jump

1   English fans in Basel, June 1981. The fears of the English authorities were for repeat, televised performances in Spain

2   Soccer Cop '82. A familiar sight on match days in Spain. Before the Finals, one English fan said, 'Anyone who picks an argument with these cops has got to be out of his mind!'

3   World Cup Task Force '82. 'Argentina, what's it like to lose a war?' sang
these fans and hundreds like them. According to *The Observer*,
'Jingoism rules in Spain

Mark . . . missed death
by a fraction

VICTIMS OF THE FASCIST MOBS

'Dead' fan saved

From CHRIS BOFFEY in Madrid

ENGLAND Soccer fans were living in fear last night after the stabbing of four Britons by a mob of screaming Fascists.

The Madrid gang's first victim, 19-year-old Mark Buckley, missed death by a fraction of an inch when a dagger was plunged into his heart.

Three hours later the fanatical right-wingers struck again, stabbing and battering three more World Cup supporters.

Witnesses of the attack on Mark heard the thugs shouting "Gibraltar is Spanish" and "Death to the English." Then they fled—leaving their victim with blood pouring over the flag of St. George wrapped proudly around his waist.

Mark, of Ripley, Derbyshire, was rushed to Madrid's La Paz hospital, where surgeon Dr. Lorenzo Espigs said: "He died for three minutes on the operating table before we were able to bring him back. We stitched up his heart—the knife had gone right in."

Mark's mum Maureen, who rang the hospital, said : "The surgeon told me that if the knife had gone an eighth-of-an-inch either way my son could have died."

As Mrs. Buckley made plans to fly out to Spain, a neighbour said: "Mark is no troublemaker—he just loves football."

The second attack by the Fascist mob—known as the New Force—was equally vicious.

They crept up on Gary Smith, Dave Moore and Robert Walton and plunged daggers into their stomachs, heads and shoulders.

Metal

Then they beat the bleeding fans with metal bars and baseball bats.

Last night Robert, 19, from Southport, was in La Paz hospital with an eight-inch gash across his stomach and a gaping back wound.

Dave, 21, from Weybridge, said : "It was the most terrifying moment of my life.

"There were about 15 youths, dressed in the fascist group's clothes.

"They kept screaming "Malvinas" — the Spanish name for the Falklands."

Broken

Dave, his Union Jack T-shirt drenched in blood, added : "I've a broken hand, broken fingers and I lost count of how many stitches they put in my head."

He and Gary, 25, from Manchester, were also treated at La Paz.

The British consul in Madrid, Mr. David Lloyd, said : "I doubt that the gang will ever be found — or that the police will try too hard."

Mark Buckley lies unconscious, a blood-spattered England flag around his waist

4 Supporting 'our boys'. The *Daily Star* reports on the near-fatal stabbing of Mark Buckley after the England v. West Germany match in Madrid

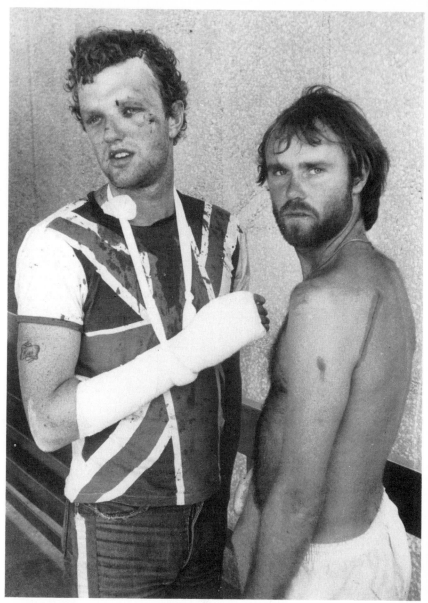

5 Victim of 'New Force'. Two English fans who were stabbed and beaten with metal bars and baseball bats as they were sleeping in a park near the Bernabeu

6 Scenes outside the Bernabeu Stadium, 5 July 1982. English
preparations for the match against Spain

7 Minutes later, Spanish police move in to disperse chanting English fans

8 Incidents before the Spain v. England game which led to complaints
from the English and apologies from the Spanish authorities. English
fans were attacked by Spanish police and members of 'New Force'
inside the Cachirulo. Outside, more policemen were in attendance

9 On the defensive in Madrid. *El Pais* reported that English fans 'were assaulted yesterday by Spanish extremists in the presence of policemen'

10 The outer fences of the Feyenoord Stadium serve as a reminder that vicious spikes and graffiti are not restricted to English grounds

11   Out and about with Villa fans abroad. Checking out the barriers in
Anderlecht

12   Segregation breaks down in Anderlecht. In the background, Villa fans
beckon the opposition to attack as the local police pick up the pieces

13   Back page fare for *Daily Mirror* readers on September 23rd 1982. The
fans at the kicking end of the action are clearly rather older than
current stereotypes of hooligan offenders suggest

14   The demon drink. Good times in Copenhagen prior to the serious
disturbances which took place in and around Idraetspark

15 The gentle art of 'mooning'. *Ekstra Bladet* told its readers that this display could be translated as 'Danish police – my arse!'

16 The flag and foreign police, constant companions at England matches abroad in the 1980s. A pre-match arrest in a Copenhagen thoroughfare

17 Standing in the *Idraetspark* seats. An English fan obliges a friendly
Danish cameraman

18 Small beginnings. English fans on the look out for satisfaction outside
the *Idraetspark*. More was to come

19 Bulldog Bobby in Spain. The Spanish newspaper *Deia* captioned this picture 'Grr'. The bulldog on his chest seems to have an effect on his temperament

Part II
THE BEHAVIOUR AND CONTROL OF ENGLISH FANS AT 'ONE-OFF' CONTINENTAL MATCHES

Introduction

The month-long World Cup Finals and the finals of the newly established European Championship, which takes place over the shorter period of two weeks, are the major international football tournaments currently staged on a regular basis. When the England team manages to qualify for their final stages, these competitions constitute a major source of concern for the English authorities. (This is only true of World Cups, of course, when they are staged in Europe.)

The English football authorities have probably reacted with mixed feelings to the national side's rather inconsistent record in international competition over the past twenty years. Poor form and tough draws during this period have often confined England fans to armchair viewing, as other nations (including, quite frequently, the 'auld enemy') have competed for the game's major prizes. During these lean years, continental travel for English fans has meant, for the most part, the short-stay, 'one-off' match, either in the European club competitions, or following the national side in the qualifying rounds of the European Championship. These are the bread-and-butter continental trips for English fans. About three or four of them per season give the authorities on both sides of the Channel palpitations. This is despite the fact that the majority of the visiting English can be expected to be on their way home after, at most, an overnight stay. A few, of course, stay longer, but in a large number of cases the return journey begins immediately after the match.

Not all the ventures into Europe of English sides carry the prospect of English-inspired disorders. Trips to Eastern Europe and the early rounds of European competition, for example, hold few attractions for the majority of English fans, even those able to afford the considerable costs involved. However, the 1982 World Cup Finals were sandwiched between two major one-off matches on the continent and serious disorders were feared at both of them. The first involved a club side, Aston Villa; the second, the national side in a European Championship qualifying match in Denmark. In the event, these two meetings produced widely differing performances by English spectators. Villa fans were praised for their good behaviour at the European Cup Final in Rotterdam, while, in Copenhagen, England fans added to their growing list of indiscretions on the continent. This section of the book concerns itself with an analysis of some of the circumstances which produced these markedly different results. It also illustrates the sorts of crowd behaviour and crowd control problems typically associated with one-off matches on the continent, and thus provides a contrast to the analysis of an extended tournament in Part I. The section – and the book – ends with some observations on the relationship between sociological research and social policy. Then, in Appendix 4, we offer some suggestions on how, in future, the authorities might best limit the incidence of hooliganism by English fans abroad. First, however, in Chapter 5 we provide a participant observer's account of a trip to Rotterdam for the European Cup Final of 1982, and in Chapter 6, of one to Copenhagen, for the Denmark–England match of that year.

Chapter Five

ASTON VILLA v. BAYERN MUNICH: CROWD BEHAVIOUR AND CROWD CONTROL AT THE 1982 EUROPEAN CUP FINAL

The final tie of the European Club Champions' Cup played at the Feyenoord Stadium, Rotterdam on 26 May 1982, brought together Aston Villa, the champions of the English First Division, and Bayern Munich, the premier club side in West Germany. The meeting promised to be rather more entertaining than those which followed the 1977 Final when, coincidentally, another English club, Liverpool, accounted for the Germans of Borussia Mönchengladbach by 3 goals to 1. Since then the European Final had been characterised largely by stereotyped, negative play and a succession of one-nil scorelines. Both Villa and Bayern, however, were sides renowned more for the quality of their attacking play than the sureness of their defences. Most commentators predicted an exciting encounter, liberally sprinkled with what the TV pundits describe as 'goal-mouth incidents' and, more importantly, a fair share of goals.

Off the field, there was also a sense of anticipation as the match approached, but of a rather different kind. Crowd trouble was widely feared. The Final had already been scarred on a number of occasions by the misbehaviour of English fans, most notably in Paris in 1975 and 1981 when Leeds United and Liverpool, respectively, were the contending English sides. The Dutch authorities, however, had special reasons for being wary of English spectators. Back in May 1974, as we noted in the Introduction, Spurs fans had run amok during their side's EUFA Cup Final defeat by Feyenoord. The visiting English had caused thousands of pounds of damage to the Feyenoord stadium and the surrounding areas, and had set about local fans with bottles and sticks, incurring the displeasure of the Dutch riot police. It was a lesson which was not lost on the people of Rotterdam or the Dutch authorities. When Spurs returned in 1981 to play Ajax of Amsterdam, their supporters brought with them what *The Sun* described as the 'sub-zero' reputation of British fans, a reputation which had induced the introduction of 'mobile sin bins, commando police, plain clothes officials and dog and horse patrols ... adding to the normal security at the Olympic Stadium.[1]

Reports of incidents which occurred before and after the match, however, suggested that travelling Spurs 'hard cases' had more than enough to cope with away from the suffocating security arrangements employed at the Ajax ground. In Amsterdam itself, groups of Dutch youths, sometimes 200 strong, were reported to be attacking and robbing English fans. In one incident at the central railway station, three Spurs fans had been stabbed and one thrown through a shop window in what a local policeman described as 'a vicious and bloody fight' which 'the Tottenham fans did not start'. It resulted, nevertheless, in the deportation of 28 of their number.[2]

Such incidents were not merely isolated examples of the actions of a latter-day Dutch resistance movement aimed, this time, at the invading English. The football scene in Holland is far from free from the effects of hooliganism as is suggested by the mazes of fences which surround many grounds (see Plate 10). In this context, it must be enough to cite two examples of the sorts of behaviour which have led the authorities to regard such defences as necessary. We have referred already to the Molotov cocktail which injured Feyenoord goalkeeper, Joop Hiele, in November 1981.[3] Then, in April 1982, the Den Haag ground in Amsterdam was set on fire by football vandals, causing damage estimated at £250,000.[4] In the same month in Belgium, Aston Villa fans were busy booking themselves a warmer reception from the authorities for the Final in Rotterdam than they might otherwise have had cause to expect as English representatives in a European competition.

In their first year in the European Cup, Villa had travelled widely up to the semi-final. Trips to Iceland, the USSR and East Germany had kept the number of travelling Villa fans and, hence, the potential for disorder to a minimum. The short trip to Anderlecht for the second leg of the semi-final, however, provided, virtually for the first time, the opportunity for a large number to follow their side into Europe. Villa officials attempted to obtain basic assurances from their Belgian counterparts before the match concerning arrangements for travelling fans. There were problems from the outset. 'We feared there would be trouble,' commented Villa secretary, Steve Stride. 'Anderlecht officials looked on in amazement when we asked that rival spectators be strictly segregated.'[5] Manchester United officials had been similarly apprehensive in 1977 before the away leg of a Cup Winners' Cup-tie in St Etienne. In France, taunts about the bread strike, then in full swing in England, had played a part in triggering the disturbances on unsegregated goal-end terraces before the match. In Anderlecht, it was reported that taunts about the Argentinians had preceded the fighting which resulted in a stoppage in play of some six minutes as fans spilled onto the playing area[6] (see Plates 11 and 12). Significantly, Charles Burgess of *The Guardian* commented in this connection that: 'It must also be said that a small group of Anderlecht supporters on the terraces behind the goal seemed intent on violence, too.'[7]

It seems inevitable that unfamiliar or non-existent policies concerning the segregation of rival fans in continental stadia will continue to be a source of concern to the English football authorities. In support of their European neighbours' reluctance to act in this regard, some English officials point to the glaring lack of crowd disorders when continental fans visit Britain. This is a little like arguing that we do not have a football spectator problem in this country by considering only the good behaviour of English fans when they visit Hampden. In both cases, it seems likely that it is the 'reputation' of the home support which acts as one of the principal deterrents to potential visiting 'troublemakers'. For the match in Anderlecht, when the Belgians refused to ensure that home fans and their guests would be kept strictly apart, Villa instructed their 170 travelling stewards to stand between the rival fan groups on the terraces. Their efforts were probably instrumental in containing the disturbances which did occur. However, they could do nothing to contain the exaggerated accounts of the disorders which emerged later in the press as Anderlecht strove to be reinstated in the competition at Villa's expense.

The use by Villa of stewards for a match abroad is a relatively new departure as far as English club sides are concerned. With no guarantee of segregation from the Belgian authorities, it was clear to Villa officials and their police advisers that the stewards' role would be vital inside the stadium. However, that was by no means the limit of the stewards' brief. They were to monitor and take care of their charges for the entire trip. Two stewards were allocated to each coachload of fans. According to Steve Stride, their duties included making sure that

> before anyone boarded any coaches leaving here, they were
> vetted to make sure they had no alcohol on them and they were
> not in a drunken state. Stewards really are briefed that they
> are in control of that coachload of people, to make sure there
> is no drunkenness or disorder, to get to their destination and
> not stop off at a pub on the way. If there was any trouble
> from our fans, stewards were to try to pacify people, really,
> the people who were causing the disorder. If things got out
> of hand, they were to tell the coach driver to drive to the
> nearest police station and get them off.[8]

After the match, Villa officials were adamant that none of the offending 'suporters' had travelled with the official Travellers' Club party of 2,000 fans which had arrived from England a matter of hours before the kick-off. In this connection, *The Daily Telegraph* reported that 'during the 24 hours preceding the match, several hundred [Villa fans] arrived independently – many drunk and looking for a fight – and obtained black market tickets in cafés near the ground.'[9] Later, Anderlecht's secretary, Michael Verscheurun, confirmed that 'the only tickets sold to Britons went to Villa but there were many sales points within Brussels where anyone could have bought as many tickets as they liked.'[10]

Villa's position with regard to the likely travel plans of potentially offending fans in Anderlecht had parallels with the experience of West Ham officials following the disturbances which occurred in Madrid towards the end of 1980. On that occasion, none of the London visitors arrested had been registered as members of the major group of travelling fans organised by the West Ham club. Villa officials blamed the disturbances in Anderlecht on the activities of part of a group of 600 fans who did not travel with the official party. Not all of those involved in the troubles came from the Midlands it was claimed, despite the fact that eight fans arrested inside the stadium were ·Midlanders. Villa Vice-Chairman, Don Bendall, later argued that 'many behind the goal where the trouble . . . flared had cockney accents',[11] although the source of this information was not made clear. Tony Barton, the Aston Villa manager, lamented the fact that 'anyone can put on a Villa scarf and cause trouble and then in the eyes of EUFA be a Villa supporter'.[12] The inference of these sorts of arguments – that the Belgian disturbances did not involve 'true' Villa supporters but, rather, alien groups of English 'thugs' masquerading as Midlanders and who had turned up solely for 'aggro' – gained limited support from the revelation after the match that the Villa 'fan' who had run onto the field during play, to be subsequently knocked unconscious by a policeman as he was being manhandled out of the ground was, in fact, a Scottish soldier on leave from Germany.[13]

Despite the plea of mitigating circumstances which Villa submitted to EUFA in their defence, the English club was apprehensive about the outcome of an enquiry into the incidents at Anderlecht. EUFA Secretary, Hans Bangerter, was already recommending that English clubs should be banned from European competition and FA Secretary Croker admitted that, 'we must be getting very close to it.'[14] It was, then, with some relief that Villa officials received the news from the EUFA Disciplinary Committee that Villa were not to be expelled from the competition as demanded by Belgian representatives. Nevertheless, their punishment was a severe one. They were fined £14,500 and ordered to play their next two home European matches in front of empty terraces and stands. On appeal, the latter aspect of Villa's sentence was reduced to just one match. The club estimated that the whole affair cost them in the region of £70,000.[15]

At the same time as Aston Villa fans were stirring the European football authorities into retributive action following the scenes in Anderlecht, the behaviour of the supporters of Bayern Munich, Villa's prospective opponents in Rotterdam, was causing concern to the German authorities. The 1981/82 Bundesliga programme had started violently in August with Stuttgart fans causing £20,000 of damage in Karlsruhe, behaviour which led to twenty arrests, and recalled the problems of the previous season when fans of Hertha Berlin set fire to and destroyed three railway carriages *en route* to a match in Aachen.[16] Then, in April 1982, immediately following the troubling scenes involving Villa fans in Belgium, West German police were reported to have seized truncheons, heavy chains and 'other lethal weapons' from supporters entering the Olympic Stadium in Munich for the match between Bayern and SV Hamburg. Other fans were arrested for attempted robbery, and police were reported to have used truncheons and tear gas to break up riots after the match.[17]

Such incidents, however, paled in comparison with those which occurred in Frankfurt on 3 May 1982, before, during and after the West German Cup Final between Bayern and Nuremberg. Before the match began, the police used water cannons to disperse fighting fans who were then reported to have rampaged through the city centre, smashing shop windows and attacking a trade union May Day march, giving Nazi salutes and chanting 'Sieg Heil!' Incidents continued throughout a day on which there were 92 arrests and 138 persons treated for injuries.[18] FA Secretary Croker was stirred by the events of 3 May into issuing a reminder about the *international* character of football crowd disorderliness. He commented:

> We are reminding EUFA and the Dutch Football Association not to look at crowd trouble as purely an English problem. [At Frankfurt] there were incidents and disturbances far in excess of anything we have seen over here. Our reputation goes before us when we have a game abroad these days. Inevitably that means there is a certain provocation. But it is a reputation we have deserved. One we have got to live down.[19]

Despite Croker's reminder, EUFA began preparations for Rotterdam with a resolve fuelled mainly by the past performances of *English* fans in Europe. In April, René Eberlé, Secretary of EUFA's Disciplinary Committee, had assured Villa officials that the European football authorities 'will have to insist that there is complete segregation in Rotterdam and that no tickets are sold to anyone but the clubs.'[20] Just over a week later, however, the commercial realities of a situation which would have left the stadium housing the Final of Europe's premier club competition half-empty for the event, led Eberlé and EUFA to think again. The Secretary conceded, again apparently paying scant regard to the reputation of Bayern fans:

> We can only control the sale of tickets up to a limit. We fear there could be trouble again in Rotterdam. If there is, the punishments will get stiffer and stiffer, until the only solution is to kick out *British* clubs.[21]

Villa were thus placed in an extremely difficult situation. No guarantees over the sale of tickets meant no effective guarantees on segregation, a fact which undoubtedly increased the likelihood of English-inspired disorders. And yet there appeared no way in which Villa could register an effective protest against the arrangements for the Final. 'What if we refused to take an allocation of tickets for a European game', Villa Secretary Steve Stride asked EUFA officials, 'and English fans were arrested for invading the pitch?' 'Then', came the predictable reply, 'Aston Villa would be fined.'[22] In the weeks before the Final and in accordance with EUFA recommendations, each of the clubs involved received an allocation of 14,000 tickets for the match. With the Feyenoord Stadium all-seated apart from two small standing terraces at either end, less than 20 per cent of each club's ticket allocation was reserved for standing spectators. It has a capacity of 56,000. Ahead for Aston Villa lay a period of intense preparation involving the carefully monitored allocation of match tickets, and extended discussions with Feyenoord officials and the Rotterdam police regarding the passage and control of Villa fans at the Final. By contrast, despite the recent disturbing performance of *their* fans, Bayern Munich felt no special provisions were necessary to cope with German fans travelling to Rotterdam.

Aston Villa linked the whole of their ticket allocation to officially accredited package tours by coach, train and plane organised by the travel firm, David Dryer Ltd, through the Aston Villa Travellers' Club. This was established by Villa in an attempt to monitor and control the behaviour of their followers abroad. Each member is required to submit two passport-size photographs and is issued, in turn, with a membership card which may be confiscated in the event of misbehaviour. By making match tickets hard to come by in England outside the Travellers' Club, EUFA, and Villa hoped to be able to account for almost all the club's travelling support. However, there were serious leakages in the system. Soon, match tickets not linked to the Villa tours began to surface. A number of London travel agencies were reported to be offering all-inclusive tours to Rotterdam, complete with match tickets. A spokesman for one such firm claimed that the high cost of these excursions made them unattractive to potential 'hooligans'. More ominous, perhaps, than the news of these luxury tours, were stories emerging from Holland that blocks of up to fifty tickets were being bought and sent to England to satisfy a thirsty black market. Villa Secretary, Stride, made enquiries himself at the Feyenoord ticket office and his request, as an 'ordinary' fan, for fifty tickets was met without question or delay.[23] This was despite previous assurances from Dutch officials that applicants in Holland would receive just two tickets apiece. Black market tickets were also on sale in the streets outside Villa Park before the home match against Everton just prior to the trip to Rotterdam. Keith Smith, Secretary of the Travellers' Club, recounted the story of a telephone conversation he had had with a 'cockney' Villa fan who, inadvertently it seems, had secured a ticket for entrance into the small standing terrace reserved for German supporters.

Further reports from Holland suggested that pre-match ticket sales there had been poor. This meant that, despite EUFA's fears about the inadequate segregation of opposing fans which might result, match tickets would probably be available in Rotterdam immediately prior to the game. Poor ticket sales, of course, are always liable to be a possibility when, as in this case, the Final is played in a neutral country. Despite their low cost, there was also a shortfall in the demand for the package deals offered by Aston Villa. About 4,000 of the club's original allocation of tickets were returned to Rotterdam a few days before the match. If 'rogue' fans were able to purchase tickets freely, then, for purposes of control, the club was keen to ensure that tickets for the 'Villa only' sections of the ground would be available to satisfy this potentially disruptive demand. Later indications, especially the reported ferry traffic between Harwich and the Hook of Holland, suggested that somewhere between 2,000 and 3,000 persons claiming to be Villa fans travelled to the game by means other than those offered by the club.

There are several reasons why the trips to Holland organised by

Aston Villa were probably unattractive to potential followers. The coach and rail tours, for example, promised to be singularly arduous. Overnight accommodation in Holland was guaranteed only for the most expensive packages. Perhaps most important of all, however, were Villa's plans to ensure that coaches, ferries, trains and planes remained 'dry' for the duration of the trip. Such arrangements, of course, had been made in accordance with the connections that are widely believed to exist between the consumption of alcohol and the incidence of crowd disorder. The – in part understandable – fears that exist in this regard tend to be heightened by the visit of British fans to the continent where they are confronted by a plethora of alcoholic beverages of a variety, strength and price with which they are unfamiliar. 'Booze-activated louts' was how Shadow Sports Minister Howell had described Tottenham fans who had misbehaved in Amsterdam the previous September.[24] 'Drunk and looking for a fight', had been *The Daily Telegraph*'s assessment of some of Villa's followers in Anderlecht.[25] Following the scenes in Belgium, the club had decided to act.

As it turned out, however, the Villa guidelines on the control of alcohol consumption by Travellers' Club members were probably more effective in ensuring that potential 'hooligan' fans sought other means of transport than they were in actually *preventing* drinking at selected points on the trip to Rotterdam. For example, the bars and duty free shops on the cross-channel ferries were open to Villa fans on both the outward and return journeys. This appeared to take many fans by surprise and the shop was consequently under-utilised on the outward journey. The threat of 'a stop and search' policy on reboarding coaches in France also seemed to deter fans from 'stocking up' with spirits for the journey through France, Belgium and Holland. This was in sharp contrast to the brisk business being done by the bars on the ferry from 0700 hours onwards. The beer- and, in some cases, wine-drinking exploits of fans in the early hours of Wednesday morning were a source of considerable consternation to the regular holidaymakers who had neither endured the drive by coach through the night from Birmingham, nor were locked in preparation for the major event which was to occur in Rotterdam later that evening. Nevertheless, there were no obvious cases of drunkenness among Villa fans as they disembarked from the ferry at Calais. However, later conversations with fans who returned to England via the Hook of Holland suggested that scenes on that route were affected rather more by heavy drinking.

As we were reminded by the press in the days before the Final, Aston Villa carried with them the hopes, not only of their own fans but also those of football supporters in the country at large. Villa, after all, were attempting to maintain an English run of success which had kept the European Cup in this country for the previous five seasons. It had been widely suggested, too, that a victory in Rotterdam would boost confidence in the England World Cup camp. In short, although they were participating in a *club* competition, there was a distinct *national* dimension to the challenge facing Aston Villa.

For the fans, the element of national identification superimposed upon their club and regional affiliations was enhanced by the prospects of travel – in the case of many of them possibly for the first time – through the unfamiliar territories of the French, the Belgians and the Dutch. As a result, Union Jacks were much in evidence on the trip, although in some cases the name of the club was sewn across the national emblem.

As was later to be the case in Spain, the high degree of nationalism which is invariably excited by trips of this sort was heightened on this occasion by events in the South Atlantic. Indeed before the departure from Villa Park on Wednesday morning, by far the noisiest and most passionate displays of national sentiment among young male fans were concerned with the early military victories being achieved by British soldiers in the Falklands. Versions of 'Rule Britannia' were lustily delivered by a group of about fifty young men, along with the more direct, 'We only hate Argentina' and a variety of cumbersome adaptations of traditional football songs to the cause in the South Atlantic. At their height, feelings were fervently expressed in a rewording of, 'What shall we do with the drunken sailor?', which had become, 'What shall we do with the Argentinians?' inviting the reply, 'Bomb, bomb Buenos Aires', and so on.

Although it might be misleading to make too much of the point, it was difficult to avoid the uncomfortable feeling that some fans saw parallels between Britain's 'mission' in the Falklands and the 'manoeuvres' Aston Villa and her fans were about to embark upon in the 'hostile' territories of Europe over the next 36 hours. Indeed, despite the nationalist fervour generated outside Villa Park about the Falklands crisis, attention occasionally returned to matters more immediately at hand. One learned, for example, that Bayern fans would need to steel themselves against taunts like, 'Two World Wars and a World Cup, too', a reference to what some Villa fans took to be the last three major engagements between the two countries.

These nationalistic themes which, in practice, revolve around the ritual degradation of foreign cultures and territories, and the simultaneous celebration of one's own, were taken up again almost immediately the group set foot on foreign soil. As the coach moved away from the ferry terminal at Calais, the young male fans who had established themselves towards the rear were soon deriding everything they saw. They were, for example, less than impressed with the delights of rural France and Belgium ('This country's a right 'ole, innit? It's all countryside. Boring!'). Local males who watched with puzzled expressions as the convoy passed were invariably labelled as 'wankers', i.e. as less than 'real' men. Those who identified the purpose of the trip and pledged their support with a wave or a clenched fist were greeted with the same. Young women attracted most attention of all, with the least attractive adding to a growing fund of 'evidence' of the 'racial' and cultural supremacy of the visitors. Those admired for their looks were loudly and crudely informed of the benefits of an instant liaison with English lads.

On an impressionistic level, the majority of Travellers' Club members who made the trip to Rotterdam were male, aged between 16 and 30, and probably from the upper sections of the working class. There was a liberal sprinkling of older spectators in the party and a few younger fans, usually accompanied by adults. Female fans, most in the company of boyfriends or husbands, made up perhaps 2 per cent of the total. Finally, despite the ethnic mix of the Birmingham area, there were surprisingly few fans of 'New Commonwealth' origin in the group.

If the overnight journey to Dover had been arduous, the coach journey from Calais to the Feyenoord Stadium was taxing in the extreme. We travelled on Coach 26 (out of 29), and its course was ill assisted by the efforts of an English 'navigator' who managed to misdirect the driver no fewer than three times. As a result, the coach fell behind schedule and the only stop of any length during an eight-hour trip was one of about 20 minutes on the French/

Belgian border. Those in the party who had recovered sufficiently from the morning's ordeal took the opportunity to aid revival with a few more beers. Experienced campaigners had had the foresight to remove their shoes during the journey which prevented undue swelling of the feet. A man who had brought a pillow to smooth his passage was no longer the subject of derision from the rest of the party. It was a very hot day for a very long trip.

Despite the discomforts of the heat and cramped conditions, most of the occupants of coach 26 attempted to catch up on lost sleep through Belgium and Holland. As the coach eventually neared Rotterdam, the party became more animated. Passing English fans in cars, vans and mini-buses hooted their allegiance and were waved and shouted at in return. Bayern fans, passing by in luxury coach or car, were roundly abused by the lads at the back who persistently urged the driver to 'catch up the German bastards' so that exchange of the international sign language of abuse might continue – two fingers from the English, raised middle finger from the Germans. The lavishness of the German travel facilities with their Mercedes, Audis and de-luxe coaches was roundly condemned as a sure sign of 'stuck up cunts'. The Villa fans were celebrating the sacrifices they had had to make in order to attend the Final. (At least two from coach 26 were unemployed and had borrowed money from their parents to make the trip.) The Germans, by contrast, were not 'real' fans at all, or so the argument went.

The appearance of the Feyenoord Stadium's floodlights in the near distance had almost the entire coach singing the current European anthems: 'When Den (Denis Mortimer, the Villa captain) goes up, to lift the European Cup, we'll be there, we'll be there!', and 'Rotterdam! Rotterdam! Well we're all pissed up and we're gonna win the Cup!' The older and more 'respectable' fans towards the front of the coach baulked a little at some of the cruder lyrics but occasionally joined in with some 'toned down' versions. Dutch motor cycle police arrived to provide an escort to the stadium. The stems which rose from the rear of their machines gave them the appearance of fairground vehicles. More derision from the lads at the back. They had all heard about the levels of policing in operation for this game. The first sight of these helmeted guards with their flashing lights hadn't impressed. 'Pigs' were mentioned.

As the Dutch authorities had promised, the coach parks backed on to the stadium itself. German vehicles had been skilfully directed by the local constabulary around to the other side. Segregation so far had been impressive. The arrangements were similar to those practised by the West Midlands force to cope with the influx of opposing fans at Cup Semi-Finals at Villa Park. Here, as in Birmingham, opposing fans were directed by the police to opposite approaches to the stadium and instructed to park accordingly. The offer of Midlands expertise in the matter had evidently been embraced by the local force, and with no small measure of success.

The 4 p.m. arrival at the Feyenoord left four hours of 'preparation' time before kick-off. Fans were instructed by the stewards (off-duty policemen employed by Villa and rewarded with free travel and match tickets for their pains) to return to the coach park half an hour after the match had ended. There would be no time, in Holland at least, for celebration, commiseration or retribution. Some fans, notably the older groups and those with female companions or children, chose simply to stay in the vicinity of the stadium, lounging on the many grass verges until kick-off approached. Most others decided that liquid refreshment was required before the match. With the city centre too far distant to engage most people's interest, the search began for a bar closer to home. Across a major road to the west of the stadium, Feyenoord FC's extensive sports grounds offered facilities for tennis, football and squash. In addition, the grounds harboured a couple of pleasant bars which appeared to be attracting the custom of Villa and Bayern fans alike.

Outside the first bar, Villa fans of all ages, bedecked in scarves, hats and club shirts moved comfortably with German fans in similar attire. Information about the available drinks from English fans who lay on the grass outside suggested that the order of the day was six, small (plastic) glasses of lager 'for under 2 quid'. On the football pitch nearby, some Villa lads had embarked on an impromptu match, complete with running commentaries from those who were watching on the sidelines. Occasionally, a police car drove slowly past to monitor the situation, keeping in tune with what appeared to be a general policy of maintaining a 'low profile'. In fact, police representatives from the West Midlands had spent many hours with their Rotterdam counterparts discussing the best ways to police English fans. The stewarding system employed by Villa, and the cooperation between two foreign police forces formed unique and indispensable parts of the whole Rotterdam exercise.

Inside the bar a group of about ten Bayern fans, probably aged between 30 and 35, were already ensconced on the right-hand side of the main saloon. Each wore a Bayern Munich shirt; some had red and white Bayern scarves. Somewhere in the region of thirty Villa fans, in club shirts, hats and some bare-chested, watched the antics of the Germans with some amusement. With each new influx of Villa supporters, the Germans responded with a barrage of songs and chants including, 'C'mon you Reds', clearly a memento of Bayern's many meetings with Liverpool over the years. This response surprised the Villa lads, short on German replies. Judging from the towers of plastic glasses near the Bayern group, their 'preparations' were well advanced.

Soon, 'chant leaders' had become informally established on each side and, despite the protests of the serving staff, began to lead their 'choirs' from precarious positions on top of tables. Just as Villa fans were threatening to overwhelm the German effort, Bayern reinforcements arrived in the shape of a group of about twenty younger fans. Their appearance was more obviously threatening than that of their compatriots already in the bar. In their late teens or early twenties, almost all the group wore a uniform of sleeveless denim jacket with Bayern insignia between the shoulder blades. In addition to a variety of scarves, shirts and emblems in club colours of red and white, many wore studded leather belts and some, studded leather wristbands. A few of the new German contingent wore heavy leather boots similar to the Doc Marten's favoured by some British fans. In contrast to the fashionable shorter hair-styles of most younger Villa supporters, many of the Bayern lads wore their hair quite long. In fact, their entire appearance was reminiscent of a 'hooligan style' popular in Engand in the early to mid-1970s. The closest approximation to such a style in this country today is probably that found in the macho mode of 'heavy metal' rock fans who are held to have a poor record of football match attendance. 'Cave men', was how one young Villa supporter described these German fans, a description which captured nicely both the brawny gait of the Germans and what the younger Villa fans took to be an outmoded terrace style.

The arrival of this new group of Bayern faithfuls galvanised the Villa ranks into ever-shriller self-praise and more penetrating degradation of the Germans and their country. Like responses came from the Bayern side. References to 'World Wars' and 'Argentina' became more frequent, prefacing a few, minor drunken scuffles which the bar's 'bouncer' managed to prevent from spreading to the main body of supporters. With tempers fraying and a serious confrontation looking likely, the situation was defused when a young Villa fan suggested a match on the nearby pitch between, as he put it, 'the Jerries and the Villa'. It proved an attractive proposition. The Bayern supporters quickly agreed that honour should be satisfied outside and the two groups moved back into the sunshine. The sides lined up on the pitch of Feyenoord's junior team with Aston Villa playing from left to right from the bar side of the ground. There had been no team selection: players simply lined up at will, an arrangement which meant that Villa outnumbered their opponents by about 50 per cent. At a conservative estimate, about thirty Villa representatives took the field against twenty followers of Bayern. Each side was cheered on by German and English fans who lined the touchlines. All in all, the affair had captured the attention of about 500 people.

With so little space for the players to work with and a high level of alcohol in the bloodstream, neither skills nor gentility were much in evidence. It was a very rough affair which lasted for about an hour. There was, however, only one free kick – awarded to themselves by the Villa lads. Opposing players were regularly flattened without ceremony, and throw-ins, corners and goal kicks were a matter of who reached the ball first when it went out of play. Because of their numerical superiority, Villa were usually in command in this department. Under a combination of pressures of this sort, the Germans succumbed to a 7–1 defeat. Someone on the touchline assured onlookers that Gary Shaw had scored a hat trick for the victorious English. A little less dubious was the feeling that this spontaneous contest between representatives of opposing factions had, for all its roughness, directed collective attention away from what had promised to turn into a potentially violent incident in a bar outside the Feyenoord Stadium.

Elsewhere, however, there had been the inevitable disagreements. During the 'match' between Bayern and Villa fans, we spoke to two bare-chested, tattooed Villa supporters in their mid-twenties who had arrived in Amsterdam via the ferry on Monday evening to head for the city's 'red light district'. First, they said they had 'bought' women for £12 for the evening. Then, later, they recounted with relish rather than regret, in the company of a number of other English fans, that they had become involved in fights with local youths outside a bar. The Dutch youths, they said, had shouted abuse at them, referring frequently to the Falklands affair.

Both these lads had been present in Anderlecht during the semi-final disturbances which, again, they described with some affection. They claimed that fans 'from all over the place' had been involved in the terrace troubles at the game that night. When asked if there were any signs of the same sorts of thing this time the Villa lads reported rumours that some 'Chelsea nutcases' had been arrested on the ferry between Harwich and the Hook. In fact, after the return from Holland, *The Guardian* reported that a coachload of London fans 'dressed in the claret and blue of Villa' and *en route* to the match had been turned back by the police at the Hook of Holland, presumably on account of suspicions about their motives for travelling. Implicit in the report and the action of the authorities in this case was the idea that these southern fans were not 'genuine' supporters of Villa but renegade English 'hard cases' in search of 'aggro'.[26]

At around 7.15 p.m., fans of all hues began drifting more positively towards the large queues which were already forming outside the stadium. Again, strict segregation of opposing spectators was clearly in evidence. A group of about twenty Villa fans approaching from the City (Bayern) end were momentarily the focus of an incident in which planks of wood were wielded by German supporters. Mounted policemen waded in to quell the disturbance almost as quickly as it had begun. The Villa fans remained within the main phalanx of German support, however, and it was clear that they had obtained tickets for the Bayern end of the ground. Around the Villa queues, small groups of young Dutch lads hung around listlessly and without apparent threat to observe the behaviour of their guests. On view outside the stadium there were just two Villa fans who were clearly so much the worse for drink that it was doubtful whether they would be capable of watching the match. These scenes were very different from those in Rome before Liverpool's first European Cup Final, when the streets outside the Olympic Stadium were littered with sleeping Merseysiders who never saw their team's triumph over Mönchengladbach.

At the turnstiles, fans were thoroughly 'frisked' by Dutch police for weapons and alcohol. A succession of wire fences then guided them towards their appointed entrances at opposite ends of the ground. Villa fans who had come with the Travellers' Club by rail had been allocated the small number of vantage points behind one of the goals All the rest, whether they had travelled by coach, air or under their own steam, were seated on upper and lower tiers around the half of the stadium to the right of the players' tunnel. Tickets allocated to fans travelling on coaches in the upper price range were for the elevated, uncovered tiers of the 56,000 capacity stadium.

In the distance, at the far end of the stadium, the knot of standing Bayern fans danced, chanted and engineered 'crowd falls' in a manner which made them hard to distinguish from English goal-terrace fans. To their right, a group of perhaps 200 Villa fans were encamped in a lower-tier seated section in the heart of the Bayern ranks. Their position was separated from the Bayern terraces by a block of seated German spectators. Chants for 'Villa!' from the English splinter group were instantly met by chants of 'Argentina!' from the German terraces. An angry surge to the left was the reply of the isolated Villa contingent. 'Sieg Heil!' with Nazi salutes, came from sections of the main gathering of Villa supporters at the opposite end.

At the mid-points of the stadium where Bayern and Villa fans were most likely to find themselves side by side, the police cause had been aided by the shortfall in ticket sales. In these sections of the ground there were rows of empty seats. A few 'neutrals' also provided something of a 'buffer' between the opposing factions, although most of the English support was concentrated in the areas of seating immediately behind the goal. Villa stewards had donned their bright orange jackets and were carefully nursing their charges into position.

Between the front rows of spectators and the playing surface, lay a succession of impressive obstacles to pitch invasion. A heavy metal fence stood before about 15 metres of concrete 'no-man's land'. This area was patrolled on this occasion by two dog handlers. Behind them, a water-filled moat and more fencing surrounded the playing area. Ingenuity will out, however. Before the start, two young Villa fans managed to gain entry to the pitch to perform pre-match rituals in front of the faithful. The club scarf was paraded, kissed and worshipped before they and their apparel were solemnly removed by the local constabulary.

The small Dutch ball boys operating in 'no man's land' had been won over to Villa's cause by the gift of hats and scarves. They conducted the terrace choirs in their songs as the plainclothes handlers with their giant *Bouviere de Flandres* dogs eyed the Villa fans with suspicion, puzzled by the array of bare chests, tattoos and the occasional claret and blue hairstyle which peppered their ranks.

Drink was available in the stadium in half-pint plastic cartons. It looked and, if allowance is made for the inferiority inevitably accorded by football fans to a foreign brew compared with those eulogised back home, it almost tasted like beer. It was a form of lager to be precise. Certainly, Villa supporters who made the endless trek back and forth to the bars, carrying six cartons with the aid of a specially designed cardboard tray, believed themselves to be *en route* to getting well and truly 'steaming'. Older, more reserved Villa fans looked on in apprehension, probably recalling some of the scenes in Anderlecht. They need not have worried. To get drunk in the Villa end that night, one would need to drink more than the 'lager' on sale to English fans. What officials later described as 'the big con' was in full swing. While fans in other sections of the ground were sinking the real thing, Villa fans were the subject of a non-alcoholic delusion.

From a commercial and crowd control point of view, the proposition of selling alcohol-free lager to unsuspecting Villa fans must have seemed irresistible to the English and Dutch authorities. Neither of their positions would be compromised. The only possible losers would be supporters who paid for a product they did not actually receive. English officials later reasoned that the mind probably takes over in such situations anyway. That is, Villa fans would get 'drunk' on the occasion and the belief that they were getting 'tanked up'. The fans, so the argument ran, were hardly being cheated at all. In any case, the urgency of securing crowd control, coupled with commercial contingencies, took precedence in the official view over the ethics of honest trading. However, whilst such a measure undoubtedly reduced the incidence of drunkenness among Villa fans *at the match*, there were many who arrived at the Feyenoord Stadium on that warm, May evening in a fairly advanced state of inebriation.

The eventual arrival of the teams on the field was greeted with rockets from the Germans and firecrackers from the Villa fans. At that point, Villa stewards turned to watch the game. It was not the affair that had been demanded by the purists. For all that, it appeared to be painfully tense and exciting for the thousands of Villa supporters who had travelled for up to 16 hours to be there. At half-time, the match was still scoreless. Villa had had most possession, Bayern the chances to score. Villa had already lost their veteran goalkeeper, Rimmer, through injury. He was replaced by the virtual unknown, Spinks, who performed heroically in the first half. Not all the Villa players earned such half-time plaudits. Peter Withe, for example, had angered many fans for trying to play 'too fancy' – like the continentals. The fans wanted more aggression in the second 45 minutes. Meanwhile, more dogs and handlers came out to surround the pitch before the interval, presumably to protect the marching bands who provided the entertainment between the halves.

At the start of the second half, Bayern laid siege to the Villa goal. That they did not score was largely due to bad luck and the sterling performance of Spinks in the Villa goal. Anxiety was beginning to be communicated through the Villa ranks in the stands. It was dissipated by chanting and singing which became louder, more desperate and almost relentless. Later, fans will claim that it was the crowd that lifted the team, that it was not anxiety but an unquenchable will to win that was communicated to the players. This will be their role in a famous victory. Some players claim never to hear the crowd during a game. Others admit to being swayed in their performances by supportive or hostile audiences. Perhaps the Villa side *did* have a preponderance of players in the latter category that night. No matter. Withe, who had been playing badly, scored.

The celebrations which ensued in the sections of the Feyenoord Stadium housing the majority of Aston Villa supporters were not diminished to any great extent by the fact that they were in seats. True, the seated character of their accommodation prevented them from engaging in the 20-yard 'sways' that are possible on half-empty terraces. But the dancing, hugging, falling, pushing, shoving and jumping that have become characteristic of goal-terrace celebrations following the scoring of goals in England were all present here. The seated sections of the ground were simply converted, as it were, to banks of very steep terracing. Inconceivable though it may seem given the pandemonium which broke out following Withe's goal, no one seemed to sustain an injury in the bout of exuberance experienced and expressed by the mass of Villa fans.

Incredibly, given the renewed German pressure and to the massive relief of the Villa contingent, the final third of the match produced no further goals. The tension was so great towards the end that some fans were unable to watch the closing minutes, choosing instead to leave the stadium or lie along the lines of vacant seating staring fixedly at the sky. It is difficult to predict what the mood of some sections of the Villa support might have been given a late goal for Bayern Munich, and perhaps eventual defeat for the Birmingham side. One had only to recall the experience of Leeds United fans in Paris in 1975 to realise how the vagaries of the match can play a part in triggering a violent response from the terraces and stands, perhaps especially when the investment by fans has been relatively large in terms of time, money and the sheer arduousness of the journey. As it was, it was the Bayern fans who slouched glumly out of the stadium, while those of Aston Villa stayed to watch their victorious team first receive and then parade the European Cup.

The tradition which dictates that fans of the winning side remain in the stadium to join in the celebrations assists the authorities in coping with post-match segregation. It serves a purpose rather similar to the tactic, widely adopted in this country, of holding away fans inside the stadium after a match while the police usher home fans out of the vicinity. On this occasion, virtually all the Villa support chose to remain in the stadium for half an hour while Mortimer and his colleagues jigged in front of them. Outside meanwhile, the disappointed Bayern fans were already being directed on board coaches or to their cars and mini-buses for the journey home or a 'wake' in the nearby city centre.

By 11 p.m., the celebrations all but over, most of the Villa Travellers' Club coaches were ready to leave, their occupants in the main too tired and drained for further revelry. As they left Rotterdam, again with police escort, small knots of Villa fans were passed hanging around bars and brightly lit service stations. They, too, seemed exhausted by the excesses of the past 48 hours. Coach 26 drove through the night to the French coast. Almost everybody slept.

Some petty theft in the middle of the night at a service station somewhere in Belgium could be put down to inadequate service. One man in a small booth found himself with the task of dealing with a hundred tired, hungry and thirsty fans in a 20-minute stop. 'He made enough, anyway', argued one of the beneficiaries, and it was difficult to argue that the station's sudden windfall of customers had not taken care of its profit margin despite the loss of some goods without payment.

There was room for coach 26 on the 4.30 a.m. crossing to Dover. On board, the bars were open again and doing good business. This time, too, the duty free and gift shops did a roaring trade, but the bottles of spirits purchased remained unopened. The ship's *bureau de change* was also choked with fans, many of whom had travelled laden with guilders and francs but had found little opportunity to spend them. The ship's restaurants and cafeterias also bulged with fans. 'It was difficult to know which queue to go to next', remarked one supporter later. It was that sort of trip. But there was little disturbance on board. A loudspeaker announcement by the ship's captain congratulated the Midlands fans both on the success of their side and their 'exemplary' behaviour during the voyage. There were loud cheers.

In contrast to the hordes of pressmen who greeted Manchester United fans on their return from St Etienne in 1977, there were no journalists on the quayside at Dover to meet the returning Villa supporters. Orderly behaviour by football fans has low news priority. The only serious incident reported in the English press concerned a pre-match city centre clash between 'armed' German fans and a group of Villa supporters. Some reports suggested the Bayern fans were carrying loaded revolvers but later accounts described them as starting pistols.[27] In this incident, nine Britons and twelve Germans were arrested for drunkenness and hooliganism. No one was hurt, and the arrested fans were jailed until the end of the match and then sent home. Kees Otteranger, the Dutch police officer in charge of crowd control at the Final, described this and a small number of other incidents as 'quite minor and no more than we would expect for any game'.[28] On 27 May, *The Birmingham Evening Mail* published the following message from Otteranger to the travelling Villa fans:

Congratulations, not only on winning the Cup, but for being

so nice while you were in Rotterdam. Everything has gone so very well. There was no fighting at all, nothing to give us any worries. We thank you all for the very sporting way you conducted yourselves. . . .

Chapter Six

ENGLISH FANS IN COPENHAGEN, SEPTEMBER 1982

Introduction

On 22 September 1982 England played a European Championship match against Denmark in Copenhagen. The previous evening, the Under-21 sides of the two countries had met in a tie in the EUFA Under-21 Championship. This 'double-header' was a repeat of the meetings between the full international and Under-21 sides of England and Denmark which had taken place, also in Copenhagen, four years earlier. In September 1978 England was successful in both matches, winning the 'senior' international by 4 goals to 3, and its 'junior' equivalent by a 2–1 scoreline. In September 1982 the two countries drew 2–2 at senior level, whilst England won the Under-21 match by 4 goals to 1.

There were reports of hooliganism by England fans in Copenhagen in 1978 but, despite the inclusion of two black players in England's Under-21 side of that year and the fact that, at the end of the 1970s the expression of hostility towards blacks was becoming an increasingly regular feature of football crowd behaviour in England, no such reaction was reported on the occasion of the Denmark–England Under-21 match of that year.[1] This was in marked contrast to what happened in Copenhagen in 1982 when demonstrations by England fans against black players in their country's Under-21 side were added to their repertoire of hooligan behaviour abroad. This new racialist dimension is one of the issues on which we will focus in this chapter. We will also look briefly at another new development of the late 1970s and early 1980s, the apparent increase in what one might call 'football-related crime'. At the end, we will discuss some of the police measures introduced to combat hooliganism by English fans abroad. We will start, however, with a short review of the events which occurred in Copenhagen in September 1978, and with an analysis of the Anglo-Danish planning exercise which led to the control measures put into effect in September 1982.

The build-up to the Anglo-Danish encounters of 1982

Whilst most observers agreed that the 1978 Under-21 match between Denmark and England had been, at best, a 'scrappy' affair, there was general consensus that their seniors had produced an encounter of incident and skill. 'Wonderful entertainment' enthused manager Greenwood after the game. On the terraces that September night in 1978, however, there was rather less cause for the English football authorities to be enthusiastic. *The Times*, for example, reported that 'England were accompanied by a large group of unruly young supporters who ransacked kiosks at the stadium and threw the contents onto the pitch. There were several scuffles on the terraces.'[2]

Despite fighting and bottle-throwing, initiated, it was reported, largely by sections of the English contingent, no arrests were made before, during or after the match. The Danish press, however, was reported to have 'strongly condemned' the unruly terrace behaviour of some of the estimated 2,000 English fans present at the senior international, and the British Embassy in Copenhagen apologised publicly for the 'violent behaviour' of these groups. They also issued a denial that British sailors visiting Denmark as part of a Nato exercise were involved in the disturbances. No incidents were reported at the Under-21 match.[3]

Four years on, the British authorities had little reason to expect a more orderly terrace performance from their fans. As we have seen, serious incidents in Italy, Switzerland, France, Belgium and

Holland had, by 1982, pushed EUFA to the brink of a total ban on English teams. There was less trouble than had been expected in Rotterdam and Spain, but it seemed possible that the experience of three weeks' hectic activity at the World Cup the previous summer might have enhanced the *esprit de corps* of what appeared to be a growing, informal English 'travel club'. As we have said, the members of this thriving band seem to be predominantly, but not exclusively, southern-based, to come primarily from working-class, especially lower-working-class, backgrounds, and to embrace a heightened sense of national identity, coupled with a readiness to resort to physical violence and vandalism against the persons and property of identifiable outsider groups which they take to be 'inferior'. 'Good times' abroad for young English supporters of this kind tend to involve rather more than mere attendance at a football match.

Despite official fears, the period before the fixtures in Copenhagen saw few of the doom-laden prognostications from the British press that have, by now, become almost a tradition prior to the passage of large numbers of England fans to the continent. There was, for example, little coverage of the 'special arrangements' made by the Danish authorities to cope with the invading English, nor of the negotiations going on between English and Danish officials aimed at restricting the prospects for disorder, especially at the match between the senior sides. However, such exhaustive attention to detail and the reliance on international collaboration to work out strategies of control are a relatively new development. Perhaps the British press was simply unaware of them?

The introduction of detailed planning and international collaboration prior to matches involving English sides abroad reflects the growing concern of the football authorities in this country that, unless misbehaviour by English supporters in and around continental stadia is effectively curbed, English teams might soon be banned from European competition. The key administrative body in this connection is the UK Football Liaison Group, established under the auspices of Sports Minister Macfarlane. Its introduction was followed by the appointment, prior to the World Cup Finals in Spain, of Leslie Walker, a retired metropolitan policeman, as offical FA Liaison Officer. In terms of his qualifications and experience, Walker seemed well-suited to this new advisory post. As an ex-Deputy Assistant Commissioner for the South and South East of London at the time of the 'Spaghetti House Siege' and later of the Brixton riots, he was well versed in public-order policing. Two years in charge of crowd control at Millwall FC in the late 1970s provided him, additionally, with a grounding in the public-order contingencies peculiar to football match situations.

The work of the Football Liaison Group began in earnest with the 1982 World Cup Finals. Before the tournament began, officials visited all the centres where the three British teams were scheduled to play, discussing arrangements for British fans with the city authorities, the local police and stadium officials. Among the specific matters raised were: the segregation of rival fans inside and outside grounds; ticket allocation and distribution; the sale of alcohol inside grounds; and parking facilities. Rather surprisingly, the Liaison Group was not used for the matches in Denmark. Instead, the task for maximising the prospects for the good behaviour and effective control of English fans in Copenhagen fell largely to Leslie Walker. He was charged with selecting, in conjunction with senior local police officers and stadium personnel, a site within the stadium from which the 500 'official' English fans might view the match safely. His brief also included seeking assurances from the Danish authorities concerning the sale of match tickets to English fans who had not travelled to Copenhagen with the official party since it was from this quarter that the most serious problems were expected.

Although it was felt that the Danish police might perceive the pre-match rituals of some English fans as strange and potentially threatening, there seemed little danger that they would over-react as the Spanish police had often done. On the contrary, they were regarded as relatively unfamiliar with serious public-order situations and hence as more liable to fall foul of the excesses of English support. In short, it was feared that the Danish police might be regarded as a 'soft touch' by some English fans. 'They [English fans] will *expect* policemen to be near them,' Leslie Walker assured the Danish authorities before the matches. 'They won't mind policemen being near them. They won't over-react.'[4] Walker's plea was for the presence of *uniformed* officers among English fans in Copenhagen's Idraetspark. The Danes chose instead to rely to a great extent on plainclothes officers. Walker's aim had been to impress on the Danish police the importance of a *preventative* rather than a *reactive* approach to the policing of English fans. He also stressed that segregation of opposing fans was an absolute priority:

> Segregation? I always go for segregation very hard and I won't leave a room until I've exhausted my arguments. As yet, I've not met anybody who has not come round to that view because, in the long run, you can throw the rule book at them and say, 'I'm telling you now that you've got to do it'.[5]

The 'rule book' referred to by Walker is the set of EUFA regulations which decree that home clubs and host countries must provide for the adequate segregation of home and away fans. EUFA regulations or not, because it lacks a penning system, segregation was always going to be a problem in the Idraetspark. The staunch wire fences that surround the pitch, however, bear witness to the fact that, on occasions, even the supposedly placid Danish fans are a danger to players, match officials and perhaps even to each other.

The majority of 'official' English fans were to be housed in ground level seats at the west end of the Idraetspark, opposite the main stand. A double-decker stand would overlook them and they would not be formally segregated from their Danish counterparts. Danish officials argued that, if disorder did break out, stadium personnel and police officers could form human barriers between rival factions. Moreover, the view of all the officers involved was that seated accommodation would be conducive to effective policing.

The English officials were moderately satisfied with these arrangements. The most serious problems were likely to occur, they argued, if English fans travelling privately managed to purchase tickets for the totally unsegregated goal end terraces. The Danes agreed. On the eve of the senior international, the Copenhagen newspaper, B.T., reported the Danish FA to be 'very nervous' about the prospects for crowd control at the match. They were also apparently anxious regarding the actions that EUFA might take against them should serious disturbances occur.[6] The Danes had good reason to be nervous. By this time, a number of English fans had already purchased tickets in the capital for these sections of the ground.

Shortly before the matches were due to take place, in what was fast becoming a kind of ritual enacted before all potentially troublesome matches abroad, the FA Secretary warned English fans who were planning to make the trip under their own steam that the senior match was already a sell-out, and that no tickets would be available either at home or abroad for spectators who travelled to Copenhagen unsupervised. For the first time for a number of matches, the FA had accepted tickets for an international match abroad. Their idea was to 'freeze out' private travellers, although past experience suggested that the plan was doomed to failure. In fact, Croker's warnings about the non-availability of tickets probably came too late. English fans began arriving in Copenhagen as early as Sunday 19 September, at least two days before the Under-21 fixture and three days before the full championship tie. At that time, tickets were still freely available in the Danish capital, and some English fans reported buying extra tickets to sell to compatriots who they knew would be arriving without tickets as the week wore on. The tickets exchanging hands in the early parts of the week were predominantly for the large uncovered west terrace, the section of the Idraetspark that caters for the more fervent young Danish supporters.

Fans arriving from England later who were not offered tickets by already established English fans could still obtain them in bars and cafés around the ground and the railway station for not much more than a couple of pounds above the stated price. In fact, a large majority of the English spectators who travelled unsupervised to Copenhagen did so in the belief that tickets would be easy to obtain there. Past experience told them that the FA's warnings would turn out to have little substance. Others appeared to believe that, with or without a ticket, English ingenuity would win over what they perceived to be feeble-minded foreign officials. As a ticketless young Manchester fan observed on the afternoon of the match: 'There's no ground in Europe you couldn't get into if you had to. Once you get there, you'll get in all right, ticket or no bloody ticket.'

Official estimates of the number of English fans who travelled to Copenhagen unsupervised and managed to gain entry to the match ranged between 1,500 and 2,000. It is, of course, difficult to determine this sort of thing precisely. What one can say with some certainty is that unsupervised fans, most of them aged between 16 and 25, outnumbered their officially accredited counterparts by a ratio of approximately 3 to 1.

England fans and the National Front

When the official parties arrived in Copenhagen on the afternoon of the senior match, some of the signs were ominous. In the first-floor window of a hotel above one of the largest 'sex supermarkets' in the city hung a large Union Jack with 'Chelsea' stitched across its middle. Some 40 or 50 Chelsea fans had been resident at the Centrum and Weber hotels since Sunday evening and, as the match day approached, more and more arrived to swell their ranks.

We travelled to Copenhagen on an official package. Once there, we were soon able to re-establish contacts made in Spain. Young members of the Stamford Bridge contingent, several of them veterans of Bilbao and Madrid, readily acknowledged their part in chanting abuse at the four black England players in the match against the Danish Under-21 side. Such antics were covered extensively in the British press. *The Sun*, for example, under the headline, 'Blacks Booed By Our Fans', reported that:

> Three young black diamonds and a slightly older stager firmly stamped their names on the future of English football in Copenhagen on Tuesday night. They played their prominent parts in an impressive 4–1 win over Denmark in the European Under-21 Championship, but throughout faced a torrent of racial abuse – from the English supporters in the sparse crowd. These mindless morons hurled their taunts in between choruses of 'When the Whites go marching in'.[7]

In similar fashion, *The Guardian* noted that 'a handful of supporters from the London area . . . took it upon themselves to boo and jeer every time one of the four black players touched the ball.'[8]

'Regis & Co Defy Race Taunts', was the headline used by *The Daily Mail* to suggest that England had triumphed *despite* rather than because of the English supporters present. The report went on to express surprise that some of Chelsea's National Front following appeared to come from Tunbridge Wells:

> A quartet of gifted black players were jeered and insulted even as they helped score the goals which launched Bobby Robson's reign as Engand manager with an Under-21 triumph over Denmark. Sadly, the abuse was as resounding as the 4–1 victory. Some of it came from beneath a Union Jack brandished

by visitors from, of all places, Royal Tunbridge Wells. The National Front seemed to be everywhere.[9]

The expression of racist sentiments in a football context is, of course, by no means new to Britain. A few years ago, the late Dixie Dean recalled the racist remarks aimed at him by a spectator at a match against Spurs in the 1930s.[10] Doubtless, other black players of the period would have similar stories to tell. However, until the late 1970s such incidents tended to be individualised, unorganised and sporadic. Then, when black players began to make significant breakthroughs into the English professional game, organised groups from the far right became prominent on the terraces as they stepped up their endeavours to recruit disaffected young working-class males to their racist cause.

The activities of these extreme right-wing groups at English football grounds have not been uniform or universal. In the spring of 1978, for example, the National Front began a leafleting campaign outside professional grounds. It was particularly active in the London area, most notably at Chelsea, Spurs, Arsenal, Millwall and West Ham. By the early 1980s, in the midst of a deepening recession, the Front's youth paper, *Bulldog*, was devoting a regular column to articles 'On the Football Front', exhorting fans to 'join the fight for race and union'.[11] A commercial development followed in October 1980. Under the headline, 'The Front Invades Soccer Clubs', *The Daily Mail* revealed a trade in NF-doctored West Ham T-shirts outside Upton Park on match days. According to the Front's official spokesman, Martin Webster, the sale of these souvenirs 'raised about £70 for party funds on a good day at West Ham'.[12]

Probably only a handful of football fans support or even understand the political aims of movements like the National Front and the British Movement in their entirety. Many more, however, perhaps especially those from the lower working class, the ones we have identified as most centrally involved in football hooliganism, appear to be attracted by the pro-white, anti-immigrant stance and proclivity for violent demonstration of these organisations. Racialism, in fact, is but an extreme expression of the general attitudes of such groups towards outsiders, although such sentiments may be heightened in time of war and/or in periods of economic crisis. Given that, it is hardly surprising that the far right currently sees the football terraces as a potentially fruitful recruiting ground. We noted earlier the way in which the NF and the BM have successfully infiltrated the ranks of Chelsea terrace fans. It seems rather more than coincidental, too, that the identification of an active BM component in the support of Leeds United in the early 1980s should have prefaced some of the worst violence and vandalism by Leeds fans, certainly since the early 1970s.[13]

In January 1981, following increasing reports of attacks on ethnic minority groups in a variety of social contexts, David Lane, Chairman of the Commission for Racial Equality, spoke of an acceleration in the recruitment drives of what he described as 'neo-Nazi' groups in a climate 'fuelled by high unemployment and economic recession.' Special mention was made in Mr Lane's remarks of the disturbing rise in the expression of anti-semitic sentiments at some London football grounds.[14] In February the same year, the FA pledged itself to investigate the growing number of allegations that racialist groups were recruiting members from among young terrace fans, although there was still a temptation on the part of some of the game's authorities to dismiss football-related racism as 'just the latest fashion'.[15]

The pre-match behaviour of English fans in Copenhagen

In Denmark, as had also been the case in Spain, it was Chelsea fans who were in the vanguard of England's violent, racist following. They were by no means alone in the expression of racist sentiments, however. Before the official party of English supporters arrived in Copenhagen, English fans had already been hard at work using spray cans to paint on walls and street signs. On the perspex surrounds of a number of cafés on Vesterbrogade, for example, one could read references to the 'Blackburn NF', the 'Manchester Nazis' and so on. Slogans like these came complete with hastily fashioned swastikas and the nicknames of the artists.

It was possible to piece together from the accounts of fans already established in Copenhagen what some of the other activities of the morning and previous evening had been. Heavy drinking and a number of raids on the tills of local cafés preceded what a young fan from the Manchester area described as 'window shopping'. Clearly, many England supporters had arrived in Copenhagen with a bare minimum of funds. Supplies of food and drink were replenished, when necessary, by stealing from supermarkets and market stalls. Although clearly much more lucrative, however, organised theft of saleable merchandise was less common. Increasingly, some fans at away matches in England have sought to put their perceived release from the restraints of the home patch to good use by embarking on the theft of marketable goods. In recent years, for example, Everton fans have stolen watches and money from the players' changing rooms at a 'friendly' match in Morecambe. Liverpool fans went one better before a League Cup tie against Bradford City in 1980 by raiding a local bank. More recently, Manchester United fans were reported to have smashed a jeweller's shop window while on an away trip to London, escaping with an estimated £40,000 worth of necklaces and rings.[16]

As one might expect, especially given the deteriorating economic and employment situation at home, criminal activities of this kind are not restricted solely to the domestic football scene. Following the match in Copenhagen, six Liverpool fans from the Huyton area were arrested in Odense after shoplifting clothes and jewellery valued at 75,000 Kroner (£4,000). In the opinion of the local police, this was a highly organised affair and not the result of spontaneous high jinks on the part of a group of drink-affected hooligan fans.[17] Serious thefts were reported as having taken place in Copenhagen before the match as well but the major losses suffered by a jeweller in the Stroget area appear to have been the result of a more spontaneous, less pre-planned raid. By all accounts, somewhere between thirty and forty English fans were at the scene of the crime. Most of them, however, were probably there in search of excitement rather than with the intention of taking part in what turned out to be a 'smash and grab' raid. 'We couldn't fuckin' believe it', said the fan from Manchester. 'They had it (some unidentified object) through the window, and they were in. We all fucked off out of it before the coppers came.'

The arrival of the official party of England fans in Copenhagen at around 1.30 p.m. on the day of the match found the early English arrivals already in advanced stages of preparation for the evening's events. A few drank spirits but the majority settled for 6-packs of the notoriously potent Scandinavian 'elephant beer' which they carried with them as they moved around the streets. However, it was not only the English who indulged in heavy drinking. Thousands of Danish fans flooded into the city via the Central Railway Station throughout the day. The overwhelming majority were males aged between 18 and 25, although some of the rowdiest among them appeared to be rather older. Many were identifiable by T-shirts depicting the Danish flag. Like the English, they moved around the capital in groups of up to twenty, 6-packs in attendance, singing their own songs and anthems.

'Unofficial' English fans continued arriving at the Central Railway Station virtually until kick-off time but were forced to vacate the area quickly in order to avoid the attentions of hostile Danes. Some were unable to do so. On 23 September, *The Daily Mirror* carried a photograph which was said to show an England fan under attack by a group of older Danes (see Plate 13). On other occasions, however, the roles were reversed. We witnessed two apparently unprovoked assaults by groups of English fans on pairs of Danish supporters around the gates of the Tivoli Gardens. On both occasions, boots and fists were used before the victims were left or ran off. More commonly, however, violence ensued when groups of Danish and English fans met head-on in the streets following drinking bouts. *Ekstra Bladet* reported of the incidents in Copenhagen in the hours before the match that:

> It had been a long day's travel as the evening drew on for the young English football fanatics. First they tried to tear down the Central Station. After, they got more drunk. They fought their way everywhere, hitting people – and getting hit. Many were arrested and never saw the match they had worked and saved for.[18]

East of Tivoli, the attractions of the pedestrian precincts of Stroget had a group of about thirty young English fans, complete with tattoos, shirts and flags, moving noisily and threateningly among the afternoon shoppers. Here, the open displays of merchandise and the ease of evading the shadowing Danish police helped to promote a spate of thefts from stores and more assaults on young Danish supporters. Periodic surges by the English down these packed avenues sent shoppers scattering. Policemen on foot and later, in desperation, in cars, served to add to rather than allay the fear and confusion.

By this time, too, (about 4 p.m.), the strains of 'Rule Britannia' and 'We're on the March with Robson's Army' were beginning to spill out from the bars around Stroget. In one of them which was catering for about twenty English supporters, two Arsenal fans in their late twenties, veterans of Bilbao and covered by discreet 'Gunners' tattoos, were holding court. They informed the assembled group that 'the Inter' (West Ham's 'Inter-City Firm') had surprisingly not made the short trip to Denmark. A couple of perhaps slightly younger Newcastle fans felt the loss of 'the Firm' was a grave blow. It was generally agreed that the West Ham lads were 'fuckin' crazy' and that their presence would have added to the general high jinks of the visit. The Arsenal lads, however, were not so sure. They drew the line abroad, they said, at 'having a good laugh'. This included, it seemed, activities like the stripping of an hotel room in Northern Spain, an incident which they vividly described. But 'the Firm', they argued, were liable to have every foreign copper eyeing the English with malice. Perhaps their absence from Copenhagen might be a bonus for English fans, enabling them to 'stir up' the locals and sample the nightlife without attracting the suffocating attentions of the local 'Old Bill'.[19]

The Arsenal lads described themselves as self-employed building workers who had 'taken a few days off'. They had travelled to Copenhagen by ferry and train, arriving the previous evening and finding cheap hotel accommodation almost immediately. One of the Newcastle fans was unemployed, and both had arrived by train that morning. They planned to 'doss down' somewhere in Copenhagen for the night but they weren't sure where. Each was travelling with the bare minimum of funds and they had picked up match tickets in the bar some two hours earlier. As had been the case in Spain, their rather incomplete arrangements appeared to be common to many English fans attending the match.

The Copenhagen daily, *Ekstra Bladet*, was also busy collecting data on the social backgrounds of English fans. Writing in a style which will not be unfamiliar to students of the popular press in Britain, the paper quoted verbatim some of the observations made by the fans about themselves:

> We sent the Vikings, but now, after 1,000 years, they are
> paying us back. The English football fanatics – called hooligans
> – hit Copenhagen yesterday. They are feared all over Europe.
> There isn't any other country where football fans run amok
> when they are following their team.

'Many of us are out of work, and for those in work a trip
to Denmark costs at least two weeks' wages plus what we
spend on drinks. But we don't mind paying. We follow our
English boys anywhere,' said Paul, 20, a builder from London.

'We come from the English working class and all the police
in Europe hate us. They expect us to fight and we can't stand
them, so we fight,' said Steve from Birmingham. 'We don't care
too much how much it costs to follow the lads so long as we
can get in to see them. It was hell in Spain but it is a bit better
here. We really want everything to be peaceful, but we are
expected to fight and it isn't too difficult to live up to that.'[20]

Outside the Idraetspark in the hour or so before the match, the
nearest bar spilled over with young English fans bedecked in flags
and match shirts. Nearby, a mobile stall selling cans of strong
Danish lager was catering predominantly for an English clientèle.
English fans, many with a considerable amount of continental
experience under their belts after the escapades of the summer,
whistled and jeered at local policemen who looked on with what
seemed to be a sense of increasing apprehension. The fans derided
the local force and its quaint uniforms. 'Wankers', agreed an apparently hardened troupe of dedicated England watchers from
Peterborough.

This sparked off a session of animated debate among the Boro
lads on the 'most bastard' police forces in England and some
reminiscences on the police in Turin, Basle and elsewhere. Altogether, there were eight of them – six semi-skilled and unskilled
manual workers, and two unemployed. Like the majority of English
fans, they had travelled by ferry and train. They had, they claimed,
lost the ninth member of their party. He had stowed away in the
boot of a van to avoid fare payment on the ferry and had not been
seen since. Those who had made it to Denmark had picked up
terrace tickets in Copenhagen since their arrival the previous day.
We remarked, not entirely innocently, that Peterborough seemed
a rather unlikely place to spawn such a healthy following for the
England team abroad. The remark was interpreted almost instantly
as a slight on weekend city-centre masculinity in 'the Boro'. We
were summarily presented with the names of a string of Peterborough nightspots and pubs at which, so we were told, an unwitting
visitor would be liable 'to have his head kicked in' for speaking

out of place. 'There's some right hard cunts in the Boro, y'know,' one of the group told us. As if to push the point home, there was already evidence of discord in their ranks. An excess of 'pop' (this time, wine) was used to explain away the by now half-closed black eye of one of the party, received following an argument with one of his mates.

As the trickle of Danish fans moving towards the Idraetspark gradually increased, so the English in the immediate vicinity of the groundside bar, now numbering about a hundred, became more vocal in their support of everything English and in their hostility towards their Danish hosts. Once again, chants about the victory in the Falklands war were a focal point of the English repertoire. Its significance was echoed in hearty renderings of 'Rule Britannia', fast, it seems, becoming something of an England supporters' anthem both at home and abroad. More menacingly, perhaps, references to the war were creeping into *football* battle hymns. Thus, in Copenhagen, there were special adaptations of the 'Sparrow Song' in circulation. In the domestic football context, the song ends with references to cockneys/scousers/geordies, etc. being 'kicked to fuck'. In Copenhagen, although the common patois of the football end with its references to 'rucks' and 'kicking' as means for ending terrace disputes remained unchanged, 'the Argies' had become the victims. The song's new but otherwise unremarkable lyrics ran:

> The Argies they went to the Falklands
> They said that they wanted to ruck.
> So the Argies went in
> And the English moved in
> And kicked all the Argies to fuck.

A number of English fans reported that the exchange of pro- and anti-Argentina slogans had been one of the main sources of conflict between English and Danish fans in the streets of Copenhagen before the match. In one of the few newspaper accounts to make out the English case after the match, *The Daily Star*, under the headline, 'Why We Fought The Danes', carried the story of a 20-year-old plumbing engineer who had cause 'to defend himself', as he put it, against Danish provocateurs. As he told *The Daily Star*:

I'm very patriotic and when they started calling me an English bastard and chanting 'Argentina, Argentina!' because of the Falklands war I thought it was about time I started to defend myself. A couple of them got cut up a bit, but there were no bottles or knives. All the continentals want to do is to give us a good thumping.[21]

The tenor of the piece in *The Daily Star* makes it difficult for the reader to assess whether the paper was condoning or condemning the action of fans like the plumbing engineer. Its problems in this regard are not difficult to see. On the one hand, the actions described are those of the typical English hooligan fan abroad, roundly condemned by the authorities and the press alike. On the other, here were groups of Englishmen defending their own and their country's honour in a manner consistent with *The Daily Star's* jingoistic coverage of the war and with the supposed new national self-image that the successful venture in the South Atlantic was widely reported to have brought. In other words, the fact began to be brought home that the hooliganism of English football fans in foreign contexts is, in part, an expression of nationalistic feelings and thus not totally dissimilar to the state-legitimated nationalism expressed and officially encouraged in conjunction with the Falklands war.

Like the Falklands war and the escalation mutually of national sentiment in Britain and Argentina, much of the hooligan behaviour of English fans in Copenhagen was co-produced, a consequence of the interaction between them and their Danish counterparts. This is not to say that English fans were not often the principal initiators of events, trying, for example, to provoke home supporters into a hostile or challenging response. Outside the Idraetspark before the match, a group of London fans in their mid-twenties goaded and jeered passing Danish fans. Later, they began throwing beer over them and lashing out at them with their feet. When young Danes stopped to remonstrate with the English, they were urged to 'C'mon and have a go'. Some were keen, too, but were dragged away by friends and, in one instance, by two policemen. This 'victory' was loudly cheered by the English, and the Danes were deemed alternately to be 'wankers' and worthy only of being 'matched with an Englishman's arse'. This was a signal for a round of 'mooning' to begin which was captured on film when a Danish cameraman arrived on the scene (see Plate 15).

Over the last few years, mooning has become a regular part of away match trips, domestic as well as continental. Its primary aims appear to be twofold: firstly to shock 'respectable' members of the community, especially females; and secondly, to impress upon the home fans that the visitors know how to throw caution to the winds at away games, that they don't, in the words of one of the London lads, 'give a fuck about anything'. On the continent, the license to moon, steal, fight, etc. is enhanced by the perceived impotence of the foreign authorities in their efforts to cope with the English. But mooning and behaviours like it are also seen to mark essential differences in national character. Danish males, for example, were endlessly described by English fans as 'boring', 'wankers' and so on, while they described themselves, warmly, as 'right crazy bastards', 'do anythin' for a fuckin' laugh', etc. 'You tell a Denmark fan to have his keks (trousers) off', one of the Peterborough fans remarked with contempt, 'and he'd run a fuckin' mile.'

During the hour or so before the kick-off, the uniformed police officers outside the Idraetspark were rather less concerned with the English penchant for mooning than they were with keeping apart the drink-affected English and their Danish counterparts. The latter were vocal in support of the home side and, in many cases, no less the worse for drink than their English guests. The Copenhagen daily paper, *B.T.*, summarised as follows the importance of the match for the Danish people, stressing the concern of the Danish authorities that it should go off without serious incident. Since it is often felt in this country that English teams are the only ones currently under threat of suspension by EUFA, it is worth quoting *B.T.*'s report in full:

> It is exciting to see if our national team can add extra spice to the match, and also to see if they can win it. Not many people believe that they can, but we all live in hope. We have played well in the latest matches against the chosen few from football's mother country. It is a big match and it can become even more important if Denmark plays well.

Appeal From The Danish FA
It is about two important points in the European
Championships, but it is also about prestige which is highly
valued by the English players who, despite being professionals,
are not playing for a lot of money tonight. The spirit among
the spectators is also important. The Danish FA has appealed
to the 44,500 Danish fans to show sportsmanship. The 500
English spectators will be in a secluded area of the lower
terraces and they could try to provoke people.
  The Danish FA are very nervous about trouble at the match.
Think back to what happened after the last home meeting
with England, and to what happened after the Yugoslavia
match. We have to think about what actions can be taken
against Danish football if there is any trouble. EUFA has sent
a Scottish representative to the match.

Big Reinforcements
All measures have been taken to prevent trouble. The police
inform us that reinforcements from *Store Kongensgade* and
an emergency squad are to handle the situation outside the
ground, and inside when it is called for. Copenhagen's
Idraetspark has increased its force to about two hundred men.
'We have had meetings with everybody involved to discuss
what to do', said stadium manager, John Mathiasen. 'We also
have your article about the problems after the Juventus match.
We will place extra men on the top part of the stand so that
we can stop people from throwing things. That's the only
thing we can do. If we go further, we have to have the approval
of the authorities. We hope it will prevent trouble, and that
anyone who starts anything will be taken out of the ground.
We're trying to place a lot of men up there so that everything
can be seen.'

Everybody Should Help
'We're also appealing to the spectators to help and call for
attention if anything is starting. It's sad that it's a minority
which starts the trouble and spoils what could be a family
entertainment. Hopefully, though, the security people will
control everything. There will be 45,000 people inside the
ground tonight which will give a net profit of 600,000 D Kr.

We hope people will enjoy themselves in the ground tonight and in front of the TV. Keep your fingers crossed for Danish football tonight.'[22]

As it turned out, *B.T.*'s reference to missile throwing at a European tie involving Juventus, proved to be prophetic regarding events at the imminent meeting with England.

Crowd behaviour inside the Idraetspark

English fans knew little of the measures taken by the Danish authorities to curb their excesses. As they filed noisily into the Danish national stadium that evening, they were in any case more likely to be ruminating on the problems of finding the correct entrance than they were on the prospects for security inside. The official party of English fans was stationed in groundside seats at the south west corner, virtually opposite the goal-line at that end of the ground. There was no formal segregation of English and Danish fans either in this or any other section. It soon became apparent, moreover, that there were English fans on both goal-end terraces. This was deducible from the fact that, as has become customary at England's matches abroad, Union Jacks had been hung over the advertising hoardings behind the goals in the hope that they might be picked out at home on TV. The largest number of English fans, however, were on the west terrace, directly adjacent to the official party. Although steel railings and stiff wire-mesh fences separated standing English fans both from the pitch and their compatriots in the seats, before the game began visiting supporters seemed to have a free passage between terraces and seats. This was evidenced later by reports from English fans who had vacated their vantage point on the terraces for one in the seats as exchanges between English and Danish fans behind the goal at the west end of the ground began to become more heated.

As far as could be made out, few of the younger English fans in the official party made a serious attempt to obtain the seats reserved for them. The seats, in any case, were of the bench variety and many of the English fans seemed totally opposed to being seated. In short, there was an attempt to recreate a terrace atmosphere *in the seats*. Before the teams came out, several members of the official party, probably in their late twenties, were standing on their seats singing, 'Rule Britannia', and urging others to do likewise. Complaints, particularly from nearby Danish supporters, were shouted down. More direct attempts to seat them were treated by some English fans as direct invitations to fight. A Danish fan, probably in his late teens, was seated to the left of the main body of English support but his view and that of his girlfriend were permanently obscured by standing English fans. About ten minutes into the match, he tapped an offending visitor on the shoulder and motioned him to sit down. Almost instinctively, the English lad, also in his late teens and sporting an England shirt, jeans and training shoes, whirled around. Taking a step backwards, he adopted the 'have a go' stance common to football grounds, city-centre pubs and nightspots in Britain − fists held low to the side, top half of the body tensed and held slightly forwards. 'C'mon, fucking make me!' he urged the young Dane. Clearly afraid, the Danish fan shook his head in incomprehension and disappeared to the back of the stand, presumably to fetch an official.

The commotion in the seats housing the English soon brought down a flurry of Danish newspaper photographers to that section of the ground. The result was a number of studies of the hostility and aggression of young English fans served up to order for the Copenhagen public next morning. In fact, all the standing English supporters highlighted in Plate 17 were watching from a *seated* section of the Idraetspark. Eventually, the police and stadium security personnel were summoned to calm the English and get them seated. However, no sooner had the officials left, than the English fans were on their feet again, shouting abuse at the complaining Danes nearby.

As the teams emerged from the players' tunnel, the police were again in action, this time to quell a disturbance on the west terrace as English and Danish fans warmed to the appearance of their respective heroes. In the seats, more strains of 'Rule Britannia' brought a barrage of missiles from Danish fans seated in the double-decker above. Beer, cans and plastic cups rained down, sometimes poured or thrown by middle-aged Danes who laughed provocatively at the visitors' discomfort. A 20-year-old fan from Middlesex reported that:

Middle-aged Danes in flashy suits started tipping beer on us from the stands. They must have poured gallons on us, and then started toasting their achievements with more beer. This carried on until police moved into the front rows and chucked them out.[23]

The fact that it was English fans who were the object of this missile attack was not without its ironies. Such a vulnerable position had presumably been chosen in order to prevent *them* from assailing local fans.

Minor scuffles between English and Danish terrace fans occurred throughout most of the match. None of them was particularly serious, however. Nor, given the lack of formal segregation, were they especially surprising. The only significant disorderly incident to occur while the match was in progress was the throwing of a smoke bomb on to the pitch. It took place following the refusal of the referee to award a penalty to the Danes. There was little doubt in the minds of officials present that it was a Danish supporter who was responsible for throwing the offending missile. It certainly emerged from a predominantly Danish section of the west terrace. Although, in all probability, the smoke bomb in no way directly endangered the players or match officials, its pungent, red smoke did obscure the vision of the principals and play was temporarily suspended while it was removed from the vicinity of the England goal-mouth.

The match itself in some ways followed quite closely the pattern of the meeting between the two nations in 1978. Again, the English defence was embarrassed by the speed of the Danish attacks. As in 1978, moreover, the visitors were hanging on at the end to a slender lead, this time of 2 goals to 1. It was at this point that the pattern of the two matches diverged. Beforehand, a young English fan had told a local newspaper that English supporters 'fear only the Danish police and Jesper Olsen'.[24] The police were to come a little later. Now was the time for the diminutive Olsen to take a hand. The Danish forward equalised brilliantly for the Danes at the goal in front of the restless west terrace, scoring so late into injury time that there was scarcely time for the match to restart. As the players left the field, the English downcast, the Danes jubilant, fights began to break out on the west terrace.

It is difficult to determine just how orderly the behaviour of English fans might have been had Olsen not equalised for the

Danes at this late stage. In Spain, England were undefeated, and conceded just one goal, a fact which may have contributed to the relative lack of serious incidents *inside* stadia at the World Cup Finals. In Copenhagen, however, judging from accounts given by English fans later, the Olsen goal together with the reactions of Danish fans to it, played a major part in provoking the disturbances which followed. What is more, the Olsen goal coincided with the removal of uniformed policemen from the west terrace to police the streets outside the stadium. From this point on, the Danish police effort was in some disarray.

The problems of late goals and the redeployment of officers outside the ground just prior to the end of major matches are well known to senior police officers in England. These are the periods when police resources are stretched most thinly. Leslie Walker, the FA's Liaison Officer, recalled after the Copenhagen match that he had warned the Danish police of the dangers of uniformed officers leaving the ground too soon, i.e. before the opposing fan groups have dispersed. Walker observed of the Danish police that:

> Because of their experience of problems when the game is over, they [the uniformed police] simply walked out with the crowd and then that violence occurred. It was plainly obvious the uniformed police had left, because there were only plainclothes left to control inside the stadium. And, indeed, I was the last person to leave the box where the Danish and English officials were, and nothing had started by then. The next day I was amazed that there had been this incident.

Somewhere in the region of 200 English fans were involved in the disturbances which began in the Idraetspark after the match, later spreading outside the ground. According to some of the fans involved, after Olsen's goal Danish supporters on the west terrace 'seemed to want to fight'. What they did in fact was to aim their celebrations at the English, some of whom, as often happens on the terraces in England, took such celebrations as gloating and hence as signifying an invitation to combat. (In an English terrace context, merely cheering a goal by one's side can be construed as being provocative.) On the unsegregated terraces in Copenhagen, this 'invitation' was heartily accepted by some of the English fans. Unfamiliar with the nuances of terrace etiquette in England, the Danes appeared surprised by the reaction they produced and were forced to retreat. This was taken by the English as yet more evidence of the 'cowardliness' of the Danes. 'It was all, "Yeah! great goal" and all this from them when they scored, but when you had a go, they didn't want to know.' For this teenage Everton fan, the Danes had proved themselves to be simply 'all fuckin' mouth'. The plainclothes Danish policemen present on the west terrace in large numbers, however, provided more substantial opposition. Long after the fighting between rival *fans* inside the stadium had ceased, they were struggling with English supporters who seemed to have little idea that their brawls with these heavily built Danes were simply the prelude to arrest by these self-same opponents.

With Danish and English fans from the west terrace and other sections of the ground using the same exits, the segregation of rival fans outside the Idraetspark was virtually non-existent. A series of fights soon erupted and fans from both sides gathered to observe the outcome (see Plate 19). At this stage, with police cars and police officers careering around the stadium in a seemingly uncoordinated fashion, policing appeared to be chaotic. When the police did manage to locate the scene of a disorder, fans quickly scattered and the officers were left to clear up the debris. Bottles, cans and stones were exchanged between groups of rival fans in missile attacks, and supporters of both sides, blood streaming from their heads, were led away to await the arrival of ambulances. The more seriously injured were taken by stretcher to hospital.

Along Osterbrogade, the main thoroughfare leading from the Idraetspark back to the centre of Copenhagen, groups of English fans, sometimes pursued by Danes, vandalised property and attacked onlookers. These and their other activities outside the stadium received ample coverage in the Copenhagen press next morning. Under the headline, 'Football Fans Run Amok After The International Match', *Aktuelt* reported that Copenhagen had been 'put to trial' by English fans. Eye witnesses reported that the English had 'vandalised everything around them as they walked down Osterbrogade and Dag Hammarskjöld's Alle.' *Aktuelt*'s account of the disturbance continued:

The English kicked everybody and everything which came in their way. A taxi-driver who was stuck sent an SOS to the taxi headquarters because he feared for his life and car. The local police station received assistance from all stations in the city and they tried – as far as they could – to follow the English fans around the city.

The number of English fans about was reduced in the course of the evening. 'We have now got over 50 fans arrested and only a few of them are Danes', reported the police at 10 p.m. last night.

After the clashes, many people were taken to hospital. Already, during the match itself, there was some fighting, but it was when the final whistle went that it really broke out.[25]

Ekstra Bladet began its account of the proceedings by noting that the disturbances had begun in Copenhagen long before the evening of the match and that '45 hooligans had tried to tear down the Central Station'. Its report went on:

Inside the Idraetspark itself police had to intervene during the warm-up and outside anyone who tried to talk to or photograph the hooligans was in danger. But the worst incident came when Jesper Olsen equalised for Denmark. About 500 English fans stood up ready to fight, knowing that the victory had been snatched.

A group of Danish fans didn't help when they threw beer bottles at their heads. The English reaction was to shout, 'England! England! England!' and to go for Danish fans with the English speciality, kicking with boots, about 15 of them kicking one Dane. Later it spread to the whole of Osterbro. About 50 hooligans were arrested.[26]

The aftermath

Back in Istedgade an hour or so after the match, it was clear that some of the English contingent who had left the match immediately on the final whistle or a few minutes before were unaware that any serious disorders had occurred. Others, and these included members of the official party of fans, recounted at length, and undoubtedly with a degree of exaggeration, their own involvement in the fights and missile exchanges outside the Idraetspark. A young, very drunken Millwall fan shouted endlessly, 'We were there! We were fuckin' there!' before uttering the valedictory lament, 'We are Millwall, no one likes us. We don't care', and wandering off to ask someone what the final score was. A couple of teenage fans from the London area now sported facial cuts, and one, a hole in the armpit of his sweater. This confirmed his identity as one of the English fighters captured earlier by a Danish newspaper photographer. Back home, he was unemployed and, yet again, a Chelsea supporter. He remarked that one of the Chelsea contingent had been taken to hospital for the treatment of unspecified injuries. The next day, other English fans surfaced on the streets of the capital with newly bandaged arms and heads.

Long into the early hours of the morning following the match, boggle-eyed young English fans in shirts and jeans journeyed to and from the live shows and sex supermarkets. There was little evidence of Danish fans swamping the area as the English had done. This fact, and the draining excesses of the early evening, probably accounts for the relative calm which settled on Vesterbro late that night. A small knot of tired and bedraggled English fans gathered in the pool room of one of the nearby bars to observe some of the locals in action. An English-speaking Dane in his early thirties, describing himself as an office worker, discussed the match. He was pleased with the performance of the Danish side but a little surprised at what he had seen inside and nearby the stadium that night. He observed that large numbers of Danish fans typically travelled to Copenhagen for major internationals and that, not infrequently, many of them drank to excess before matches. However, he claimed that the extent to which Danish fans had contributed to the disorders at the English match was unusual. He had an explanation for this: 'The English, say the newspapers, have the vandals, so the Danes who want to fight, they come to see the English.' Later, Leslie Walker also noted what he described as 'a worrying new phenomenon' at England matches abroad:

It was quite clear to me in Denmark – and this is more worrying to me than trying to control our fans or the numbers going – that many young Danes at the stadium were looking for trouble. I looked at them beforehand, and Danish officials told me that these fans were not the sort of people who usually go to football matches. They were there for a punch up. That worries me because I think there is some evidence that other countries are now latching on to this violence. They're coming onto 'our territory'. It's like Chelsea, isn't it? The idea of Chelsea supporters is: 'Well, if they don't want trouble, they shouldn't come to Chelsea'.

As a result of incidents before, during and after the match in Copenhagen, more than a hundred English fans were arrested. Of these, just six were held in custody for more than a day, in each case on a charge of theft. It is, of course, by no means unusual for miscreant fans to be held by foreign authorities for a short period only. In countries such as Spain, they are sometimes held for longer periods, even for crimes they have clearly not committed, but more usually foreign authorities are quick to rid themselves of English hooligans, often without bringing charges. In Denmark, English hooligans were fined for their misdemeanours and immediately released.

In addition to the hundred English, fifteen Danish fans were arrested as a result of incidents connected with the international. This fact, together with what could be easily observed in the Danish capital on the day of the match, lent credence to the claim of Stephen O'Meara, the British Vice-Consul in Copenhagen, that 'not all the blame is being put on the English supporters'.[27] Of the British press, however, only *The Daily Star* took a similar view – in fact, it was in that paper that O'Meara's remarks were reported – suggesting that:

A proper investigation into the scenes which led to around 100 arrests will for once show England's notorious supporters to have been the victims. And at least a fair measure of responsibility lies with the totally inadequate policing organised at the stadium by the Danish authorities.[28]

Reported under the headline, 'Innocents Abroad', *The Daily Star* account went on to describe the activities before the match of what it referred to as 'drunken Danish fans' who were 'clearly spoiling for a fight'. Reference was made, too, to the situation after the game in which, according to *The Daily Star*, it was 'English fans who were being assaulted from two sides'.[29]

As far as most British commentators were concerned, the scenes reported to have taken place in Copenhagen constituted yet more evidence that English fans are now quite beyond the control of the football authorities in virtually any European context. Headlines such as, 'England Fans Riot',[30] and 'Thugs Day of Action'[31] – the latter misleadingly hinting at a parallel between hooliganism and organised industrial protest – were the fare which greeted returning England fans on the morning after the violence and property damage in Denmark. Some English football officials, however, felt strongly that the British press had misrepresented the incidents in Copenhagen. According to Leslie Walker, for example:

> Denmark was not a major incident in terms of misbehaviour abroad. It was very limited. It was after the match and, indeed, I think the press and the media did a disservice because it was nowhere near as bad as people thought it was by the pictures.

Clearly, according to the official view, incidents *outside* the stadium are less significant than incidents *inside*. Depending as they do on the referee's version of events and on the reports of their official match observers, EUFA was likely to share this point of view and hence not to look too harshly on the events which took place outside the Idraetspark. At any rate, they would have been mainly reliant on the press for any knowledge of such incidents and unable to take them into account in determining their course of action. This point is an important one because the apportionment by EUFA of blame for the Copenhagen disorders was a matter of considerable moment to the English football authorities. Thus far, the ultimate sanction – expulsion from European competition – still remained just a threat but it was a very worrying one to the FA. Not surprisingly, they were keen to make their case to EUFA very strong and very clear. FA Press Officer, Glen Kirsten, admitted towards the end of September 1982 that the fact that EUFA might at any time ban English sides from European competition was a 'constant worry' to the English authorities. At the same time, however, he pointed out that the arrangements for matches involving English sides abroad were something that the visitors could do very little to influence. He suggested that the control of the sale of tickets for matches involving the England team was a particularly pressing problem:

We appealed to the Danes not to sell match tickets on the day of the game and only approved travel agents received tickets from us. The total number was 500. Yet it seems that there were somewhere around 2,000 English fans in Denmark and it makes you wonder where they got the tickets.[32]

EUFA was swift to comment on the disturbances in Copenhagen. René Eberlé, the Secretary of the Disciplinary Committee, expressed himself to be 'sick about all this. In the end, it will kill football if you can't stop it.'[33] More ominously, he warned that, in his opinion, the next step would have to be 'no more tickets for English fans'.[34] If they believed it was possible to devise a system for preventing maverick English fans from purchasing tickets for major matches abroad, the FA would probably have agreed with the sentiments expressed by Eberlé.

For some time before the disturbances in Copenhagen, the FA had lobbied for the confiscation of offenders' passports. Such an idea, however, has been repeatedly discounted by the Minister for Sport on the grounds that the rights of British citizens in this matter must be protected at all costs. Nor, it seems, is the Foreign Office willing to give the names of offending fans to the FA. The football authorities are still awaiting details on the fans arrested in Basle in 1981 but the Foreign Office have refused to release them on the grounds that it would be 'unfair to the individuals, and an intrusion on their liberty'.[35] 'For all we know', commented the FA Secretary after the disruptive scenes in Copenhagen, 'people who were arrested in Switzerland could have been in our official allocation for the Denmark match and then arrested again in Copenhagen. We have no way of knowing.'[36]

For Frank Taylor of *The Daily Mirror* things have already moved beyond reparation by the intervention of either the British government or the FA. In his view, it is simply time that EUFA stopped 'pussyfooting' around the problem of England's violent fans. EUFA, is, he thinks, the only body capable of halting 'this violent trend' in spectator misbehaviour. The European body is, he argues, faced with two possible courses of action in this regard:

[It] can either insist that when England play abroad, admission is by ticket only and that the tickets are sold through the home Association and the English FA, none to travel agents and none for 3 days before the match. Or they must tell England they are no longer wanted in European competition.[37]

EUFA's Disciplinary Committee met to consider the Copenhagen match on 7 October 1982. No action was taken either against the English football authorities or English fans. Instead, a fine was levied against the Danish FA because a Danish fan was proved to have interrupted the match by throwing a smoke bomb on to the field of play.

English football officials were clearly relieved on hearing the committee's decision. They had already moved with their own plans for the forthcoming round of continental matches. More particularly, they had decided to accept no tickets for the forthcoming Under 21 international against West Germany or for the European Championship tie to be played in Greece. Both matches went off with relatively few disturbances. It was very clear, however, particularly in Greece, that English fans are increasingly becoming the target for continental hooligans who have their own reputations to defend. *The Sunday Times* reported that:

> A savage incident in Athens when one of their buses was bombarded and its Greek driver cruelly beaten up, showed that they [English fans] have become merely a target for the hooligans of Europe. Luxembourg, Turin, Basle, and Copenhagen have taken their toll. However aggressive, however innocent, they will be in danger every time they go abroad. As ye sow. . . .[38]

The full extent of the planned Greek reception, however, was only revealed some time after the match. According to a report in *World Soccer* in December 1982:

> As the game drew near, a dozen 'hooligan' clubs from around the country joined forces to warn the visiting English hooligans that they better behave. The 'Zountex' hooligans said, 'If the English hooligans dare to cause trouble, we will take hostages'. One group, '13 Cannibals', said they would use pistols if need be.
>
>   'Greek fans, don't be afraid. Despite our differences, we will unite under the Greek flag to show that Greece is not Denmark or Luxembourg,' a statement from Gate 7 Olympiakos, Gate 13 of Panathinaikos and Gate 21 of AEK read. The 'Panthers'

of Panionios said, 'we will send back the hooligans to England, dead.'

The Neofascist Panathinaikos fans (NOPO), who claim 400 members, also sent out a warning to English hooligans and the 'Red Killers' of Pananaiki said, 'We may fight against each other, but on November 17 we will strike against the English.'[39]

Estimates suggest that less than a hundred English fans attended the match which was staged in Salonika at the insistence of the Greek authorities. Perhaps it was as well that fans from the Shed, the Shelf, the North Bank and elsewhere decided against making the long trip to Greece in large numbers. If they had, disorders of a severity far surpassing those in Basle, Luxembourg, Turin, Copenhagen and Spain may well have occurred.

CONCLUSION:
TACKLING THE PROBLEM

Sociological research and social policy

One does not need psychic powers to anticipate that a question
which is probably in the minds of most readers concerns the implications for social policy of the research reported here. It is a
question which expresses understandable concern and it deserves
a clear and unequivocal answer. We shall develop such an answer
in general terms in this concluding chapter. A set of more specific
proposals – we do not conceive of them as anything more than a
preliminary and provisional means for coping with limited aspects
of the problem – are set forth in Appendix 4. Since the relationship
between policy and research is more complex and contentious than
many people seem to allow, it is necessary to spell out some of the
basic assumptions on which our proposals are predicated. The first
step is to outline, very briefly, our general position on the research
process.

We hold, in common perhaps with the majority of researchers,
that the principal objective of any piece of research is the advancement of knowledge. Through the constant interplay of reasoning
and observation (the theoretical and the empirical), the aim is to
construct an explanation of a given phenomenon which either
supplements existing knowledge or which, when compared with
previous accounts, proves more compatible with the available
evidence. In other words, the aim of research is the production of
an explanation that represents an advance in terms of 'object-

adequacy', a conceptualisation with a greater degree of 'fit' with the phenomenon under study.[1] Explanations of this kind are an essential prerequisite for successfully intervening in any aspect of the world, unless, of course, one is lucky and hits upon appropriate actions by chance.

In order to be able to construct *more* object adequate explanations – the comparative is significant – it is necessary for researchers to possess a conceptual framework and to use an approach to social research which help them in their attempt to rise above the everyday involvements and commitments characteristic of social life. Of course, the nature of the research task, its funding and the interests of the investigators involved, militate against the possibility of conducting social research which approaches the ideal of 'perfect' object adequacy. What *is* possible, in our opinion, is to *limit* the distorting effects on perception of values and ideologies, and of sectional and self interests. In doing so, one can hope to reduce the bias which results from the jaundiced or, conversely, the romanticising eye. This is what we have tried to do in our case studies. Readers will have to make their own judgments on how successful we have been.

The research process has the advancement of knowledge as its principal goal but is impeded and distorted by being too closely tied to ideological concerns. By contrast, the construction of social policy presupposes a commitment to the pursuit of what is judged to be a more desirable state of affairs. That is, it is predicated, to a large extent, on ideological commitments. It involves selecting the kinds of actions regarded as necessary in order to move from an unsatisfactory state, A, to a more satisfactory state, B. In a word, social policy is a question of relating means to ends. The selection among competing means-ends strategies is made on the basis of their 'cost-effectiveness' measured in terms of a range of material and ideological priorities. But, and this is a central point, in a differentiated and stratified society such as ours, one party's desired state of affairs is liable to differ more or less drastically from that sought by another. This means that social policy programmes are always liable to be contested and that the choice among them is closely tied up with the distribution of power.

Our discussion so far has focused upon what we take to be a central distinction between research and policy formation. But what of the connections? There is no doubt that research can have implications for social policy, but these implications do not necessarily point in a single direction. Nor can any piece of research, whether in the social or the 'natural' sciences, tell us *in and of itself* what should be done with its findings. For example, a breakthrough in nuclear physics would not, *per se*, tell us how the new knowledge ought to be exploited. Should it be applied for military or peaceful purposes, or for both? Current debates about precisely these sorts of issues clearly testify that knowledge alone cannot tell us what to do or, indeed, whether we should do anything at all. What is true of research in the physical sciences is equally true of research in the social sciences.

To put it bluntly, people tend to approach the findings of sociological research with views already highly charged by prevailing ideological commitments, that is, with pre-formed views of how society is and how it ought to be. In short, the implications drawn from sociological research tend to be heavily influenced by the reader's own world view. It is entirely possible that two parties may read, understand and accept a piece of research as an adequate appraisal of a particular phenomenon. However, because they have different views on the direction in which society should move, they may diverge substantially on the use to which the findings should be put. This is not to say that research has nothing more than the potential to reinforce existing prejudices and ideologies. Research findings may not be able to tell us which courses of action to follow but they can tell us something about the limits of the possible. They may even persuade us to concede the unrealistic nature of certain objectives and, in consequence, lead us to adjust our sights.

Whatever aims a particular set of research findings are used to support, the possibility of achieving them is crucially dependent on: (i) the degree to which they are realisable: and, given this, (ii) the willingness of those who adhere to them to accept the consequences, whatever they may be, of attempting to achieve them. One can only make such appraisals and devise appropriate policies on the basis of adequate knowledge – hence the need for research. Ideally, the research should form an ongoing process in the sense that the means-ends strategies employed in a particular policy should be the subject of continuous monitoring. Furthermore, policy objectives and the means employed to secure them should be continuously re-appraised in the light of whatever findings such monitoring yields.

Consistently with this general line of argument, we hold that our research does not, in itself, indicate what, if anything, ought to be done about football hooliganism. It does not tell us whether we should construct policies designed to eradicate it, curb it, maintain it at its present level, or – unlikely as it may sound to some – encourage its growth.[2] Nor does it tell us whether the side-effects of particular policies are an acceptable price to pay. No doubt readers will have their own views on what the priorities are, and on what should and should not be done. In this regard we are no exception, for to claim that our research is characterised by a high level of detachment is not to relinquish the rights and concerns of citizenship. We are both researchers *and* citizens, and, as citizens, we have our own visions of the directions in which we want society to move. We would be naive, however, to believe that the power we have to realise our visions of a 'better society' equates with that of those in political office, the media, or what has generally become known as 'the establishment'. Nevertheless, we feel bound to try to influence the way in which our findings are interpreted and put to use, if only to distance ourselves from those – whether in politics, administration or the media – who will undoubtedly seek to use them in the service of goals which differ radically from our own. It is in this spirit that we embark on the discussion which follows and in which we have devised the proposals set forth in Appendix 4.

Short-term and long-term strategies

It should be clear from our discussion of football hooligan violence at the beginning of this book that we do not regard hooliganism at matches at home or abroad as something which in any simple sense is 'caused' by football or the context in which football matches are played. That is, the social roots of football hooliganism do not lie solely in the complex interactions between the media and fans. Nor do they lie simply in the interaction between fan groups and the agents of social control, or in the dynamics of crowd processes. All these factors have a part to play. Thus, the sensitive management of crowds and more responsible reporting of hooligan incidents can *limit* the prospects for disorder. Indeed, in the short term at least, strategies in these areas probably constitute the authorities' most effective response to football-related disorders, perhaps especially those involving English fans abroad. In the longer term, however, much more ambitious policy initiatives will have to be pursued and sustained in order to modify the social structures which play an important part in producing and reproducing an adherence to what we described earlier as a violent or aggressive masculine style. Although we disagree with aspects of their analyses, some of the long-term recommendations of Roger Ingham and his colleagues seem to be broadly along the right lines.[3] They at least attempt to deal with the wider social context, though, in our view, their programme is too narrowly based on the need to overcome material deprivation. Of course, a commitment to improve material conditions *must* be a crucial element in any realistic scheme. However, it is also necessary to recognise that hooligan standards are generated by a complex *interaction* between material conditions, the community structures of the lower working class and the location of these communities in the wider society. Unfortunately, limited space precludes a lengthy discussion of our own long-term proposals in this volume.[4] All that can be attempted here is to develop some short-term strategies designed to alleviate the pressing problem of the violent behaviour of some English fans abroad.

There are obvious dangers, of course, in introducing a distinction between short-term and long-term policy objectives. Our view is that no short-term 'holding' initiative is likely to be productive unless it moves in harness with longer-term strategies. But, as Ingham rightly points out with reference to the hooligan problem here at home, the distinction between short-term and long-term policy initiatives is often misrepresented as synonymous with policies that are practical and impractical, possible and impossible. That is, long-term measures are dismissed as utopian and this is used as a justification for doing nothing or for increasing the strength of what Ingham calls the 'knee-jerk' response, i.e. the reflex call for the ever harsher punishment of offenders.[5]

There is also a less prominent tendency, particularly in certain academic circles, to view short-term policies as merely expedient, to dismiss them as being, in principle, insufficiently radical. In short, there exists in practice a divide between the authorities, who tend to be overly concerned with the immediate to the detriment of the longer term, and some academics and others who have tended to train their eyes on the horizon and to be rather dismissive of prevailing anxieties. This clearly constitutes something of an impasse. Let us briefly consider the responses of each of these two groups.

In recent years, given their preoccupation with finding a 'quick solution', and under pressure from sections of public opinion often 'ventriloquised' by a sensationalising press, the authorities have reacted to the problem of football hooliganism with a mixture of anger and frustration.[6] Such sentiments have found expression in the implementation of ever-more-aggressive policing and the harsher sentencing of hooligan offenders. Policies of this kind are increasingly geared, not only to match days, but also towards more stringent law enforcement in lower-working-class communities. As a strategy for curbing hooliganism in its various guises, this method has been exhaustively tried, and found to be wanting. Some of the reasons for its failure are not difficult to find. A major weakness is that it attempts to modify the offending behaviour by employing means similar to those which have played a central part in its production. That is, physical coercion is a principal ingredient in the socialisation of lower-working-class lads and is central to the values they adhere to. The institutional confinement of a 'short, sharp shock' sentence is more likely to reinforce than to dissipate the macho tendencies of violent hooligan offenders. It also runs the risk of criminalising the more marginal cases. Furthermore, these sorts of 'hard line' approaches are more likely to intensify than to break down the hostility towards the authorities and outsiders which is a feature of sections of many lower-working-class communities.

In the face of the growing clamour in recent years for harsher punishments for hooligan offenders, most academics who have studied football hooliganism have tended to minimise the violence often involved. Some point to statistical 'facts' about hooliganism and argue that the phenomenon is almost exclusively a non-violent ritual.[7] Others have been more concerned to examine the media treatment which, they claim, by exaggerating and distorting what is largely a harmless phenomenon, plays fancifully on the anxieties of working people.[8] In our view, these sorts of approaches are characteristic of what Ian Taylor has recently described as a rather weak strain of liberal criminology.[9] Not only do they tend to devalue the experiences of 'ordinary' football supporters, and of ex-fans who have stayed away on account of hooliganism, they also pay little heed to the more direct victims of hooligan behaviour. As Jock Young has observed of street crime, it is a common mistake of theorists of this school to imagine that street criminals are a species of inner-city Robin Hood when, in reality, the victims of their crimes are usually poor and otherwise incapable of defending themselves.[10]

Not all the victims of football hooliganism fit this description. However, most of those who fight and sustain injuries at matches are from disadvantaged social groups. It is also undoubtedly the case that the image of football and its popularity as a spectator sport have suffered in recent years as a result of hooliganism. This is an important point, and one which has, again, been studiously ignored by many recent academic writers on the subject. Professional football in this country is ailing for a variety of complex and interrelated reasons which no short-run initiative of whatever description could hope to cure. Changing leisure preferences and the failure of clubs to respond adequately to change are just two of the major reasons why gates continue to slump. Nevertheless, the evidence suggests that, for *some* potential fans at least, the threat or the experience of hooliganism *does* contribute to their reasons for not attending matches. We should add that this goes for working-class men and women, as well as for the so-called 'new consumers' from the higher social classes much discussed by writers of the Left.[11]

In the present hostile climate towards football in this country, expulsion from European competition because of hooliganism by English fans would undoubtedly prove a serious blow, perhaps even a fatal one. It would certainly threaten the fabric of the lives of many committed football fans, *whatever* their social backgrounds, to say nothing of the livelihood of players, managers, coaches and the game's multifarious ancillary staff. We are of the opinion that the game as a whole and the interests of the majority of fans should take precedence over the satisfactions that a minority gains from engaging in violent and destructive activities abroad. In our judgment, what is required in the first instance is a short-term holding operation designed to ensure the survival of central aspects of a valued sporting tradition which, if not defended, may perish. It is in this light and against the background of imminent crisis that the proposals set forth in Appendix 4 are offered.

The views we have expressed so far will probably be regarded as startlingly uncontroversial in most quarters. However, they will not find favour with everybody. For example, we may well be accused by some of our academic colleagues of being sucked into a simple 'law and order' approach to social problems. It is an understandable point and one which needs to be confronted. In reply, it must be enough for the moment to say that it seems likely that many of our potential critics on this score will be sympathetic either to variants of the essentially non-interventionist positions we criticised earlier or committed to what we regard as free-floating and therefore unrealistic long-term aims. Ironically, however, it is precisely the kinds of romanticised accounts of football hooligan violence and of 'street' crime in general which they have produced which have in recent years left the vacuum which the populist and punitive criminologies of what Taylor has described as the 'New Right' have rushed, successfully, to fill.[12] For reasons we set out earlier, our own short-term proposals will steer carefully clear of the crude, punishment-oriented approach, but they will not shy away from the need for firm but sensitive strategies of control.

Our aim of limiting the activities of English hooligan fans abroad will probably also not be welcomed by political groups of the extreme Right. There is evidence, some of which is presented in our case studies, which suggests that organisations like the British Movement and the National Front regard hooligan fans, not without justification, as potential recruits to their cause. Whilst they have made headway with the followers of particular clubs – Chelsea and Leeds United come immediately to mind – in general they have met with only limited success. A possible reason for this is the fact that, even though hooligans across the country share views of the world and act in ways that make them appear attractive to right-wing groups, the behaviour they engage in at football matches is expressive of very narrow local identifications and involves a form of intra-class conflict. As a result, they are difficult to forge into a unified political movement.

However, the qualities of football hooliganism which tend to thwart the more ambitious plans of the extreme right at *club* level are not present to the same extent at matches involving the *national* side. That is because the national team is symbolically more appropriate from the standpoint of such groups and has more potential as a unifying rallying point. It is, after all, the *England* side and hence, according to the thinking of such groups, ought only to contain players who conform to *their* ideas of 'Englishness'. As was witnessed in Copenhagen, the presence of increasing numbers of black players in English representative sides and the fact that, at this level, they are less protected by club loyalties, has not been lost on the followers of these racist factions. In our view, right-wing exploitation of this emerging feature of football in this country constitutes a threat to the game and to sport as a means for promoting racial harmony. It is a problem, moreover, which appears likely to grow. As such, it is an area calling out for sociological investigation and for remedial action based on the results of that research. This is an issue of immense importance, but lack of space again prevents us from taking the discussion further here.[13]

Summary

So far, we have outlined some of the main reasons why we have decided to formulate a series of short-term recommendations to limit the prospects for disorder by English fans abroad. It is important, of course, to stress that, even if our proposals are adopted and implemented by the FA, this will not 'solve' the problem of football hooliganism. All that will happen – to the extent that such measures are successful – is that the opportunities for groups of English fans to engage in disorderly behaviour at continental matches will have been severely curtailed. They may or may not continue to engage in hooligan behaviour on the continent in *non-football* contexts but they will almost certainly continue with their *football* and other forms of hooliganism here at home.[14] That is likely to be the case with any measures – such as those we have outlined in Appendix 4, however non-punitive their orientation – which are solely concerned with *controlling* the problem. In order to move towards a *resolution*, measures which are simultaneously *deeper* and implemented over the *longer-term* will be required, that is, measures which tackle the problem of hooliganism at its *social roots*.

   As we have said earlier, we do not have the space here to outline such a policy at length. It is, however, possible to discuss what we have in mind in brief and general terms. We have argued that the more violent forms of football hooliganism are the expression in a specific context of an aggressive masculine style which is prevalent in *certain sections* of the lower working class. This raises the question of how it has come about that the differences between these groups and other sections of society should be of a kind that lead the former to behave in ways that are regarded by the latter with horror and distaste. Our view of the matter derives largely from a particular interpretation of recent history. In the course of the twentieth century, the upper strata of the working class have become increasingly 'incorporated' into the wider society. That is, the standards to which they adhere have in many respects moved closer to those of the dominant social groups. By contrast, while they have not been entirely unaffected by this process, the lower strata of the working class have remained relatively untouched. They constitute, in effect, something of an 'underclass'. More particularly, they remain locked in structures which constrain many of them, especially the males, to engage in modes of behaviour that are more openly violent than the dominant norms demand. This violence is mainly expressed in fighting with others from similar communities but, since they find themselves at the bottom of the social 'heap', they are also led to be hostile towards the authorities and more established groups. As a result, they are often resistant to official interventions, and bring their aggressive tendencies into play in various forms of anti-authority behaviour.

The recalcitrance and resistance of these sections of the lower working class will have to be taken into account in any long-term policy which aims to reduce their tendency to resort to physical violence. It is also worth pointing out that violent anti-authority demonstrations of the kind witnessed in 'inner city' areas up and down the country in 1981 seem more likely, under present circumstances at least, to 'persuade' the authorities to improve the material conditions of poor communities than any recommendations of the sort we might make. This, of course, is simply an observation based on some of the outcomes of the 1981 disturbances.[15] It serves as a reminder of the fact that the members of communities who lack the power to secure redress for their grievances through formal channels are liable to resort to collective violence.

As we have already said, however, improvements in material conditions *alone* will not be enough to bring about the changes we describe. Moreover, any attempt to modify the values and lifestyles of the members of these sections of lower-working-class communities will necessarily involve parallel modifications, not only in the existing distribution of resources but also in the dominant modes of thought. For example, a policy aimed at integrating the lower working class into the wider society on more equal terms would require the more powerful and prosperous majority to accept the concept of 'positive', or perhaps more accurately 'counterbalancing' discrimination. That is, they would be required to forgo some of the material and status advantages that they currently enjoy in order to facilitate the massive intellectual and material investment in lower-working-class communities that such a programme would demand. That, in its turn, would require the formation of a social structure which did not have a relatively impoverished 'underclass' as a constituent feature.

We realise, of course, that the chances of making headway with initiatives of this kind are rather slim in the present social and economic climate. (Indeed, if our analysis is correct, current social and economic policies – and, let it be said, this was also true of those of previous governments – are likely to *worsen* rather than alleviate the sorts of social conditions which help to generate violent, hooligan behaviour.) Nevertheless, it remains the case that unless dominant groups are prepared to participate in the sorts of social transformations we have described, problems such as football hooliganism are liable to be with us for a very long time. That is because policies which are oriented solely towards control might succeed in *redirecting* hooligan behaviour but they cannot hope to *eliminate* it.

The measures outlined in Appendix 4 are, of course, control measures, though of a relatively non-punitive kind. In our view, if they are adopted the opportunities for serious violent behaviour by English fans abroad will be severely curtailed. However, that will not mean that the problem of football hooliganism has been 'solved'. Any step towards resolving the problem will require a blend of short-term, holding initiatives and long-term measures which address the social roots of the phenomenon. Nor will this be an easy task. Short-term palliatives frequently run the risk of coming into conflict with crucial aspects of long-term programmes. What we have tried to do in this book is to make a contribution towards securing a reorientation of social policy towards a research-based and more harmonious blending of short-term and long-term initiatives. Without this, hooliganism in its various guises is a phenomenon that specific interest groups will continue to use as a justification for 'law and order' policies. Meanwhile, the rest of us will have to continue experiencing the consequences both of hooliganism and of the deteriorating spiral towards more repressive forms of social control.

APPENDIX 1

CROWD DISORDERS ABROAD REPORTED IN ENGLISH NEWSPAPERS IN WHICH NO ENGLISH TEAMS OR FANS WERE INVOLVED

Argentina	c. 1936	*match unnamed* during 'crowd uproar', policeman shot and killed referee.
	1965	*Independiente v. Internazionale Milan* stones thrown at Inter manager and players.
	1968	*River Plate v. Boca Juniors* 74 died and 150 injured when Boca fans threw lighted newspapers on to fans in the lower tiers, causing a panic.
Austria	c. 1965	*Rapide Vienna v. Benfica* riot led match to be abandoned.
Belgium	1981	*match unnamed* riot by Winterslag supporters.
Bermuda	1980	*Hotels International v. Alabama University* beer bottles thrown at American team; turnstiles raided and around £1,000 stolen.
Brazil	1982	*San Luis v. Fortaleza* 3 died, 25 injured when police fired shots at an angry crowd.
Canada	1927	*Hokoahs (Austria) v. Scottish FA XI* fighting between teams led to pitch invasion that 'bordered on a riot'.
China	1979	*match unnamed* 2 fans jailed for 2 days after stoning visiting team's bus and using 'filthy language'.

	1981	*People's Liberation Army XI v. Guangdong Province* main gate of Nanking stadium 'charged by group of troublemakers', preventing players from leaving; missiles thrown, car windscreens smashed.
	1983	300 fans dispersed by police after a riot outside the Chinese national team's dressing room. 'Several' arrests made.
Colombia	1982	*Deportivo Cai v. Club America* 22 killed and 200 injured in panic started when 'unruly fans' in the upper tiers threw bottles, firecrackers and urinated on those below them.
Egypt	1966	*Zamalek v. National Sporting Club* 300 hurt when soldiers tried to quell an 'angry crowd'.
France	1980	*Strasbourg v. Nantes* police used batons to disperse a 'mob' who set fire to rubbish on the pitch and who tore up seats to throw onto the field.*
Gabon	1981	*FC-105 (Gabon) v. Union Sportive (Cameroon)* match in Libreville ended in street riots in which cars were stoned and set on fire.
Germany (Federal Republic)	1931	*Hertha Berlin v. Fuerth* pitch invasion by Hertha fans; Fuerth player attacked, leading to his hospitalisation.

* An article printed in *The Yorkshire Post* on 15 September 1975 dealt with the problem of football hooliganism in France and is worth quoting here. It reads:

In France, soccer hooliganism has not taken on the proportions of England's problems, but it has been a headache for many years. The worst offenders are the fans of southern clubs – particularly Corsican sides Bastia and Ajaccio and Marseilles Olympic. Following a near riot in a match between Bastia and Marseilles some years ago, French officials decreed that all the pitches should be surrounded by high wire fencing. Strong police reinforcements are always on hand for matches which are likely to end in violence, and the French Federation cracks down hard on clubs whose fans do not behave. Clubs are fined large sums and pitches are regularly suspended for one or two home games, depriving fans of matches and forcing the club to play away from home.

1965   *Werder Bremen v. Partizan Belgrade*
pitch invasion.

1971   *Borussia Mönchengladbach v. Internazionale Milan*
Italian player felled by beer can.

1979   *Hamburg v. Bayern Munich*
70 hurt as Hamburg fans celebrate championship victory.

1981   *Karlsruhe v. Stuttgart*
£10,000 worth of damage caused; 20 arrests.

1981   *Aachen v. Hertha Berlin*
on their way to the match, Hertha fans set fire to the train, gutting three carriages.

1982   *Hamburg v. Bremen*
16-year-old boy died from injuries received when rival fans attacked each other with stones and firework rockets.

1982   *Oberhausen v. Dortmund*
fans attacked each other with stones; several fans and policemen injured.

1982   *Bayern Munich v. SV Hamburg*
24 arrests during match; police seized truncheons, heavy chains and other lethal weapons from fans; posters bearing slogans like 'Death to FC Bayern' also seized; more arrests in post-match violence and attempted robbery; police used truncheons and tear gas to break up rioting.

1982   *Brunswick v. Bayern Munich*
after their team had lost 2–0, about 40 Bayern fans rampaged through a bar, breaking windows and stealing beer glasses.

1982   *Munich 1860 v. Bayern Munich Amateurs*
19 arrests when rioting broke out during match.

1982   *Bayern Munich v. Nuremberg*
138 injured when Bayern fans, shouting 'Sieg Heil!' attacked a May Day rally.

Greece   1980   *Olympiakos v. AEK*
30 arrests after fans rampaged through the suburb of Nea, Philadelphia, smashing shop windows, attacking riot police, and causing £5,000 worth of damage in the AEK stadium.

1980   *Paok v. Panathinaikos*
        35 injured, 6 arrested when 10,000 crowd
        pelted match officials with stones and bricks.
        Police used tear gas to disperse
        demonstrators.

1982   *Panathinaikos v. Olympiakos*
        9 arrests when 1,000 fans demonstrated in
        Athens, smashing shop windows and
        damaging cars.

1983   *Aris v. Panathinaikos*
        fan stabbed and killed when he was attacked
        after the match by three opposing fans.

Guatemala   1980   *match unnamed*
                        3 fans shot dead and dozens injured at play-
                        off for the Guatemalan League
                        Championship.

Holland   1982   *Den Haag v. Haarlem*
                        Den Haag stadium set on fire by vandals after
                        4–0 defeat.

India   1931   *unnamed match in Banglahore*
                    45 arrests, 65 injured in riots during and after
                    a match between a Hindu and a Moslem
                    team.

            1982   *North Korea v. Kuwait in the Asian Games*
                    Referee had 30 stitches inserted in cuts to his
                    head after being kicked and beaten with
                    sticks at the end of the football semi-final.

Ireland*   1913   *Ireland v. Scotland*
                        Scottish players attacked after match.

                1919   *Glentoran v. Belfast Celtic*
                        pitch invasion; bottles and stones thrown at
                        players, match officials and police;
                        vandalism to stands; players kicked and
                        beaten; 'disorderly march' through town
                        after match; Republican songs sung
                        throughout.

* Includes incidents reported in Eire and Ulster, and those reported before the
partition.

	1920	*'Cliftonville Riot'* fighting between rival mobs; repeated baton charges by police.
	1920	*Glentoran v. Belfast Celtic* pitch invasion, stone throwing, revolver shots fired, bullet wounds sustained by 4 fans, baton charges by police.
	1920	*Oban Rangers v. Millwall Athletic* referee felled by blow; fearing a riot, the police intervened and were attacked by crowd.
	1930	*Shelbourne v. Waterford* referee attacked by Shelbourne fans.
	1955	*Derry City v. Linfield* fighting between rival fans.
	1970	*Waterford v. Celtic* running battles on terraces; bottles, sticks, fists and boots used.
	1979	*Dundalk v. Linfield* clashes before, during and after match; shop windows, cars damaged; more than 30 police and dozens of fans injured.
	1979	*Northern Ireland v. Republic of Ireland* stone thrown at Republic player, who needed 3 stitches in head wound.
Italy	1920	*Viareggio v. Lincques* police intervened in fight between teams at the end of the match, one of them shooting the referee dead. The crowd then rioted, taking revolvers from the police and cutting telephone and telegraph wires at the railway station.
	1955	*Naples v. Bologna* riot, 152 injuries.
	1959	*Naples v. Genoa* 65 injuries as a result of pitch invasion.
	1963	*Salerno v. Potenza* pitch invaded by 2,000 fans, followed by riot in which one fan was killed by gunfire and some 20 more injured; 40 arrests; 15 policemen injured.
	1963	*unnamed match in Naples* 50 'angry spectators' invaded pitch and were beaten off by police.

	1965	*Milan v. Naples* fighting between fans; stones and firecrackers thrown; more than 40 arrests.

1965 *Milan v. Naples*
fighting between fans; stones and firecrackers thrown; more than 40 arrests.

1973 *unnamed match in Naples*
2,000 fans stormed dressing rooms after match, throwing stones; dispersed by police using tear gas.

1975 *unnamed matches in Naples and Milan*
police use tear gas to disperse 'turbulent fans'.

1979 *Roma v. Lazio*
33-year-old mechanic died after being hit in the eye by home-made rocket fired from flare gun.

1981 *Internazionale Milan v. Real Madrid*
pitch bombarded with firecrackers, bottles and other missiles; police had to protect Real players after match.

1982 *Roma v. Bologna*
Young Roma fan dies in fire started on train by 'hooligans'.

Lebanon 1964 *unnamed match in Beirut*
spectator, angered at decision by the referee, shoots and kills one man with a pistol and wounds another.

Malta 1975 competitive soccer banned following attacks on match officials by players and spectators.

1980 *Malta v. Poland*
match abandoned after spectators threw stones on pitch.

Mexico 1983 *Mexico Youth v. Scotland Youth*
violence and missile throwing by spectators following the Scots' winning goal.

New Zealand 1981 *New Zealand v. Kuwait*
refereee mobbed and linesman injured.

Nigeria 1983 *Nigeria v. Ivory Coast*
mounted police break up a 'riot' after a pitch invasion during a match in Lagos. The match was abandoned.

Peru 1964 *Peru v. Argentina*
318 die, 500 injured in panic following crowd eruption after disallowed goal.

Portugal	1970	Benfica banned from using their stadium following incidents in a league match when 5,000 fans invaded the pitch. Referee chased into dressing room; police clashed with spectators.
Spain	1950	*Celta v. Atletico Madrid* match abandoned after referee hit by stone.
	1980	*Barcelona v. FC Cologne* bottles thrown at Cologne dugout.
Turkey	1964	*Turkey v. Bulgaria* Crowd trouble in which 84 were hurt.
	1967	*Kayseri v. Sivas* 44 killed, 600 injured in 'uncontrollable' rioting during and after match; stones thrown, vehicles set on fire; pistols, knives and broken bottles used as weapons in inter-fan group fighting; order restored by troops, using bayonets; rioting spread to Sivas.
USSR	1960	*Moscow Central Army XI v. Kiev Dynamo* following pitch invasion in which they chased the referee and stopped the match, 4 drunken fans jailed for total of 11½ years; 2 additionally banned from living in Moscow for total of 5 years.
	1982	*Moscow Spartak v. Harlem* 69 died, 100 injured when crush barrier broke and fighting broke out among drunken fans.
Yugoslavia	1955	*Odred v. Split* mob attacked referee; Odred suspended.
	1955	in matches in Belgrade, Zelenik and Kujazevac, fans fight each other armed with knives, hammers, metal bars and chains.
	1982	*unnamed match in Sabac* referee drew gun when, after match, local players and spectators attacked him with broken bottles and umbrellas.

1982   in other matches: one referee almost lost an
        eye after being hit with a stone; another
        suffered a broken rib after being attacked by
        fans; another had his nose broken; another
        was beaten and his car destroyed; yet another
        was stripped naked and thrown into a
        thorny bush.

APPENDIX 2

CROWD DISORDERS ABROAD REPORTED IN ENGLISH NEWSPAPERS IN WHICH ENGLISH FANS WERE RECORDED AS THE AGGRESSORS

West Germany 1965 *SV Hannover v. Manchester United*
pitched battle on the terraces, spreading on to the pitch, between British soldiers and German fans.

Belgium 1974 *AS Ostend v. Manchester United*
United fans brawled in city centres, smashing windows and damaging cars; 33 arrests.

Holland 1974 *Feyenoord v. Spurs*
Spurs fans went 'on the rampage' before the match and 'rioted' during it; more than 70 arrests; 200 injured.

France 1975 *Leeds United v. Bayern Munich*
Supermarket ransacked before match; £10,000 damage to stadium; assaults on French and Germans.

1977 *St Etienne v. Liverpool*
Liverpool 'gangs' stole from shops and service stations, and beat up 'ordinary supporters' on the trip.

1977 *St Etienne v. Manchester United*
serious terrace disorders; 33 needed hospital treatment.

Luxembourg 1977 *Luxembourg v. England*
England fans caused £15,000 damage to stadium; went 'on the rampage' through the town.

West Germany	1978	*Borussia Mönchengladbach v. Liverpool* fighting, vandalism, theft. '500–mile rampage through Europe' by Liverpool fans.
	1979	*Borussia Mönchengladbach v. Liverpool* brawling, assault, theft: 18 arrests.
	1980	*VGB Stuttgart v. Liverpool* brawling in bars; damage estimated at £1,000; 7 arrests.
Spain	1980	*Castilla v. West Ham United* West Ham fans spat and urinated on Spanish supporters; fights, running battles with police; 26 arrests. 18-year-old West Ham fan allegedly deliberately run down and killed by Spanish coach driver; West Ham fined £7,700 by EUFA and ordered to play the second leg of the tie 'behind closed doors'.
Italy	1980	*England v. Belgium* fights between England and Italy fans; baton charge and use of tear gas by police; 6 fans needed hospital treatment; FA fined £8,000.
West Germany	1981	*Bayern Munich v. Liverpool* 25 Liverpool fans arrested.
Switzerland	1981	*Switzerland v. England* fights between England and Switzerland fans; missile throwing, vandalism, theft; 20 injuries, including stab wounds; 55 arrests.
Norway	1981	*Norway v. England* street fights, missile throwing.
Holland	1981	*Ajax v. Spurs* 60 Spurs fans fought with 200 local black youths; 32 arrests, 25 of Spurs fans; two young Britons hospitalised with knife wounds.
Belgium	1981	*Winterslag v. Arsenal* fighting, missile throwing.
Eire	1981	*Dundalk v. Spurs* missile throwing.
Spain	1981	*Real Madrid v. Glasgow Celtic* 'drunken riots'; 16 arrests.

Australia   1981   *England Youth v. Argentina Youth**
                             two stabbed, dozens injured in 'brawling'
                             between England and Argentina fans.
                     1981   *England Youth v. Rumania Youth**
                             16 arrests for disorderly conduct.

---

* There is doubt in these two cases over whether the England fans in question
  were English or Australians of English descent.

APPENDIX 3

CROWD DISORDERS ABROAD REPORTED IN ENGLISH NEWSPAPERS IN WHICH ENGLISH FANS OR PLAYERS WERE RECORDED AS VICTIMS

Hungary	1908	*Manchester United v. unnamed Hungarian team* pitch invasion; players attacked during match and when leaving the ground.
France	1933	*Nice v. Wolves* 'civil disturbance' quelled by gendarmes; Wolves manager, Buckley, took team off pitch.
Sweden	1946	*Malmö v. Wolves* bus carrying Wolves players pelted with stones after match by 'hundreds of angry supporters'.
France	1960	*Rheims v. Burnley* missiles thrown.
Italy	1965	*Roma v. Chelsea* Chelsea players struck by missiles during match; crowd riot; Chelsea team bus stoned.
Jamaica	1965	*Jamaica v. Arsenal* match suspended on account of brawls between teams; demonstrations by crowd; riot squad called out.

Rumania	1979	*Arges v. Nottingham Forest* bottle thrown on pitch by fan.
Germany	1980	*FC Nuremberg v. Manchester United* riot police with dogs rescued 50 United fans 'surrounded by thousands of baiting local supporters clearly looking for trouble'.
Greece	1980	*Salonika v. Ipswich Town* Ipswich players, fans and officials stoned before the game.
Italy	1980	*Juventus v. Arsenal* bonfires lit on terraces by Juventus fans; Arsenal fans attacked with stones and coins.
United States	1980	*Tampa Bay Rowdies v. Nottingham Forest* Forest fan's eyeball shattered by glass from beer bottle thrown by Tampa fan after match.
Spain	1981	*Seville v. Southampton* Southampton's Kevin Keegan struck by bottle thrown from the crowd.
	1982	*Valencia v. Manchester United* United fans reported to have been attacked by Spanish police and local fans inside the stadium. Outside, coaches were stoned and damaged.
Greece	1982	*Greece v. England* English fans attacked on buses in Athens, and England players stoned during training sessions.

APPENDIX 4
A PROVISIONAL SCHEME FOR LIMITING THE OCCURRENCE OF HOOLIGAN BEHAVIOUR BY ENGLISH FANS AT CONTINENTAL MATCHES

The 'games model' approach

In order to devise an adequate strategy for curbing hooliganism by English fans abroad, one needs to have a clear appreciation of the network of relationships formed by the parties involved at various levels in the production and control of such behaviour. That is because they exert a series of constraints on one another which have a more or less fundamental bearing on the problem. The different parties also sometimes act in ways that are mutually contradictory or fail to engage in expected actions.

We have found the 'games model' approach developed by Norbert Elias to be an extremely helpful device for the analysis of such problems.[1] It is based on the idea that, in order adequately to comprehend the actions of individuals and their outcomes, one must go beyond an examination of attitudes and intentions, and locate the individuals within the network(s) of relationships that they form with others. As Elias puts it: 'one can understand many aspects of the behaviour or actions of individual people only if one starts out from the study of the patterns of their interdependence . . . in short from the figurations they form with each other.[2]

The model that is of particular relevance to us is a variation on what Elias calls the 'two-tier game'.[3] In this scenario, all the 'players' are interdependent and their fates irrevocably intertwined. At the same time, not all of them play directly with each other. Such, moreover, are the discrepancies in power between them that the game may be fruitfully conceived as taking place on two distinct yet interconnected levels. The players on the upper tier have more power – both collectively and individually – than those on the lower tier. Nevertheless, certain players on the lower tier are able to engage in modes of behaviour to which exception is taken by all the players on the upper tier and even by the majority of those on the lower level. Given the inequality of power between the groups on the upper and lower tiers, how is this possible? The paradox is largely resolved by examining the structure of the relationships formed by the players on the upper tier. The competing priorities of these players are sufficiently diverse and the relationships between them sufficiently conflictful to have the unintended effect of creating opportunities for certain players on the lower tier to engage in what is judged to be 'deviant' action. In short, despite the power resources at their disposal, the lack of unity of the players on the upper tier reduces their power in relation to those on the lower level and hence their ability to control them.

This model exemplifies in a simplified form a central dilemma of the football authorities, the football clubs and the government for, despite all the power resources at their disposal, they have been unable to halt the occurrence of football hooliganism, whether abroad or at home. Indeed, their actions have sometimes intensified and exacerbated the problem, and sometimes displaced it, e.g. into the streets surrounding football stadia. Let us take the analysis one step further.

The network of relationships involved in the enactment and mediation of hooliganism by English fans abroad can be illustrated with the help of a diagram (see Figure 4). This diagram inevitably oversimplifies the complexity of the network in at least three ways: it is a static representation of a dynamic 'game'; it stresses only the more immediate and significant chains of interdependence; and it takes no account of conditions specific to particular matches, e.g. the way in which the Falklands War and its coverage by the media played a part in sparking off hooligan incidents in Belgium, Spain and Denmark. Despite these oversimplifications, however, the diagram is useful for analysing the dilemma posed for the authorities by football hooliganism by English fans abroad. Let us use it to 'flesh out' the games analogy a little further.

The object of the 'game' is that one set of 'players' (principally the English FA) should engage in forms of action that substantially reduce the opportunities for disorderly behaviour at and in conjunction with 'one-off' matches on the continent. However, they are opposed by other 'players' who wish to engage in these disorders, and by others still who, knowingly or not, act – or fail to act – in ways which facilitate their continuation. As a body, the FA is far more powerful than the hooligans, yet it remains seemingly impotent to prevent or even significantly to reduce these recurrent outbreaks of disorder. Despite its apparent powerlessness in this regard, it is nevertheless regularly subject to criticism in Parliament and the press. For its part, EUFA has preferred to vent its anger, not on

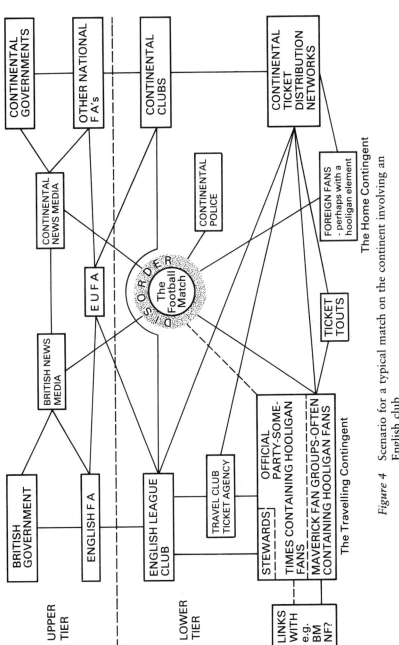

Figure 4   Scenario for a typical match on the continent involving an English club

its affiliate member, but on football clubs whose supporters are perceived to have been the culprits. From the standpoint of the English FA, the only feasible way of curbing these disorders on the continent – it cannot be expected to engage alone in the long-term actions necessary for tackling the problem of hooliganism at its social roots – is to devise a policy which will discourage the attendance of would-be hooligans at such matches and which it will be able to implement largely on its own. This, then, becomes the central policy objective.

Recognising what is and is not possible is the basis of any practical strategy. One needs to know the bodies from which co-operation can be expected and to what degree. One also needs to know those which might be obstructive, perhaps by failing to take actions which they might reasonably be expected to take, and how this can be circumvented. Let us, accordingly, review some of the mediators that are likely to affect the FA in its attempts to formulate and implement such a policy. Four of those singled out in Figure 4 seem to us to be crucial: the British government, the media, continental clubs, and EUFA. As in Elias's model of a 'two-tier' game and although, along with the FA (and with the exception of the continental clubs), they occupy positions in the upper tier and have the power resources to go with such positions, the degree to which they act in concert with the FA is one of the crucial determinants of the latter's power to handle the problem of hooliganism by English fans abroad.

(i) The government

While the government looks to the FA for action, it refuses – rightly from the standpoint of maintaining an important civil liberty – to contemplate the imposition of restrictions on the extent to which individuals convicted of football-related offences abroad can use their passports. Moreover, the Foreign Office refuses to supply the FA with information on football fans apprehended or charged on the continent. The recent conference of European Ministers of Sport may lead to greater international co-operation in this field, but there seem to be few grounds at the moment for anticipating significant movement. The FA is, therefore, forced to rely on its own resources for ascertaining who the offending fans are.

(ii) The media

The media are not non-participant narrators of hooligan incidents. On the contrary, they have played a part of some significance in the emergence and subsequent development of football hooliganism as a social problem.[4] The popular press, in particular, has acted as a dual catalyst in this process: firstly, as the often self-fulfilling harbinger of hooligan incidents, and secondly, as a central contributor to the moral panic which has advertised football matches as contexts where hooligan behaviour can be engaged in with relative impunity. Clearly, the success of any FA scheme will be heavily influenced by its treatment by the media.

(iii) The continental clubs

Continental clubs that have played host to English football teams have tended to approach the attendant crowd arrangements with a relative lack of concern. Perhaps understandably, their primary administrative aim has been to sell the maximum number of tickets. Advice which has counselled vigilance, such as the need for strict segregation of rival fans and for tickets to be sold only through formal channels, has not always been acted upon, especially if it was liable to detract from the profitability of an occasion. It is also possible that, in some cases, this complacency may have been encouraged by the fact that the clubs in question have had relatively little experience of the kinds of crowd problems that are a regular feature of match days at many English grounds. Or perhaps they think that spectator misbehaviour is a problem for the police and not for them? In any event, it is clear that a *sine qua non* for the success of any scheme is co-operation from the continental clubs regarding crowd segregation, etc.

(iv) EUFA

Even a cursory examination of EUFA's record in handling crowd disorders in recent years shows that its officers have tended to perceive clubs as responsible in an area where their responsibility is open to doubt. As a result, they have punished what they regard as the offending clubs rather than sought to develop and consistently implement effective *preventative* strategies. That is – and despite their formally exacting regulations on crowd control – the European authorities have seemed incapable or unwilling to adopt, implement and sustain with careful monitoring a feasible pre-emptive strategy at European matches designed to secure the segregation of opposing fans and to facilitate effective crowd control. This means that any FA initiative in this field will have to secure the co-operation of EUFA or, possibly, find a way of minimising dependency on it.

These, then, are the sorts of constraints within which the FA will have to operate in constructing a policy for limiting the opportunities for hooliganism by English fans abroad. As in our discussion of the 'two-tier games model', its room for manoeuvre will be seriously circumscribed and its power correspondingly reduced to the extent that it is unable to count on effective co-operation from bodies such as the government, the media, EUFA and the continental clubs. We have tried to take this into account in constructing our plan. At the same time, we have attempted to develop a set of proposals which minimise the FA's dependency on other bodies. Let us now consider our proposals in some detail.

General desiderata

In order to be successful, a scheme for limiting the occurrence of hooligan behaviour by English fans at continental matches will need to:

(i) incorporate a means for controlling the distribution of tickets. More particularly, since it is essential to eliminate the supply of tickets to touts and, hence, to the 'maverick' fans who tend to be at the centre of disorders, there will need to be a strictly controlled and limited number of ticket outlets;

(ii) establish standard procedures for organising travel arrangements;

(iii) involve a means of supervising and monitoring package trips;

(iv) ensure that EUFA's rules on crowd segregation are refined and enforced;

(v) contain a means of identifying the culprits when disorders occur and, where they play a part as well, breaks in the chain of official responsibility;

(vi) be sufficiently subtle to distinguish between hooligan and orderly fans. In some circumstances, this is a relatively easy distinction to draw, in others it is less so. As a result, a degree of expertise – based partly on formal training but more importantly on experience – will be necessary to ensure the effective operation of the plan;

(vii) penalise identified hooligans via specific measures and not, as usually happens today, by measures which punish either the *club* or *all* travelling fans. Probably the simplest thing to do in this regard would be to bar offending fans from participating in future trips. For this to be successful, however, it will be necessary to ensure that seriously violent or disorderly fans are identified at the time of a disturbance;

(viii) penalise clubs or travel agencies where they have been negligent in operating their part of the scheme.

In our view, if consistently implemented, the scheme we have devised will go some way towards meeting these desiderata. To this end, it is designed to maximise the degree of control exerted by the Football Association over continental trips. That is, it involves an attempt to circumvent undue reliance on the British government, EUFA and the continental clubs. In order for the scheme to operate effectively, of course, it will be imperative, as our earlier discussion makes clear, for the FA to gain the co-operation of the media, especially the popular press. Above all, the media will have to be briefed on the fact that the scheme is not an immediate panacea and that its effects are likely to be cumulative. However, since disorders are likely to continue to occur (e.g. in the early stages of the scheme, normally peaceful English fans might retaliate against the aggression of continental supporters, or new clubs may enter European competition), it is crucial that such hiccups should not be construed by the media as cues for writing off the scheme. If that does occur, the FA should not give in to pressure to abandon its initiative.

An outline of the scheme

Our provisional scheme involves five principal elements, namely:
  (i) a system of 'colour coding' for match tickets;
  (ii) a scheme of ticket distribution linked to membership of travel clubs;
  (iii) careful organisation and monitoring of travel arrangements;
  (iv) a new role for stewards;
  (v) effective segregation at the grounds of host clubs.

These five elements are best viewed, not in isolation from one another, but as interrelated features of a tightly knit package. For purposes of exposition, however, we shall examine each one in turn, apart from elements (i) and (ii) which, because they are so closely interconnected operationally, need to be considered together.

(i) Colour-coded tickets and distribution linked to travel club membership numbers

The use of a colour-coded ticket scheme means that we envisage that all major games involving English clubs and the national side abroad will, in future, become 'all-ticket' affairs. (Of course, the overall scheme need not be applied to matches where only a few English fans are likely to attend, e.g. those in Eastern Europe). By a 'colour-coded ticket scheme', we mean simply that the tickets for different fan groups would be of different colours since this will form an easy and effective means of identification. When a neutral ground is used to stage a match, then three colours could be used. The 1982 European Cup Final can serve as an example. Had our scheme been operated in that case, blue tickets could have been used for Villa fans, red tickets for Bayern fans, and green ones for neutral spectators. (When no neutral parties are involved, only two ticket colours would be necessary.) The proportion of tickets allocated to the fans of each club or country, and, where necessary, to neutral fans, should be determined by EUFA in consultation with the national FAs and clubs involved. It would also be useful if the English FA could oversee the arrangements for ticket distribution and perform a liaison function between clubs and the relevant European authorities. In that way, a better balance between local autonomy and central control will be secured than would be the case with a system either operated solely by the clubs or solely by the FA. In the case of international matches, of course, the role of the FA would, of necessity, be central.

Tickets would be made available only to the FA Travel Club or to those of particular League clubs. Fans should be able to join such travel clubs for a small fee. The travel clubs will then be in a position to ensure that only *bona fide* members receive them. In most cases, the tickets would be sold in conjunction with stewarded motor coach, rail (and air) tours. Exceptions to this rule would be possible, of course, at the discretion of the FA and particular clubs. The point is that the travel clubs would have to be accountable for *all* their travelling members.

In addition, we recommend that match tickets not intended for English supporters should also carry a prominent warning to the effect that the holders of them *will not be admitted to the ground if they are a travelling English supporter*. If necessary, the English authorities should negotiate the right to produce the different sets of match tickets, above all in order to ensure that the warning is prominently displayed. (The impact of the scheme might be reinforced by printing the converse of the warning on the tickets for English supporters.) The warning would serve three purposes: firstly, and in conjunction with the already existing limitations on the sale of tickets to personal applicants at continental grounds (which would have to be strictly enforced), it should further deter ticket touts from buying tickets abroad for re-sale in England (traditionally, it has been touts and ground sales that have led to the outflanking of such segregation plans as have been operated by continental clubs); secondly, the warning ought to deter most English fans from purchasing such tickets, should they be on offer; and thirdly, English fans who did manage to buy them would have a clear warning of the fact that, if detected, they would not gain entrance to the ground. Ignorance of local procedures or language problems, for example, would hardly provide a viable excuse in these cases, as sometimes happens today.

It can be anticipated that these precautions might not, initially at least, prevent some of the wrong tickets falling into English hands. Indeed, it is to be expected that some hooligan fans will perceive the new scheme as a *challenge* and may thus be *encouraged* to seek tickets for the non-English sections of a ground. Two points are important to make in this connection: firstly, publicity for the printed warning should be extensive in order to direct would-be travellers towards the official package tours. However, it should be matter of fact and not suggestive of 'another hooligan clamp-down' since past experience shows that, when hooligan fans are faced with direct challenges to their powers of ingenuity, e.g. by official bans, they are ready and willing to take up the challenge (we realise, of course, that the necessary co-operation might be difficult to obtain, but neverthe-less consultation with the press is essential in order to produce publicity of a sufficiently moderate character); secondly, those English fans who do obtain tickets for the non-English sections of a ground should *under no circumstances* be admitted *to any part*. (Our thoughts on how a 'lock-out' policy might be successfully implemented come a little later.)

(ii) *The distribution of match tickets*

The scheme that we envisage would involve the distribution of tickets for club and international matches abroad by one or a small number of closely supervised ticket agencies. League clubs which have already established travel clubs for dealing with package tours of this kind should be required to continue using them, and clubs which gain entry to European competition which do not have such organisations should be required to form them. Perhaps the FA could also revive its own Travel Club for purposes of international matches? But whatever is done in this connection, the object should be to maximise control over the distribution of tickets.

Applicants for membership of a travel club would be required to provide their names, addresses, dates of birth and two passport-size photographs. One of the photographs would be retained by the travel club. The other would be affixed (heat sealed) to the travel club membership card and presented to the applicant. The new member would be assigned a membership number which would be constructed on the basis of his/her initials and date of birth, e.g. Charles Edward Green, born on 19 May 1960, would be given the number CEG 1951960.

The cardholder would then be eligible to apply for tickets for continental matches. Successful applicants would receive their travel documents but match tickets would not be distributed until the travelling party set foot on foreign soil. At the point of departure, the stewards would be required to check the travel membership cards and passports of all the members of their respective parties in order to determine whether or not the membership numbers coincided with the names and dates of birth on the passports. Precautions along these lines should make it difficult for successful applicants to pass on or sell their tickets to someone else. If they did, the persons involved would be discovered prior to departure from England and could be prevented from taking further part in the trip. More importantly, the scheme would make it extremely unlikely that an individual or group could acquire a large number either of 'legitimate' match tickets or of illegitimately acquired tickets for the 'non-English' sections of a ground. Let us move on now to consider some of our ideas about travel arrangements.

(iii) *Travel arrangements*

Although this is not exclusively the case, our research suggests that the most troublesome fans at matches abroad are either 'mavericks' who travel on their own or fans who travel on tours in the lower price ranges. The former should be prevented completely from gaining access to matches by our scheme, so we will concentrate in what follows on packages which rely principally on road or rail transport.

Although the balance of advantages between them is not clear cut, we tend, on the whole, to favour road over rail transport for travel to continental matches. Travel by rail is not without its attractions – cheaper packages; the easier movement of larger numbers of fans; greater freedom of movement for passengers whilst in transit; and the obvious advantages that accrue when stadia are sited close to mainline stations. However, long periods of rail travel also have their drawbacks. Continental rail travel can be unpredictable and extremely uncomfortable as a result of the long spells between stops. Moreover, rail transport lacks the flexibility of coach travel since, with the latter mode, stops can easily be made when passengers become restless. It is important to stress in this connection that stifling forms of control carry with them the danger of leading usually orderly fans into *dis*orderly forms of behaviour. Care has to be taken, therefore, to minimise the discomfort caused on trips.

On balance, we also favour coach over rail travel because it provides greater opportunities for stewards to become familiar with their charges. This should help them to develop a friendly relationship with their 'clients', as well as providing ample opportunity for them to identify the more seriously 'troublesome' factions should they be present. Rail travel would not make the 'new role' for stewards that we are proposing insuperably difficult, but behaviour problems are less likely to arise and more easy to supervise on coaches. Of course, coaches should continue to avoid stops in major towns and cities. Since the sale of alcohol at cafés is almost universal on the continent, drinking during stops is almost inevitable. This should not cause undue problems as long as stops are fairly frequent but short, and as long as stewards enforce an embargo on the carriage of alcohol on the coaches, particularly wines and spirits. (Once the scheme was underway, stewards could be allowed to use their own judgment in the case of well-behaved fans, being given the latitude, for example, to allow each person to bring on board small quantities of beer.) Let us turn now to a brief discussion of the way in which we see this 'new role' for stewards developing.

(iv) A new role for stewards

Sensitive but firm stewarding plays a central role in the operation of our plan. We recommend that stewards should travel with all parties of English fans on trips abroad. Exceptions to this rule may be feasible in the case of groups of fans travelling by air on more expensive excursions which include overnight or longer stays abroad. In these cases, as is the custom already, the presence of travel couriers should be sufficient for purposes of supervision and liaison. On other packages, the ratio of stewards to supporters is something which would undoubtedly vary according to factors such as the size and reputation of the travelling contingent, the reputation of the host fans, and the character and reputation of the local police. Given the importance of making an immediate impact without, at the same time, overdramatising problems of control and thereby incurring the risk of provoking confrontations, one might consider a ratio of, say, one steward for every 50 fans to be appropriate. For 'special' cases or exceptional circumstances, however, e.g. when the travelling fans and/or those of the opposing team are known to have an established hooligan following, a ratio of one to 25 might prove necessary.

The stewards should also be clearly recognisable as such. The wearing of a prominent badge or an armband should be sufficient during the part of the trip spent in transit. At the ground, however, a bright steward's 'bib' would be more helpful. Stewards would then be easily identifiable by the local authorities and by distressed English fans or fans simply requiring information or directions. This kind of identification might also prove advantageous should stewards be required to assist in re-establishing segregation in the event of a breakdown in the plans of the host club.

We propose that at least one steward should be assigned to each coach (in the case of rail travel, at least one to each carriage), with a number in reserve ready to take up places as and when the occupants of particular coaches (carriages) become identified as seriously troublesome. Stewards should also be issued with a list of the names and travel club membership numbers of their charges and we recommend that they should be issued with match tickets by the club or its agents just prior to departure. However, to reiterate and develop a point made earlier, match tickets should not be issued to fans until, say, the first stop on foreign soil. In the course of the trip, stewards will be required to familiarise themselves with their parties. This can be done unobtrusively simply by checking the composition of their groups after each stopping point. Coaches should be easily identifiable in order to help ensure that no change of personnel takes place during the trip.

In addition to performing this largely observational role on the outward and return journeys and in the ground itself, it may be on occasion necessary for stewards to act in a co-ordinated fashion to defuse potentially troublesome situations. In order to achieve such co-ordinated action, the appointment of a number of 'senior stewards' is probably required. It would be the task of these senior personnel to oversee the activities of the other stewards but, in addition, they would be in a position to liaise with host officials, both those of the club and, more importantly, the local police.

It should be emphasised that this 'incident prevention' aspect of the stewards' duties is subordinate to what we see as their primary function, namely that of monitoring proceedings, so let us return to this. If they observe any of their charges acting in a seriously disorderly or violent manner, or if information to that effect is relayed to them by a fellow steward or local official, they should, at first, simply take note of the fact. Then, on the next occasion when they check the occupants of their coach, they should quietly confirm the identity of the fan in question and record his membership number, together with details of the 'offence'. Since applications for tickets for matches abroad according to our scheme are tied to travel club membership and hence to name and date of birth, the FA and the League clubs will, as a result of these procedures, be in a position to ensure that offending fans are denied access to future matches as long as they (the FA and the clubs) see fit. By this means, the football authorities will also build up over time their own list of offending fans.

Given the centrality of their role in the overall structure of our scheme and the sensitive nature of the tasks they will be required to perform, the quality of the stewards chosen is self-evidently of paramount importance. They must be authoritative but not authoritarian; able to defuse difficult situations with diplomacy and tact rather than by resort to intimidation. We should make it clear that it is *not* our intention that stewards should interfere in any way with the essential character of football match trips abroad. These are exciting and highly charged experiences for any committed football fan. Simple overenthusiasm or even lack of knowledge or experience of local customs can often result in minor indiscretions. Stewards must be able to distinguish between rough good humour and overenthusiasm of this sort and *seriously* violent or destructive hooligan behaviour. (In this latter connection, they should above all have a clear recognition of the way in which injudicious and heavy-handed official intervention can sometimes help to transform the former into the latter.) They should be prepared to adopt the role of a sort of informal 'buffer' to mediate between boisterously noisy but non-violent young English fans and local supporters, and sometimes, between them and the local police who are apt, as happened occasionally in Spain, to misinterpret what are nothing other than harmless rituals.

The recruitment of a sufficient number of stewards who have – or less likely who can be trained into – these sorts of qualities is obviously not going to be easy and needs to be given careful thought. Since, under our plan, the FA will have the task of appointing stewards for away internationals, one possible course of action would be for the FA to assemble a squad of stewards who could then be utilised for club matches abroad as well. There are two immediate advantages to such an approach: firstly, this squad of specialist stewards would gain experience very quickly; and secondly, there would be fewer problems of 'split loyalties' in the reporting of offenders as might occur if the clubs' own stewards officiated abroad on an exclusive basis. Of course, there is nothing to prevent clubs from using their own stewards for matches abroad, and it may be that a mixture of FA and club stewards would achieve the best results. In any case, should, say, four English clubs find themselves playing away legs in Europe in the same week, the use of club stewards would be imperative. In these sorts of circumstances, it might well prove advisable to spread the FA stewards across the ties, depending on the sizes and reputations of the contingents involved and the distances to be travelled.

Given the fact that the FA stewards might be required to supervise a number of trips at short notice and in quick succession, it can be anticipated that suitable candidates for the job will not typically be in full-time employment. (It may be advisable, of course, to employ the 'senior stewards' on a permanent basis.) Experience in 'handling' people of all backgrounds, especially the young, and 'practical knowledge' of crowd control and group supervision would obviously stand stewards of the kind we have in mind in good stead. We will say a little more about stewarding later on.

(v) Segregation arrangements by the host clubs

As we suggested earlier, many continental clubs have, to date, remained unaware or unconvinced of the importance of effectively segregating rival fans either inside or outside grounds at potentially troublesome matches. In our view, this is one of the major issues on which the English authorities will have to seek the vigorous and sustained backing of EUFA, a backing which often seems to have been lacking in the past.

Given the English authorities' experience of crowd segregation and English hooligan styles, we recommend that police and football officials from this country should continue to liaise with host clubs on the continent – as happened with notable success, for example, for the 1982 European Cup Final – and that plans for the segregation of fans *outside* grounds should be similarly pursued. Care should be taken, however, to prevent the measures adopted becoming either stifling or provocative since that could be counterproductive. (Again, the success of the low profile adopted by the Dutch police for the match in Rotterdam comes readily to mind.) We further recommend that English officials should continue to play a leading role in choosing the most appropriate sites inside grounds for occupation by English fans. Ideally, such sites should not be too exposed to attack (by missiles, for example) from the rear or from the side. Nor, ideally, should they overlook, or be overlooked by, opposing spectators. We realise, of course, that these are difficult matters for the officials involved to judge and that it is impossible to take every eventuality into account in advance.

Some senior and experienced English stewards, together with English police advisers, might also be profitably used to enforce the rules prohibiting the entry of English fans into what have been designated as 'non-English' sections of grounds, i.e. to help in the identification of English fans, if any, who are attempting to gain entry using tickets intended solely for host and neutral fans. Of course, some English fans attempting to gain entry in this manner will be easily identifiable by the ticket collectors of the host club. Others, however, may be more difficult to spot, but they should sport an identifiably *English* style, even if it is more cosmopolitan than the stereotypical 'skinhead' or flag-bedecked mode. English officials with knowledge of the more recent 'hard case' styles should be readily able to detect English infiltrators. If there is uncertainty in particular cases, then the fan or fans in question could simply be challenged. After all, at some grounds in this country, police sometimes use regional accents as an identifying criterion in their 'vetting' of turnstile entrants. In addition to these tasks, stewards might also be used informally or under the direction of local police to aid with spectator segregation. Also, if, as we anticipate to be likely in the early stages of the scheme's implementation, fans do turn up without the proper tickets and are refused entry to the ground, the presence of English stewards might provide a useful 'cooling' influence and help in other ways to control the sorts of confrontations that might occur.

The operation and notional costs of the scheme: the 1981/82 season as a case study

Obviously, particular matches have to be assessed on their merits and the characteristics of European competition vary from year to year. Nevertheless, an examination of one season should provide some indications of the likely strains on the scheme and give an idea of the costs likely to be involved. Table 5 lists the away legs of European ties involving English clubs during the 1981/82 season. It also includes estimates of the numbers of travelling English fans in each instance, and of the numbers of stewards that, had our scheme been in operation, we would provisionally regard as having been necessary.

We are almost bound to have overestimated the numbers of travelling fans in some cases and to have underestimated them in others. Such errors probably cancel each other out. We have probably also overestimated the numbers of stewards necessary on some trips. For example, Villa's trips to Iceland and East Germany, and Swansea's visit to the latter country, would probably have required no stewarding beyond normal courier services. In other cases, we have tried to make allowances for fans who travel in the upper range of package tours where, similarly, courier facilities

Table 5: *European fixtures involving English sides during the 1981–82 season**

Competition	Match	Estimated no. of travelling fans	Stewards
European Champions Cup Round 1	Oulu Palloseura (Finland) v. Liverpool	>250	5
„	Valur Reykjavik v. Aston Villa	>250	5
Cup Winners' Cup Round 1	Ajax v. Spurs	1000	30
„	Lokomotiv Leipzig v. Swansea City	>250	5
EUFA Cup Round 1	Panathinaikos v. Arsenal	250	5
„	Aberdeen v. Ipswich	1000	*NA
„	Grasshopper Zurich v. West Bromwich Albion	>250	5
„	Limerick v. Southampton	>250	5
European Champions Cup Round 2	Alkmaar (Holland) v. Liverpool	500	15
„	Dynamo Berlin v. Aston Villa	>250	5
Cup Winners' Cup Round 2	Dundalk (Eire) v. Spurs	600	20
EUFA Cup Round 2	Winterslag v. Arsenal	1000	30
„	Southampton v. Sporting Lisbon	>250	5
European Champions Cup Round 3	CSKA (Sofia) v. Liverpool	>250	5
„	Dynamo Kiev v. Aston Villa	>250	5
Cup Winners' Cup Round 3	Eintracht Frankfurt v. Spurs	1000	30
European Champions Cup Semi-Final	RSC Anderlecht v. Aston Villa	2500	60
Cup Winners' Cup Semi-Final	Barcelona v. Spurs	500	15

* Matches in Britain to be dealt with by the authorities in the normal way.

Competition	Match	Estimated no. of travelling fans	Stewards
European Champions Cup Final	Aston Villa v. Bayern Munich (Amsterdam)	12000	100
England matches	Hungary	>250	5
	Norway	2000	50
	Switzerland	2000	50
Estimated total number of stewarding duties required			455

alone might be sufficient. Fortunately, when the system is most likely to be under the greatest strain in terms of the number of matches being played simultaneously or within a couple of days of each other, i.e. during the early rounds of European competition, travelling support is likely to be at its lowest levels.

Let us assume that the FA established a pool of, say, 60 stewards, and let us further assume that 50 of them would be available at any one time. Spread not too thinly across the 19 ties and with the aid of club stewards, a complement of this size would probably have been sufficient to cover European club competition throughout the 1981–82 season, with the glaring exception of the European Cup Final. On occasions such as this, with as many as 12,000 to 15,000 travelling fans, the 'one-off' nature of the occasion may allow for increased recruitment of stewards from among club supporters, or, perhaps the borrowing of stewards experienced in European competition from other clubs. In any case, numbers of trouble-some fans in such cases are liable to be small relative to the size of the whole travelling contingent. This should allow room for manoeuvre at an early stage of the trip and make it possible to ensure that the more experienced FA stewards were placed in charge of the more disorderly coaches (carriages). For matches such as this which involve very large numbers of travelling fans, it would probably be necessary to have all the available FA stewards on duty.

Both the clubs and the agents for the national side, of course, are in a position to break-up overly large groups of young fans who apply for places on the same coach. Whether this is done or not should be left to the discretion of the agents and officials involved. Whilst we would not recommend that entire coaches (carriages) should be given up to groups, say, within the 17–25 age range, we also think it would be unnecessary to place undue restrictions upon well-behaved young fans who, quite naturally, are keen to travel to matches with groups of friends. In some instances, too, it might be advantageous for the controlling agencies to have groups of troublesome fans concentrated on a small number of coaches (carriages) rather than scattered throughout the entire travelling party.

On the basis of the figures in Table 5, we estimate that around 450 stewarding duties (FA and club stewards) would have been necessary under the guidelines of our plan for the whole of the 1982–82 season. (Hopefully, of course, the success of the plan would mean that lesser numbers of stewards would be needed as time went on.) The fact that FA stewards would be on stand-by at various times during the season, and that their role would require considerable responsibility and expertise, means that they should be remunerated for their services. Some of the stewards appointed by League clubs could be treated in similar fashion. However, current practice suggests that a free trip to see their side play abroad is sufficient reward for most club stewards. Taking these facts into account, let us work on a costing of £150 per steward per match. On this basis, the total cost for stewarding for the 1981–82 season, including stewarding England's international matches abroad, would have been close to £70,000 (£150 × 455). Making allowance for additional costs and administration, a rough estimate would place the total somewhere in excess of £100,000 for the season.

These admittedly sketchy calculations suggest that the scheme would not be cheap to operate. However, our costing for a season begins to look reasonable when account is taken of what the cost to our national sport would be of a European ban on the England team. The financial losses incurred by West Ham and Aston Villa when EUFA instructed them to play the home legs of European ties 'behind closed doors' also help to place the sum of £100,000 in perspective.

Anticipated effects of the scheme

One clear advance that would follow if our scheme were adopted would be that the FA and the clubs would, henceforward, have greater ability to control their travelling supporters. Indeed, an early effect should be to reduce the tendency for 'hard cases' to travel to matches under their own steam without tickets or with tickets for inappropriate sections of a ground. In time, if consistently implemented, the scheme should stop the tendency of such 'fans' to travel at all. Quite often, groups like these are not even club supporters, and they are at least as interested in causing disorder as they are in watching football. Another likely medium- and long-term effect of the scheme would be a steady growth in the ability of the FA and the clubs to identify and exclude offending supporters. Perhaps, too, as behaviour abroad improved – especially if the improvement was given prominent coverage in the popular press – an increase might take place in the number of orderly English fans who travel to watch matches on the continent.

We anticipate that, in the early stages of the scheme, disorder might continue to occur as the scheme is tested by fans and the authorities alike. After this 'settling in' period has passed, however, disorder may still periodically occur if:

(i) the FA or club officials fail to abide by important aspects of the scheme;

(ii) host clubs fail to ensure effective segregation of the opposing fans, or place English fans in sites where they are exposed to missile-throwing (we regard this as more likely);

(iii) clubs whose fans have a 'hooligan' reputation gain entry to European competition for the first time, or for the first time after the introduction of the scheme;

and (iv) continental hooligans are the initiators or sole perpetrators of disorders.

In any event, we would not expect the effects of the scheme to have a simple linear and progressive character, i.e. for a continuous reduction in disorderly incidents to occur without ups and downs.

Even though it may be possible via a scheme such as ours to stop fans who are 'looking for trouble' from gaining entry to European matches, there is, of course, at present no way of preventing them from travelling to the towns and cities where English sides are competing abroad. However, to the extent that they deny hooligan fans entry to matches – and we think it likely that they would, in a short space of time, prove effective in this regard – our proposals should ensure that, if and when disruptive behaviour does occur, it will take place principally *outside football stadia*. As a result, it should become clear to the government, the media and the general public alike that the causes of football hooliganism lie mainly outside the game; and that it will only be possible to tackle them effectively *at that deeper level*. In short, if put into effect, our proposals might help to demonstrate that football hooliganism is a problem which the football authorities *cannot realistically be expected to tackle on their own*.

NOTES AND REFERENCES

Introduction

1 This concept was introduced by Stanley Cohen in his *Folk Devils and Moral Panics*, London, MacGibbon & Kee, 1972.

2 The rise of football hooliganism to 'social problem' status in the mid-1960s was probably connected with concern about the prospects for spectator misbehaviour at the 1966 World Cup Finals staged in England. See S. Cohen, 'Campaigning against Vandalism', in C. Ward (ed.), *Vandalism*, London, Architectural Press, 1973, p. 232.

3 We have, in fact, conducted crowd surveys at the Leicester City and Coventry City grounds. The Coventry survey was designed to elicit reactions to the club's all-seater stadium and 'differential pricing scheme', and was carried out for the Football Trust.

4 Another very popular myth about football hooliganism, but one we have not mentioned in the text, is that the phenomenon is the product of the early 1960s. In fact, crowd disorderliness at soccer matches in England – though not its perception as a serious 'social problem' – has a long history. However, its incidence and the rate at which it has been reported have tended to vary over time. More particularly, the reported rate – and probably the actual incidence as well – was relatively high before the First World War, fell during the inter-war years but never even remotely approached zero-point, stayed low until the late 1950s, then started rising, relatively slowly at first and much more rapidly from the mid-1960s. See our *Working Class Social Bonding and the Sociogenesis of Football Hooliganism*, a report to the SSRC, 1982; and our *The Social Roots of Football Hooligan Violence*, London, Routledge & Kegan Paul (forthcoming).

5 See Appendix 1.
6 Reported in the *Leicester Mercury*, 26 November 1955.
7 *The Times*, 18, 19 September 1967.
8 This is probably, in the main, a consequence of the social composition of the travelling support i.e. the 'hooligan' fans who operate in a domestic context in countries such as Germany, Holland and Italy have not yet, like their English counterparts, started regularly travelling abroad.
9 Stuart Weir, 'The Sewer Rats', *New Society*, 1980, vol. 52, p. 319.
10 *The Sunday Mirror*, 27 July 1980.
11 See Appendix 2.
12 See Appendix 3.
13 Richard Holt, *Sport and Society in France*, London, Macmillan, 1981, pp. 135–6.
14 J. M. Lewis, 'Sports Riots: Some Research Questions', unpublished paper presented to the American Sociological Association General Meeting, 1975.
15 *The Times*, 19 October 1971.
16 Paul Harrison, 'Soccer's Tribal Wars', *New Society*, 1974, vol. 29, p. 604.
17 J. A. Harrington, *Soccer Hooliganism*, Bristol, John Wright, 1968, p. 25.
18 E. Trivizas, 'Offences and Offenders in Football Crowd Disorders', *British Journal of Criminology*, 1980, vol. 20, no. 3, p. 282.
19 Harrison, op. cit., p. 602.
20 Peter Marsh, Elizabeth Rosser and Rom Harré, *The Rules of Disorder*, London, Routledge & Kegan Paul, 1978, p. 69.
21 *Oxford Mail*, 9 January 1981.
22 This research is reported in our SSRC report (1982) and will be discussed in greater detail in our *The Social Roots of Football Hooligan Violence* (forthcoming).
23 See ibid. for a fuller exposition of our theory of the sociogenesis of lower-working-class masculine violence.
24 D. Robins and P. Cohen, *Knuckle Sandwich*, Harmondsworth, Penguin, 1978, pp. 77–8.
25 Harrison, op. cit., p. 604.
26 E. G. Dunning, J. A. Maguire, P. J. Murphy and J. M. Williams, 'The Social Roots of Football Hooligan Violence', *Leisure Studies*, 1982, vol. 1, no. 2, p. 141.

Chapter 1: Preparations for Spain

1 *Leicester Mercury*, 20 November 1981.
2 *The Financial Times*, 12 June 1982.
3 *The Guardian*, 27 November 1981.
4 *The Daily Telegraph*, 18 January 1982.
5 *The Daily Telegraph*, 2 December 1981.
6 England, Scotland and Northern Ireland.
7 *The Sun*, 11 June 1982.
8 *The Times*, 18 February 1982.
9 *The Daily Express*, 4 December 1981.
10 *The Daily Mirror*, 11 March 1982.
11 *World Cup Special Magazine*, May 1982.
12 *The Daily Express*, 4 December 1981.
13 *The Guardian*, 1 December 1981.
14 The Travel Club 'experiment' was abandoned by the FA in 1981.
15 *The Daily Express*, 20 November 1981.
16 As we explained in the Introduction, our findings suggest that class is more important than age as a determinant of football hooligan behaviour. That is, the majority of 'hard core' football hooligans seem to come from the socio-economically lowest sections of the working class. They tend, of course, to be young but many are over 21 and, as our case studies show, they are by no means unknown in their forties.
17 *Leicester Mercury*, 3 December 1981.
18 *The Times*, 3 March 1982.
19 *The Times*, 18 February 1982.
20 *The Daily Express*, 20 November 1981.
21 *The Daily Record*, 9 March 1982.
22 *The Times*, 3 March 1982.
23 *The Financial Times*, 12 June 1982.
24 In a letter to the authors.
25 This was not, of course, the first time that the outbreak of war led people in the football world to examine their consciences. See Anthony Mason, *Association Football and English Society, 1863–1915*, Brighton, Harvester, 1980, p. 255, for a discussion of their reaction to the onset of the First World War.
26 *Sunday Standard*, 16 May 1982.
27 Ibid.
28 *The Times*, 20 May 1982.
29 *The Guardian*, 20 May 1982.
30 *The Times*, 21 May 1982. Our italics.
31 'World Cup Preview', BBC Television, 11 June 1982.

32 *The Daily Express*, 18 June 1982.
33 The disorders at the Anderlecht–Aston Villa match are discussed in Chapter 5.
34 *The Daily Mail*, 11 June 1982.
35 *The Guardian*, 14 June 1982.
36 *The Sun*, 14 June 1982.
37 Quoted from a letter to the authors.
38 *The Daily Mirror*, 15 January 1982.
39 *The Daily Telegraph*, 18 January 1982.
40 *The Observer Colour Magazine*, 23 May 1982.
41 *The Daily Telegraph*, 18 January 1982.
42 *The Daily Mail*, 14 June 1982.
43 In conversation with Brian Burnett of the Department of the Environment, June 1982.
44 For an account of the use of sporting events to promote political aims see, for example, G. Whannel, *Blowing the Whistle: The Politics of Sport*, London, Pluto, 1983.
45 *The Glasgow Herald*, 26 April 1982.
46 *The Daily Star*, 18 January 1982.
47 'World Cup Preview', BBC Television, 11 June 1982.
48 A good example was an article by Allan Laing, 'Everything You Ever Wanted to Know About Spanish Policemen', *Glasgow Herald*, 28 April 1982. A brief comparison of English and Scottish press treatment of the difficulties fans were likely to encounter in Spain, suggests to us that the Scottish press gave far more assistance and useful advice to prospective travellers than did the English which tended, prior to the Finals, to concentrate on sensationalistic, 'harem-scarem' type stories.
49 *The Daily Star*, 9 March 1982.
50 *The Sunday Times*, 25 April 1982.
51 *The Glasgow Herald*, 28 April 1982.
52 *The Daily Mail*, 20 January 1982.
53 *The Observer Colour Magazine*, 23 May 1982.
54 *The Daily Mail*, 20 January 1982.
55 *The Daily Star*, 14 June 1982.
56 *The Sunday Post*, 7 March 1982.

Chapter 2: English fans in northern Spain

1 That is, our trip to Spain would have been cancelled had the England team withdrawn, even though, in our opinion, a lot could have been

learned about football hooliganism, crowd behaviour and crowd control from studying a World Cup Finals minus England.

2 *The Daily Express*, 15 June 1982.
3 *The Guardian*, 15 June 1982.
4 *The Daily Mail*, 15 June 1982.
5 Given the limited nature of our information about the occupations of some of the members of our sample, there are liable to be, as in all such exercises, a number of errors in Table 2. However, they probably cancel each other out and certainly do not detract from the general thrust of our findings.
6 In August 1982, Chelsea FC took the unprecedented step of writing to supporters rebuking the racialists among them. In an open letter under the heading, 'Racial Policy', the Chairman described the attitude of the club as 'colour blind and unprejudiced' (reported in *The Sun*, 26 August 1982).
7 *Egin*, 17 June 1982.
8 *El Diario Vasco*, 17 June 1982.
9 *Tribuna Vasca*, 17 June 1982.
10 *Deia*, 17 June 1982.
11 Ibid.
12 *El Diario Vasco*, 17 June 1982.
13 Ibid.
14 *Egin*, 17 June 1982.
15 *Deia*, 17 June 1982.
16 *El Diario Vasco*, 17 June 1982.
17 *Tribuna Vasca*, 18 June 1982.
18 *Deia*, 19 June 1982.
19 *The Guardian,* 17 June 1982.
20 *Deia*, 17 June 1982.
21 *El Pais*, 17 June 1982.
22 *Tribuna Vasca*, 17 June 1982.
23 *Egin*, 17 June 1982.
24 *The Guardian*, 9 January 1982.
25 Nigel Fielding, *The National Front*, London, Routledge & Kegan Paul, 1981, pp. 78, 86 and 92 (emphases added).
26 Émile Durkheim, *The Division of Labour in Society*, New York, Free Press, 1933.
27 See p. 16.
28 *Egin*, 17 June 1982.
29 Ibid.
30 *Tribuna Vasca*, 17 June 1982.
31 *Deia*, 18 June 1982.
32 *Egin*, 22 June 1982.

Chapter 3: The behaviour of English fans in northern Spain in non-football contexts

1 *El Diario Vasco*, 23 June 1982.
2 *Deia*, 18 June 1982.
3 *Deia*, 19 June 1982.
4 *The Sunday Times*, 20 June 1982.
5 *El Diario Vasco*, 17 June 1982.
6 *El Diario Vasco*, 24 June 1982.
7 The 'Huyton Baddies' are a group of older criminally inclined 'hard cases' whose members originally hailed from the Huyton area of Liverpool, but who, in recent years, have tended to recruit from a wider area of Merseyside. Their exploits are well known both to the police and fellow spectators in the North West, although their penchant for violence and vandalism is by no means confined solely to the football context.
8 *El Diario Vasco*, 22 June 1982.
9 *The Daily Telegraph*, 18 June 1982.
10 *Tribuna Vasca*, 25 June 1982.

Chapter 4: English fans in Madrid

1 *The Daily Mirror*, 30 June 1982.
2 *The Sunday Times*, 4 July 1982.
3 These figures are based on estimates provided by the Spanish authorities and the English and Spanish press whilst we were staying in Madrid.
4 There was some discrepancy between these early accounts and the official reports published later. According to the latter, 10, and not 11, German fans were expelled from Spain, and the 'Iranian' person may, in fact, have been an Austrian.
5 *El Pais*, 30 June 1982.
6 *The Guardian*, 29 June 1982.
7 *Marca*, 27 June 1982.
8 *The Guardian*, 30 June 1982.
9 *El Alcazar*, 30 June 1982.
10 *El Pais*, 2 July 1982.
11 *The Daily Mirror*, 1 July 1982.
12 *The Daily Star*, 1 July 1982.
13 *The Daily Mirror*, 2 July 1982.
14 *Diario 16*, 4 July 1982.
15 This was probably not all bravado on the Hull fan's part for, on 6

September 1983, the following appeared in a report in *The Yorkshire Post*: 'Police have launched an enquiry after weapons were recovered from a coach carrying Hull City supporters to Saturday's match at Gillingham. An air-rifle barrel, a rounders' bat, knives and razor blades were seized shortly before the coach left Hull.'

16 *The Times*, 7 July 1982.
17 *The Sunday Times*, 4 July 1982.
18 *Diario 16, El Alcazar*, 6 July 1982.
19 *Diario 16*, 7 July 1982.
20 *The Daily Express*, 8 July 1982.
21 *The Daily Mirror*, 6 July 1982.

Chapter 5: Aston Villa v. Bayern Munich: Crowd behaviour and crowd control at the 1982 European Cup Final

1 *The Sun*, 11 September 1981.
2 *The Evening Standard*, 17 September 1981.
3 See p. 7.
4 *The Times*, 6 April 1982.
5 *The Guardian*, 23 April 1982.
6 *The Daily Telegraph*, 23 April 1982.
7 *The Guardian*, 23 April 1982.
8 In conversation with the authors.
9 *The Daily Telegraph*, 23 April 1982.
10 *The Guardian*, 2 April 1982.
11 Ibid.
12 *The Guardian*, 1 May 1982.
13 *The Guardian*, 24 April 1982.
14 *The Times*, 23 April 1982.
15 In a letter from Steve Stride.
16 *The Guardian*, 26 January 1981.
17 *The Times*, 26 April 1982.
18 *The Guardian*, 3 May 1982.
19 *The Daily Mirror*, 7 May 1982.
20 *The Guardian*, 23 April 1982.
21 *The Guardian*, 1 May 1982. Our italics.
22 In conversation with the authors.
23 Ibid.
24 *The Times*, 18 September 1981.
25 *The Daily Telegraph*, 23 April 1982.
26 *The Guardian*, 27 May 1982.

27 *The Birmingham Evening Mail*, 27 May 1982.
28 *The Daily Mail*, 28 May 1982.

Chapter 6: English fans in Copenhagen, September 1982

 1 See, 'Football and the Fascists', Centre for Contemporary Studies (mimeo), January 1981.
 2 *The Times*, 21 September 1978.
 3 *The Times*, 23 September 1978.
 4 In conversation with the authors.
 5 Ibid.
 6 *B.T.*, 22 September 1982.
 7 *The Sun*, 23 September 1982.
 8 *The Guardian*, 24 September 1982.
 9 *The Daily Mail*, 23 September 1982.
10 Nick Walsh, *Dixie Dean*, London, Pan, 1978, p. 121.
11 Reported in 'Football and the Fascists', op. cit.
12 *The Daily Mail*, 27 October 1980. The designs on most of these T-shirts drew explicit links between support for West Ham United and commitment to the National Front. One, for example, carried the club's crossed hammers emblem with the letters, NF, at the centre of the cross, and the words, 'West Ham National Front' above and below the emblem.
13 An article in *The New Musical Express* (20 June 1980) described Leeds as 'an important centre for extreme right wing recruitment.' It went on to describe the activities of 'about 30' BM members at a recent Leeds United home match, suggesting that they were distributing leaflets at Leeds home games and also attracting 'fringe support'.

   We should stress here that our argument is *not* that it is only persons from lower-working-class communities who are racist. That, patently, is not the case. What we *are* saying is that the life experiences and values of many persons from these communities make them more amenable than most to exploitation by groups like the British Movement and the National Front.
14 *The Times*, 2 January 1981.
15 The remark was attributed by *The Guardian* (3 March 1981) to Graham Kelly, Secretary of the Football League, speaking at The Football Trust's One-Day Conference on Football Hooliganism in March 1981.
16 *The Sunday Express*, 3 March 1983.
17 *The Sunday Times*, 26 September 1982.
18 *Ekstra Bladet*, 23 September 1982.

19 According to *The Daily Telegraph*, (16 August 1983) the West Ham ICF comprises 'a 500-strong gang of hooligans who [have] been responsible for major outbreaks of violence at football grounds around the country. . . . Members of this gang [have] . . . calling cards printed to leave in the pocket or on the bodies of their victims. They read: "Congratulations, you have just met the ICF". Shunning the regular football 'specials' and coaches, they [infiltrate] groups of fans by not wearing team colours, ready to cause trouble at a given signal.' Arsenal fan, Jock Dickinson, was stabbed to death in May 1982 by unidentified ICF members in a fight between West Ham and Arsenal fans. A 'calling card' was pinned to his chest.

20 *Ekstra Bladet*, 23 September 1982.

21 *The Daily Star*, 24 September 1982.

22 *B.T.*, 22 September 1982.

23 *The Daily Star*, 24 September 1982.

24 *Ekstra Bladet*, 22 September 1982.

25 *Aktuelt*, 23 September 1982.

26 *Ekstra Bladet*, 23 September 1982.

27 *The Daily Star*, 24 September 1982.

28 Ibid.

29 Ibid.

30 *The Sun*, 23 September 1982.

31 *The Daily Mirror*, 23 September 1982.

32 *The Daily Express*, 29 September 1982.

33 *The Daily Star*, 24 September 1982.

34 *The Daily Mail*, 24 September 1982.

35 *The Times*, 29 September 1982.

36 Ibid.

37 *The Daily Mirror*, 24 September 1982.

38 *The Sunday Times*, 21 November 1982.

39 *World Soccer*, December 1982, p. 25.

Conclusion: Tackling the problem

1 See Norbert Elias, 'The Sciences: Towards a Theory', in R. Whitley (ed.), *Social Processes of Scientific Development*, London, Routledge & Kegan Paul, 1974, pp. 21–42; and 'Problems of Involvement and Detachment', *British Journal of Sociology*, 1956, vol. 7, no. 3, pp. 226–52.

2 That, it seems to us, is an implication which could be drawn from the work of Peter Marsh and his colleagues. See their *The Rules of*

Disorder, London, Routledge & Kegan Paul, 1978; see also, Peter Marsh, *Aggro: the Illusion of Violence*, London, J. M. Dent, 1979.

3 Roger Ingham (ed.), *Football Hooliganism: the Wider Context*, London, Inter-Action Imprint, 1978, pp. 83–102.

4 See Dunning, Murphy and Williams, *The Social Roots of Football Hooligan Violence* (forthcoming).

5 Ingham, op. cit., p. 84.

6 For examples of the way in which newspapers purport to speak *on behalf of* the public, see S. Hall et al. (eds), *Policing the Crisis*, London, Macmillan, 1978, ch. 3.

7 See Marsh et al., op. cit.

8 See for example, G. Whannel, 'Football, crowd behaviour and the press', *Media, Culture and Society*, 1979, vol. 1, pp. 327–42.

9 For a more lengthy analysis of the failings of recent liberal criminologies and the resurgence of 'popularist' criminologies of the Right, see Ian Taylor, *Law and Order: Arguments for Socialism*, London, Macmillan, 1981, pp. 1–9.

10 See John Lea and Jock Young, 'The Riots in Britain 1981: Urban Violence and Political Marginalisation', in D. Cowell et al. (eds) *Policing the Riots*, London, Junction, 1982, pp. 5–20.

11 Although their findings might be disputed on a number of methodological grounds, the consistency with which newspaper and football club surveys highlight 'hooliganism' as a major factor in the decline of football match attendances strongly suggests that it *has* played a significant part in football's demise as a popular spectator sport in recent years. Moreover, the findings of a survey by the Football League's Marketing Department suggest that proportionally more fans from the unskilled and semi-skilled occupational groups have been lost to the game over the last decade or so than from any other occupational grouping. See 'The Changing Face of Football', Football League Marketing Department, 1981.

12 Taylor, op. cit., p. 9.

13 See 'Football and the Fascists', Centre for Contemporary Studies (mimeo), January, 1981.

14 Recent newspaper reports already suggest that disorderly behaviour by British subjects abroad is by no means confined to football match trips. *The Times*, for example, reported on 8 August that the Spanish authorities had decided to form a special police squad, the 'Green Berets', to cope with disorderly behaviour by British holidaymakers in Benidorm. On one night in the Spanish resort it was reported that 34 people were held and there was not enough room for them all in the cells. At the moment, however, the Spanish authorities do not regard vandalism and violence by their visitors from Britain as a serious

problem. Out of the 800,000 Britons who visit Benidorm each year, less than 1,000 are arrested.

15 We are thinking particularly here of the 'success' of the Toxteth riots in attracting government funds to the area and in leading to the appointment of a 'Minister for Merseyside' in 1981. Clearly, these initiatives do little more than scratch the surface of the problems in communities like Toxteth. Nevertheless, it is hard to disagree with Whannel when he asserts that, 'Since the riots of 1981, it has suddenly become much easier to obtain funding for inner city projects. Nothing loosens the purse strings like panic'. Whannel, *Blowing the Whistle: The Politics of Sport*, op. cit., p. 92.

Appendix 4

1 See Norbert Elias, *What is Sociology?* London, Hutchinson, 1978, p. 71 ff.
2 Ibid., p. 72.
3 Ibid., p. 84 ff. We have collapsed here what Elias called the 'oligarchic' and 'increasingly democratic types'.
4 This issue is treated at greater length in Dunning, Murphy and Williams, *The Social Roots of Football Hooligan Violence*, (forthcoming).

INDEX

West Ham fans, 46, 53, 54, 61, 65
West Midlands police, 133

xenophobia, 113, 114

'Yer Man', 25ff.

'Zusism', 7